PAINTING SKIES IN PASTEL

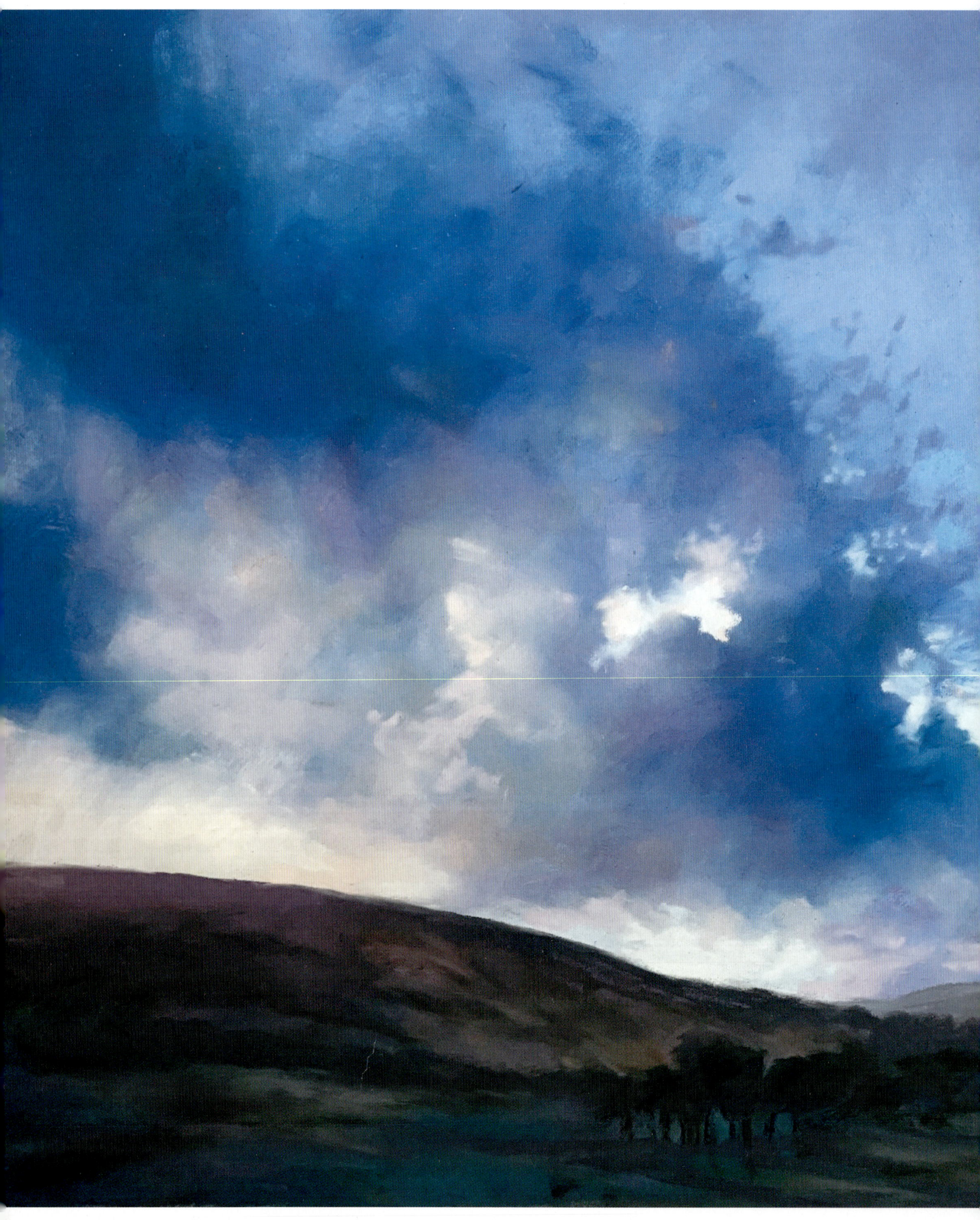

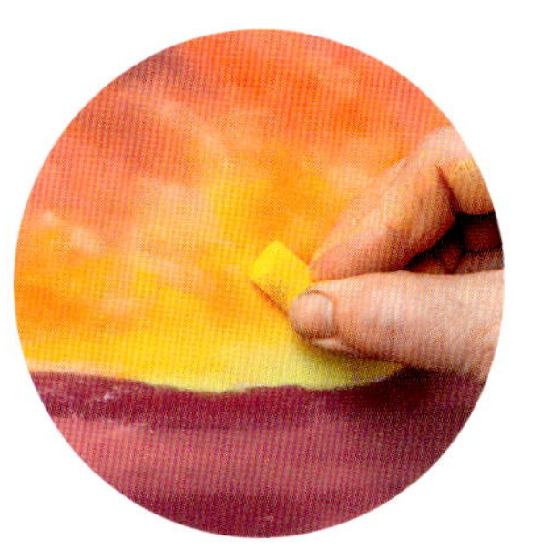

PAINTING SKIES IN PASTEL

Creating dramatic clouds
and atmospheric skyscapes

Sandra Orme

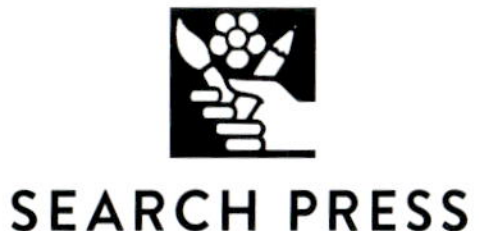

Search Press

Dedication

*To my family, with thanks for
all the years of support.*

Acknowledgements

*Many thanks to my editor Edward Ralph
for his patient guidance, Mark Davison for
the wonderful photography and all the
welcoming team at Search Press. Thank you
to Chris Farrow at www.originalgiclee.co.uk
for additional Fine Art photography.*

Page 1:
As the Sun Sets
45 x 65cm (17¾ x 25½in)

Pages 2–3:
Evening Comes to Axe Edge
40 x 30cm (15¾ x 11¾in)

CONTENTS

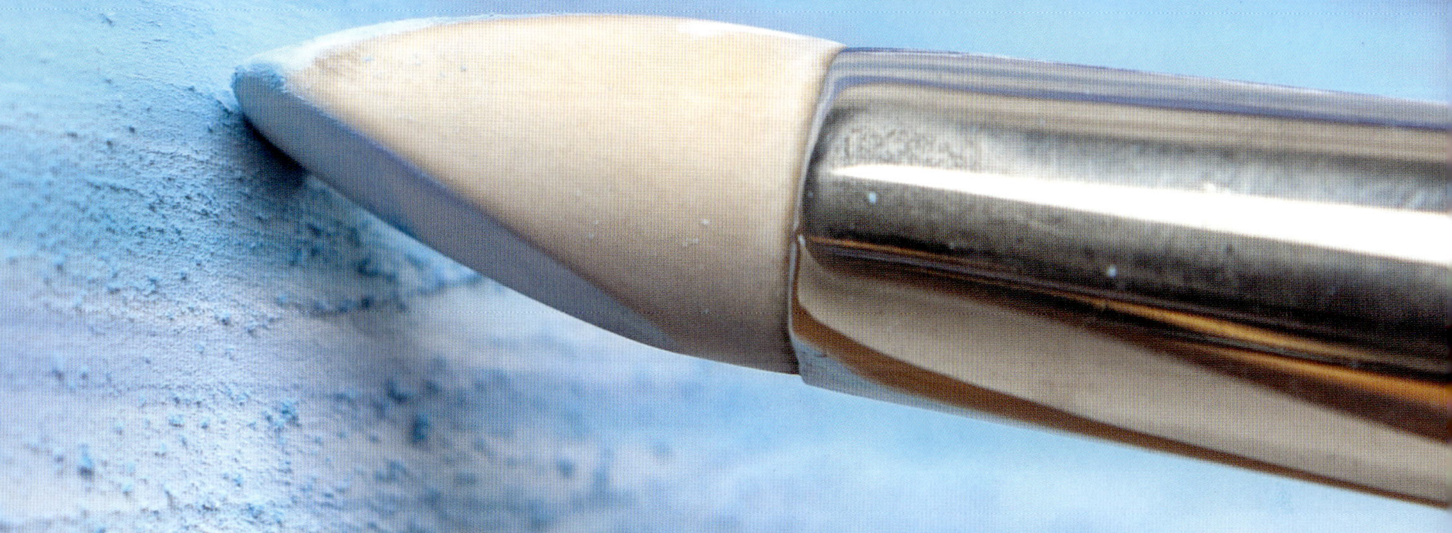

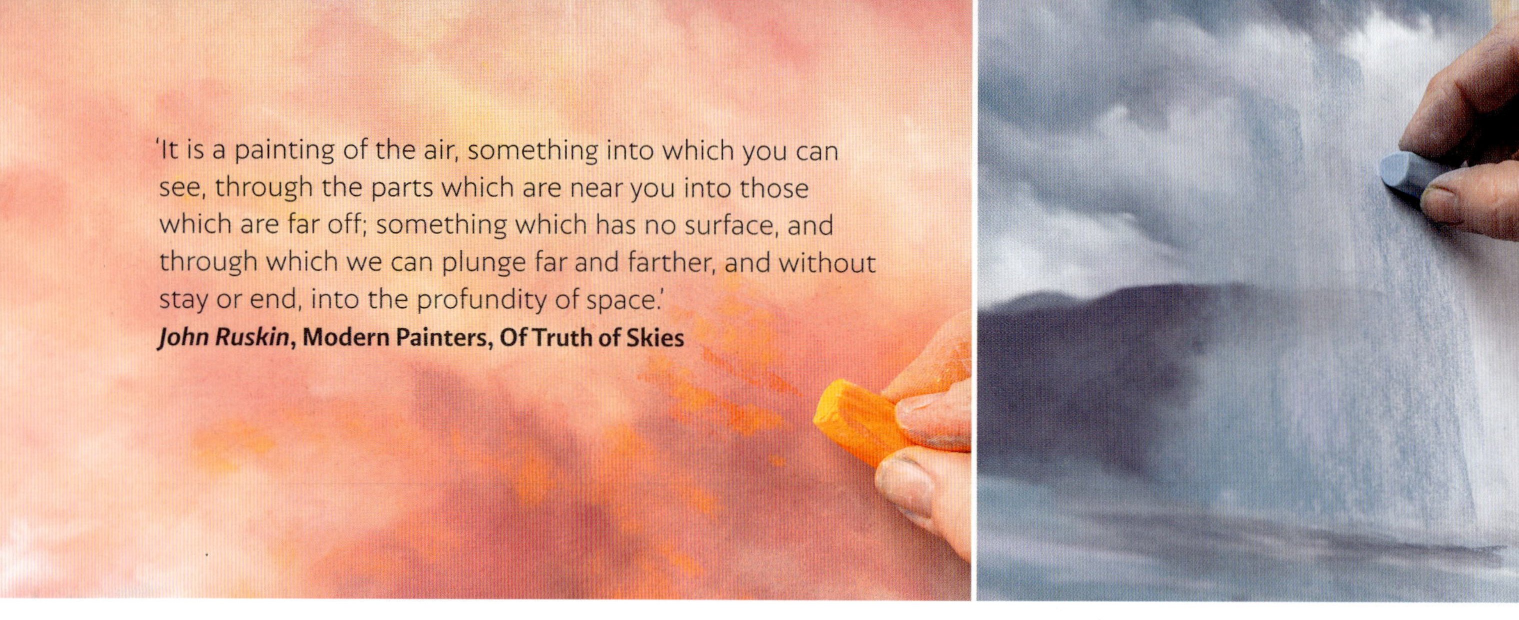

Introduction

LIVE IN AN OLD QUARRYMAN'S cottage perched on the side of a steep hill above Buxton, high up in the hills of the Peak District in the UK. The row of old stone cottages sits on one side of a short, narrow lane that was dug out of the hillside. Steps on the other side of the lane lead up to the sloping gardens which in turn back onto open fields and footpaths that take you up onto the moors.

We moved here during a brief summer heatwave in 2002. After leaving the oppressive and airless humidity of London in August, we were woken, on our first morning in Buxton, by the cold; shivering under our thin duvet. As summer became autumn, then winter, I discovered the dramatic extremes that the weather in Buxton has to offer: rainfall, temperatures, snowfall – along with phenomena I had not previously experienced, like a peculiar, dazzling, bright fog and stinging, horizontal hail; the wind whipping clouds past the kitchen window and down the lane.

I became keenly aware of the weather in a way I had never been before, and as I acclimatized I grew to love the variety. As I type, rain is spattering against the window, the wind is testing the slates on the roof and I am distracted by watching the hills across the valley appear, disappear, then reappear as another storm gradually passes over.

I tell you all this to explain why my obsession with the sky was almost unavoidable. My initial responses to beautiful Derbyshire were artworks based on favourite walks, well-known moorland tracks and rock edges. Slowly, gradually, the power and presence of the weather began to inform the art I produced.

I found myself focusing on light – not just the movement of light across moorland, but also the light within the clouds themselves. The way the clouds shifted and roiled, how they gathered on the distant horizon above Kinder Scout, how beams of light sliced through them, or a curtain of rain darkened the hilltops as it moved across the moor towards me.

I witnessed the wind stretching dark cloud to thin threads over the hills as the sun set, endless tints and shades growing then fading beneath the surface of the swirling storm clouds. I saw the seasons shifting around me as the sunset slowly moved across the sky to set directly opposite my home in midsummer.

Now, when I am working in my studio, built in our garden above the lane, with views down the steep valley, I feel the constant presence of the sky and the moors that surround it. I'm aware of the wind twisting around the studio as I watch the weather shift and change before descending over the town. I can become absorbed studying the mist weaving up from the valley bottom and climbing up into the sky. Despite the daylight bulb over my work, I sense the light outside altering, darkening or brightening. The weather is elemental and infuses all that I do.

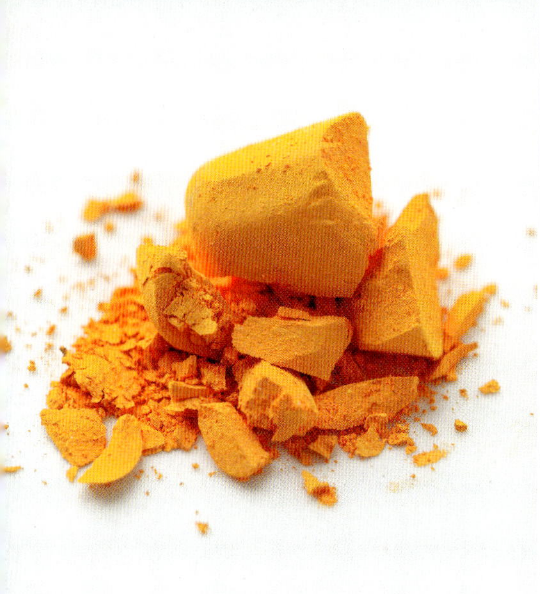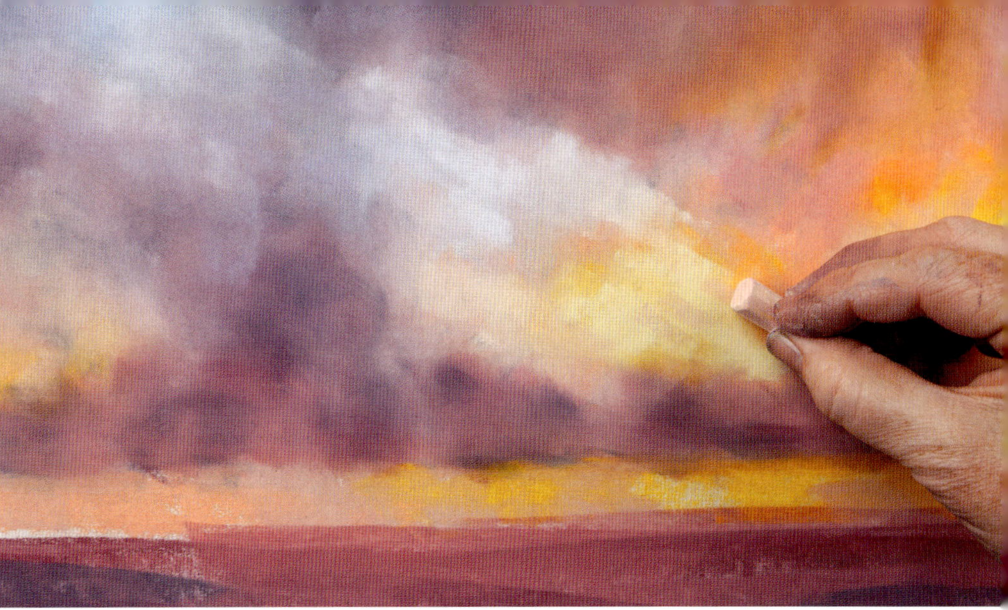

Recreating skies, with their endless variety of forms, colours and possibilities, presents both challenges and inspiration. For me, the first challenges were technical. During and since my Fine Art degree, I have explored a number of different art techniques, but have always been more at home with 'dry' media. Exploring at first with charcoal, and progressing to pastel, I blended, pushed and smoothed the colours into cloudforms. It felt right. I experimented with a number of different pastel paper surfaces, and as I developed my own way of working with layers of pastel, I found that a soft but strong tooth was an ideal paper to work on.

The next challenge was to get the structure and feel of the sky right. There is a flow and arrangement of cloud structure that needs to be captured. Each different type of cloud formation has a balance and different parts of the sky work together to create the impact of the whole. The immediacy and power of pastels is capable of conveying the drama of many different types of sky, which is perfect for communicating a sense of time and place. That is what I want to share with you in this book.

The book is divided into three parts: the first exploring the materials and techniques we will use; the second the projects, where you will learn to apply the techniques; and finally the pastel sky clinic, where I share more of my secrets and answer common questions. The clinic can be dipped into at any time when you want to practise or focus on a particular aspect of clouds. It will also help you resolve any struggles you find within your own sky studies.

I will take you through different combinations of light, movement and sky types – from sunsets to storms. We will address developing depth and colour along with texture and movement. You will learn to control disparate elements and bring these into a whole that captures the mood of different days. We will reflect on technical, practical issues of painting the skies, through to more intangible elements like creating atmosphere and mood. Above all, we will create beautiful skies.

'Sometimes gentle, sometimes capricious, sometimes awful, never the same for two moments together.' *John Ruskin*, **On Skies**

ANATOMY OF THE SKY

'Now this is nature! It is the exhaustless living energy with which the universe is filled.' *John Ruskin*

The skies above are endlessly changing and ever-inspiring. I will never tire of trying to capture fleeting clouds, shapes and colours, feeling even more respect for those artists working before we had cameras, who relied solely on memory and sketches.

There is a multiplicity of cloud types to study, explore and recreate; from high cirrus clouds to rain-bearing nimbus. However, naming and identifying all the cloud variations is not the purpose of this book. Instead I hope to guide you on a journey through different skies and give you an understanding of how to recreate this variety in pastels.

This painting, *The Last Rays, Glen Wyllin Beach*, is a complex sunset that includes a variety of cloud types and some of the key issues we will consider. Once you have worked your way through the book, I hope you will feel confident and ready for the challenge of creating your own dramatic skies with many different clouds.

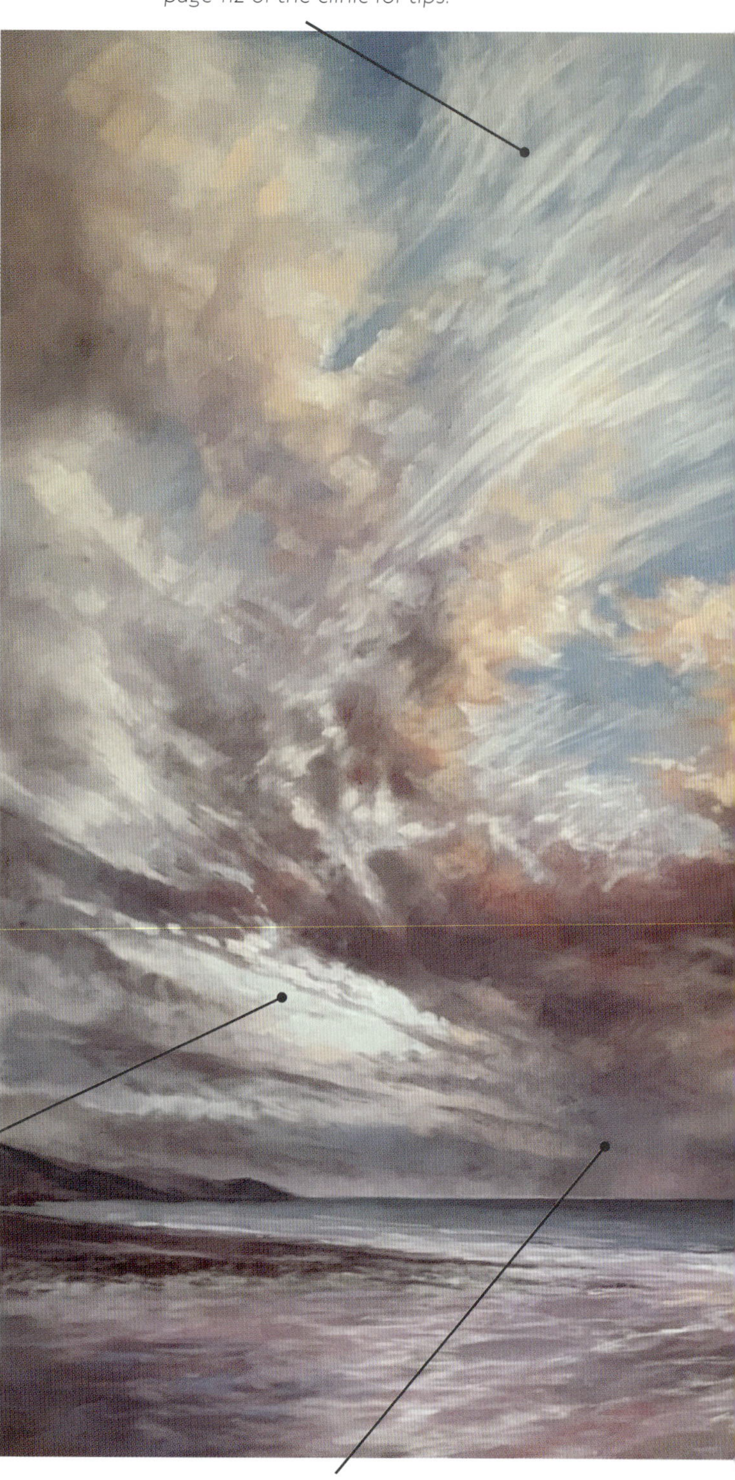

Cirrus clouds

*Delicate and windswept, almost transparent.
See Windy Weather on page 62 and
page 112 of the clinic for tips.*

Cloud windows

*We explore making 'cloud windows' – the gaps
through which you can see the sky beyond the
cloud – in Stormy Sunset on page 86.*

Nimbus clouds

*Low-level nimbus clouds are often rain-bearing –
this example shows a distant haze of rain on the
horizon. They appear in Cloudburst on page 50.*

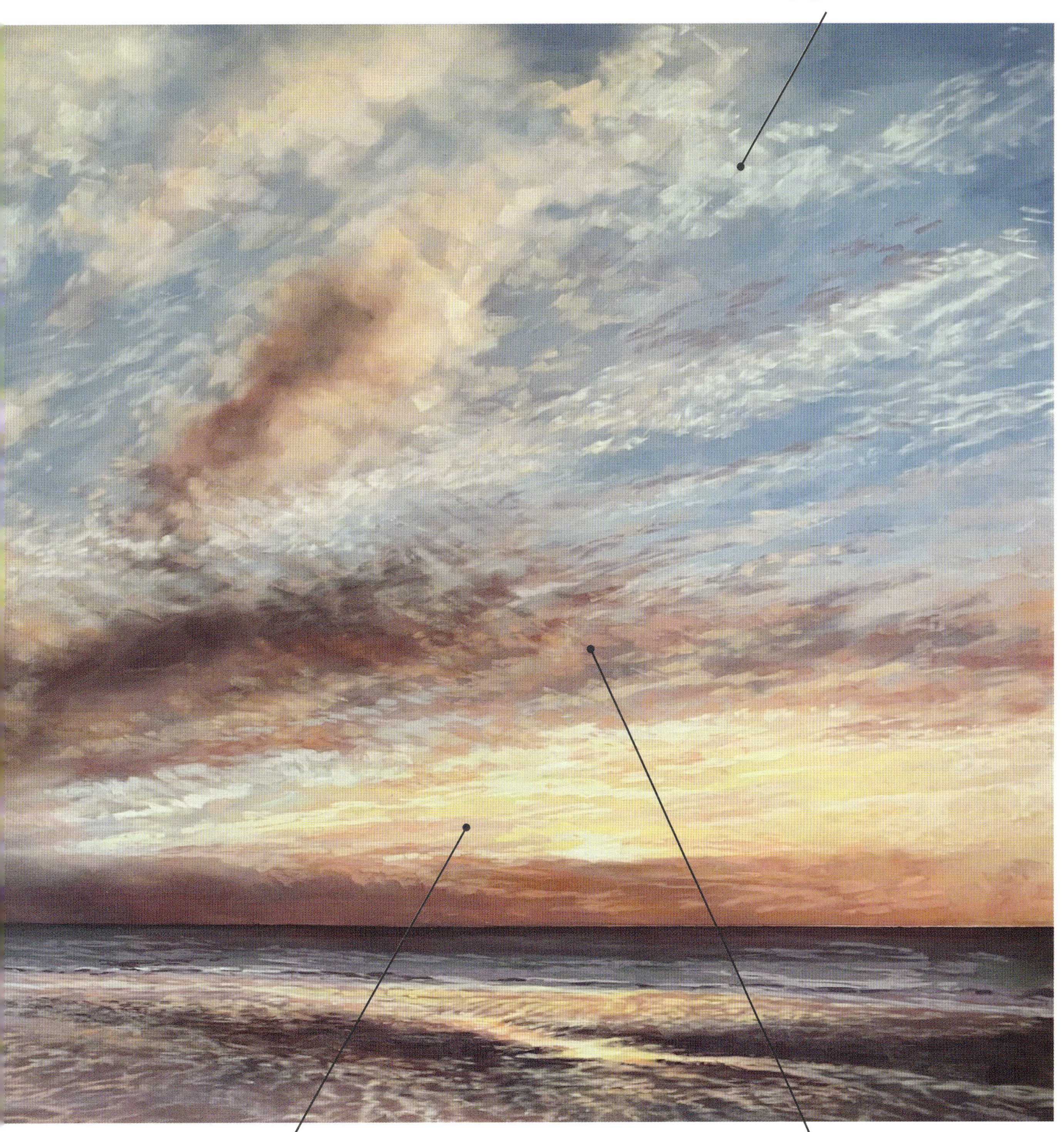

Soft and delicate highlights

You will learn to work on building delicate layers of soft colours in Delicate Sunrise on page 98.

Colour transitions

We will look at creating and controlling clean colour transitions in dramatic skies, in the Stormy Sunset project on page 86 and Delicate Sunrise project on page 98.

Altocumulus clouds

Mid-level clouds that form beautiful broken patterns, here they are capturing the warm light from the sun. We will also explore these in white in Blue Sky, White Clouds on page 38.

What do you need?

ARTWORKS MADE WITH ARTISTS' GRADE pastels, if handled properly, with good framing and hanging conditions, are among the most stable and long-lasting we can create. Unlike some types of paint, pastels do not darken, fade or crack as they are pure pigment mixed with a neutral binder; and so your art will last many lifetimes.

The key elements of pastel art are the 'three Ps': pastel, paper, pressure. Selecting good quality materials, from the pastel set you choose to the paper on which you work, is an investment in helping you create beautiful work more easily – and also in the future of the work you produce. Whether you plan to sell or savour your art, when you use artists' grade pastels you can be confident that your artwork will remain as vibrant as the day you made it.

This is one of the joys of pastel: the immediacy and permanence of the work. As you are working, you know that it won't dry differently; the textures and colours that you mix and explore as you toil will remain and will look the same, whether you come back to it the next day or the next year.

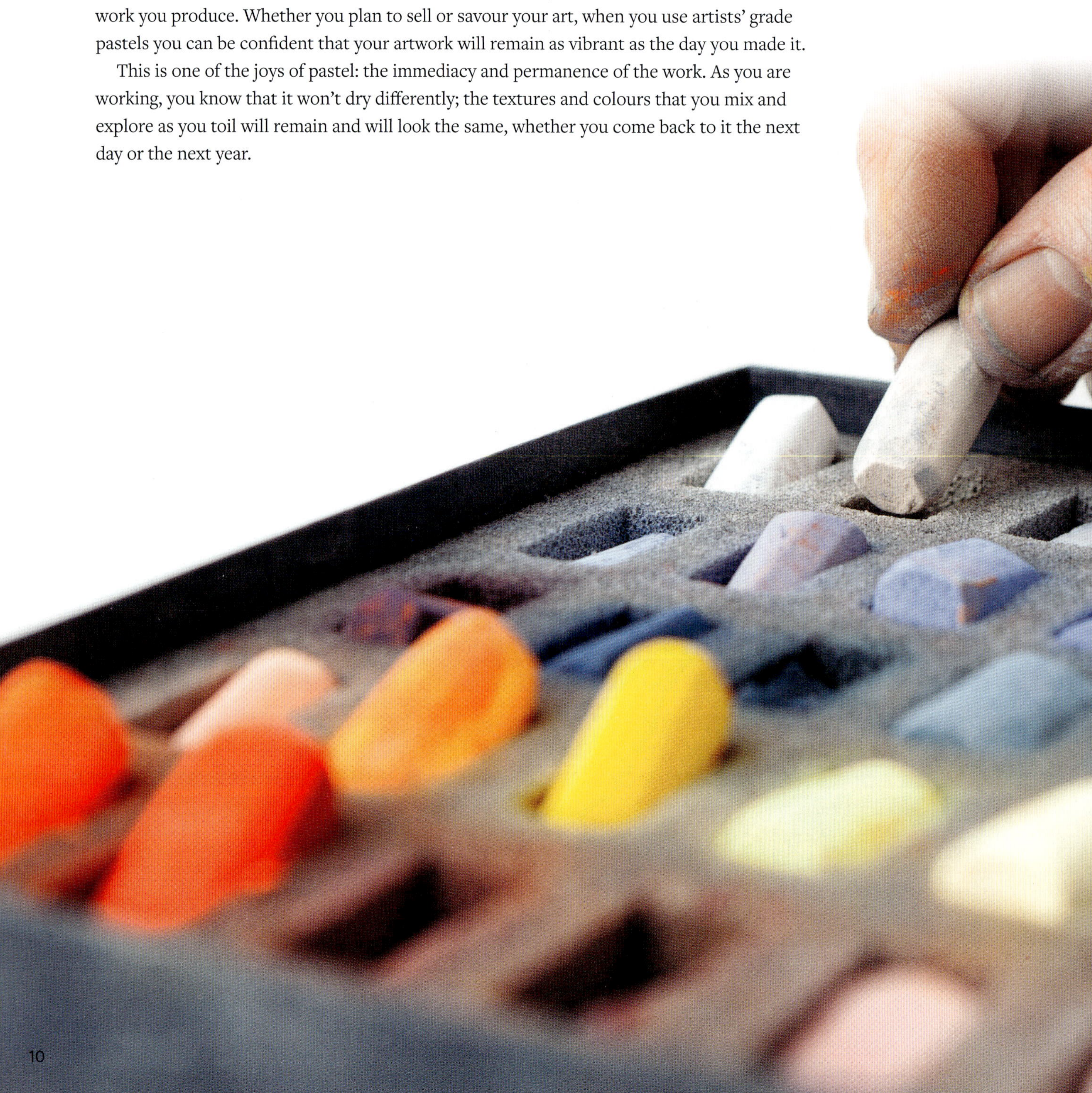

WHAT PASTELS TO USE?

I use what are known as soft pastels – sometimes described as chalk-based pastels. These range from cheap chalky sets to the top-end artists' grade brands with a high proportion of pure pigments. You can use whichever soft pastel range you like, but I recommend you invest in quality.

I have tried many different brands of pastels over the years and favour the Unison Colour Soft Pastels range, which I find beautifully smooth and soft, and with a buttery and creamy consistency, neither too crumbly or too firm. This quality is key because it allows you to create layers. Cheaper students' range pastels can be chalkier and powdery. Some are even gritty, with a sandy feel to them. This might be okay for other ways of working in pastel or the initial part of my process – even cheaper pastels will bind to the surface of any good quality pastel paper that has a distinct tooth – but as you work through the projects, you will discover how important the quality of pastel is. You will be learning to build layer upon layer, mixing and blending on the surface of the paper. Unison Pastels will bind not only to the paper but to each other; and as the tooth is gradually filled, this characteristic becomes essential.

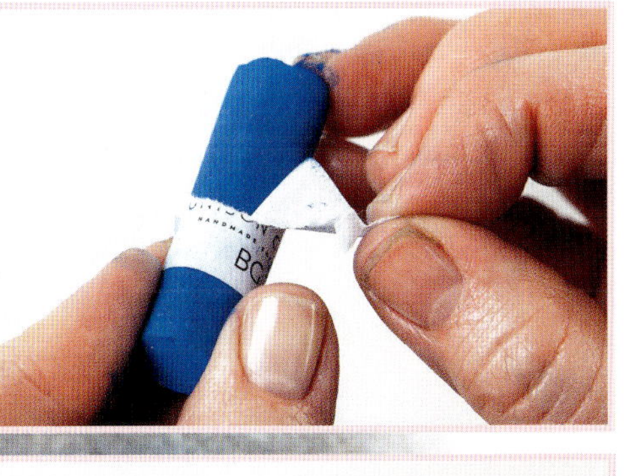

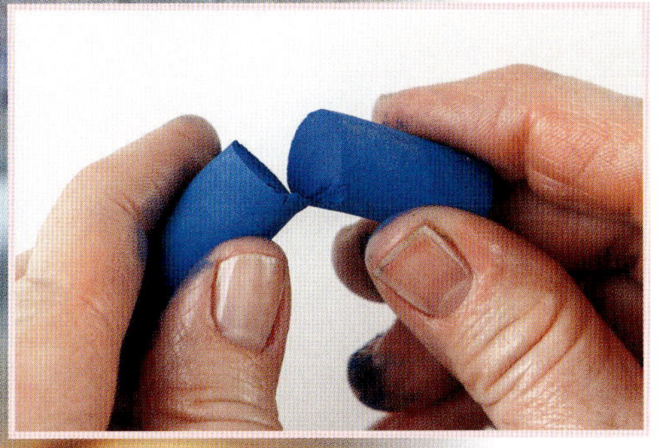

Preparing pastels for use

Most pastels are bought as large sticks. We will be using the pastels on their side for most of the stages of work, and a full size stick is too large for this purpose. If you are using full size Unison Soft Pastels, you will need to remove the paper (see left, top), and snap it in two (see left, bottom). You can then use the side of the half-pastel. This is important because working with the tip of the pastel applies more pastel to the surface than the side. Using the tip will therefore fill the tooth too quickly in the first stages.

Those of you who can't bear to take the wrapper off your gorgeous new pastel and then snap it in half (you know who you are) may find this painful. But a half-stick size is the perfect size for the marks we want to form on the paper. I know this can be excruciating to contemplate, but it really is for the best!

My choice of pastels

Although we are mixing many tints and hues on the surface of the paper, we need the right set of colours to combine together to create our clouds and different types of sky. I have worked with Unison Colour to select a gorgeous combination of pastels to form a bespoke Sandra Orme Sky Set, which includes the colours listed below. This set forms a great base of sky colours from which to build to let you create most skies from a cloudy day through to blue skies or a sunset. I will be working from this set to produce all the work in these tutorials, so if you use another set, you will need to look for similar hues.

I recommend you purchase some Unison Pastels so you are able to get the best results with the tutorials. If your budget won't stretch to a full set, choose the project you want to try and buy a few appropriate colours from those listed here. If you can use these along with your existing pastels, they will help bind all of your pastels to the surface.

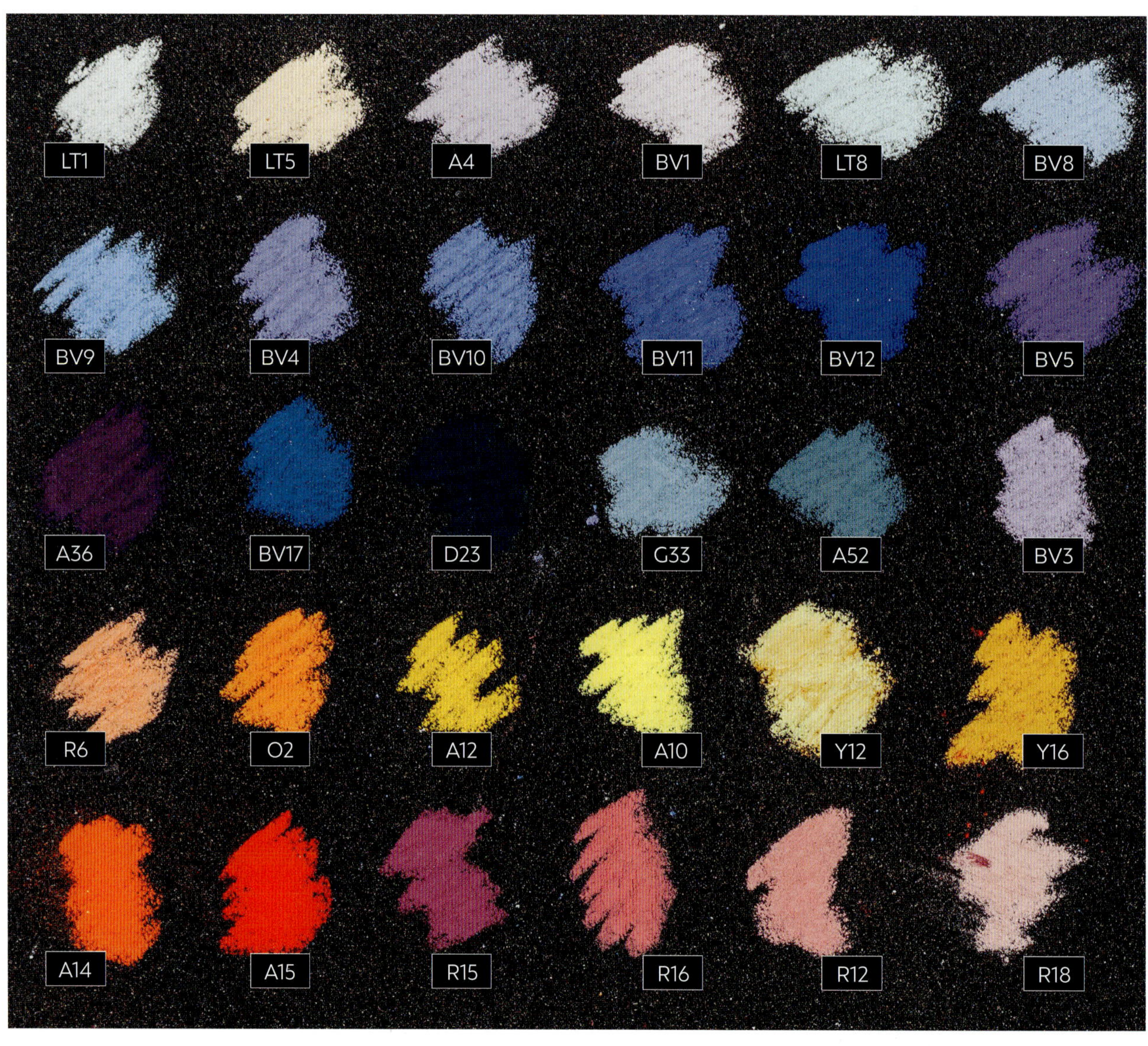

Exploring the Sky Set

I've developed my preferred colour palette to ensure it's as versatile as possible. There are combinations and groups of colours that will help you to create a range of different skies, including blue skies, sunsets, sunrises and storms.

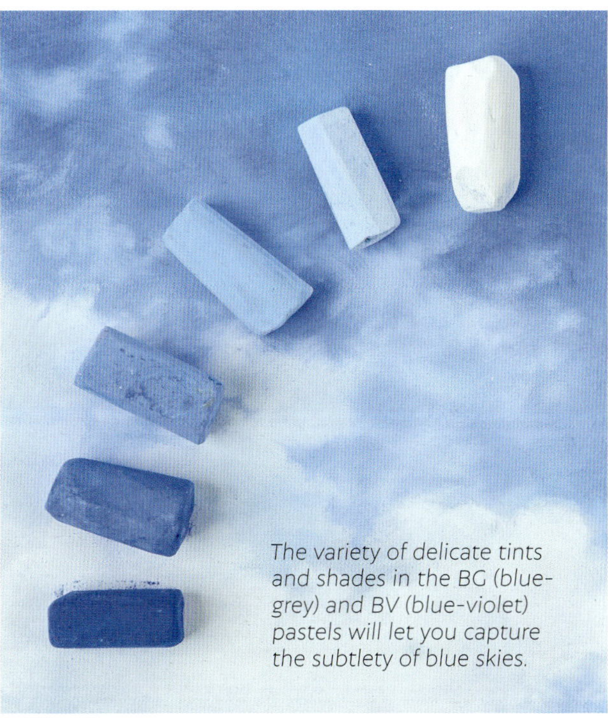

The variety of delicate tints and shades in the BG (blue-grey) and BV (blue-violet) pastels will let you capture the subtlety of blue skies.

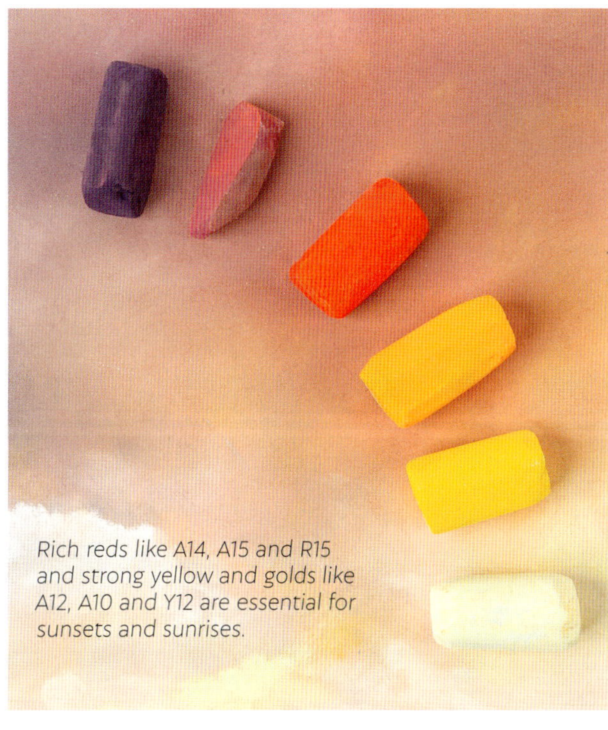

Rich reds like A14, A15 and R15 and strong yellow and golds like A12, A10 and Y12 are essential for sunsets and sunrises.

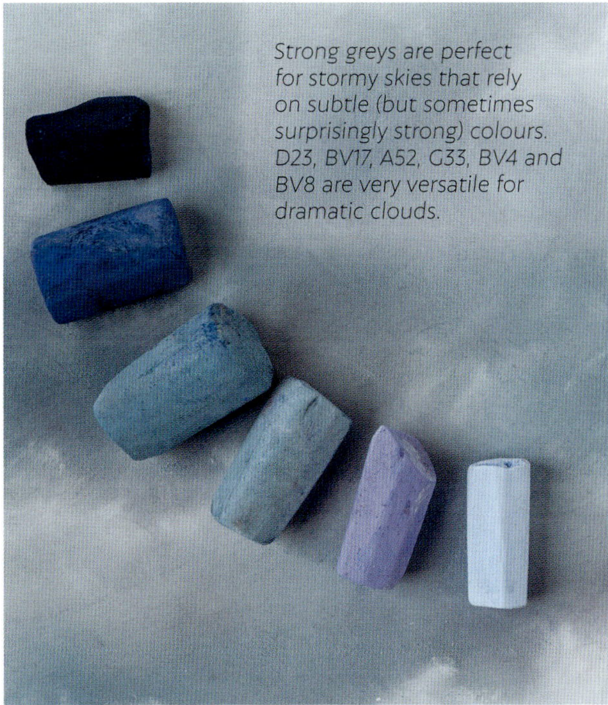

Strong greys are perfect for stormy skies that rely on subtle (but sometimes surprisingly strong) colours. D23, BV17, A52, G33, BV4 and BV8 are very versatile for dramatic clouds.

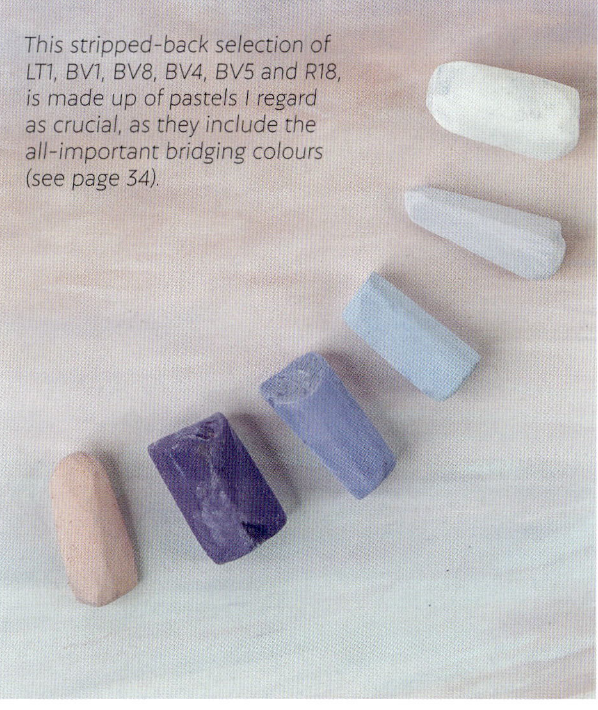

This stripped-back selection of LT1, BV1, BV8, BV4, BV5 and R18, is made up of pastels I regard as crucial, as they include the all-important bridging colours (see page 34).

THE IMPORTANCE OF PAPER

As you will have read, layers are central to the 'painterly' way I work with pastels. It is vital to choose the right paper for what you are trying to achieve.

A comment I regularly hear is 'I've tried pastels and just can't get on with them' – and nearly every time, it's because they are using something like sugar paper or everyday branded pastel paper in pads. These are all papers that lack any useful 'tooth'. Tooth is the textured surface of the paper and the correct tooth is essential for successful pastel art. Attempting to work on generic 'pastel paper' with more than a few layers will end in failure. After two or three layers, the colours will begin to fall off the paper and it all becomes hugely frustrating.

There are many different kinds of artist's grade pastel paper with a variety of tooth – ranging from rough to smooth. For these tutorials and for all my own sky work, I use Clairefontaine Pastelmat. This is a paper with a very fine tooth. It feels deceptively soft and smooth to touch. However, when you apply a little pastel to it, the pastel won't blend or move on the surface – in fact, it takes many layers of pastel to get movement on this paper. Because of this tight adhesion, it allows you to control and retain colour exactly where is has been applied, and then go on to create movement and light. When working on an image which is detailed, colour-filled and involves careful control of layers – a sunset, for example, Pastelmat is vital. You can buy Pastelmat in pads or large sheets, and in a variety of colours.

I recommend that you buy paper of at least 40 x 30cm (15¾ x 11¾in) size, as you need to work at this scale or bigger to be able to control and create the details needed. The colour of the surface isn't vital as we are working with so many layers that you won't see the paper at the end. However, if you find it useful to have a base colour to work against, choose a colour that is harmoniously linked to the piece you are working on. For example, don't work on a blue sheet when trying to create a mostly orange sunset.

From top to bottom.

Fisher 400 – mixed media surface, so can be used with other media prior to pastelling.

Senellier pastel card – with a very obvious tooth, this is very textural; ideally, don't blend on this paper.

Clairefontaine Pastelmat – my go-to surface; its soft but firm tooth gives superb control and definition.

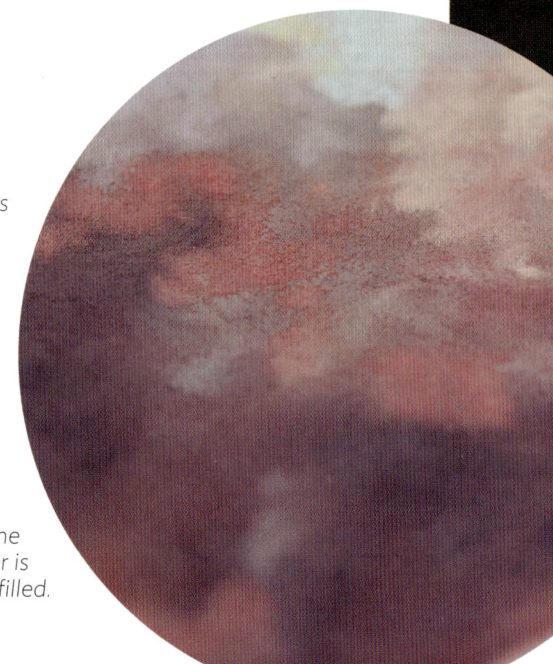

As pastel is applied, the 'tooth' of the paper is gradually filled.

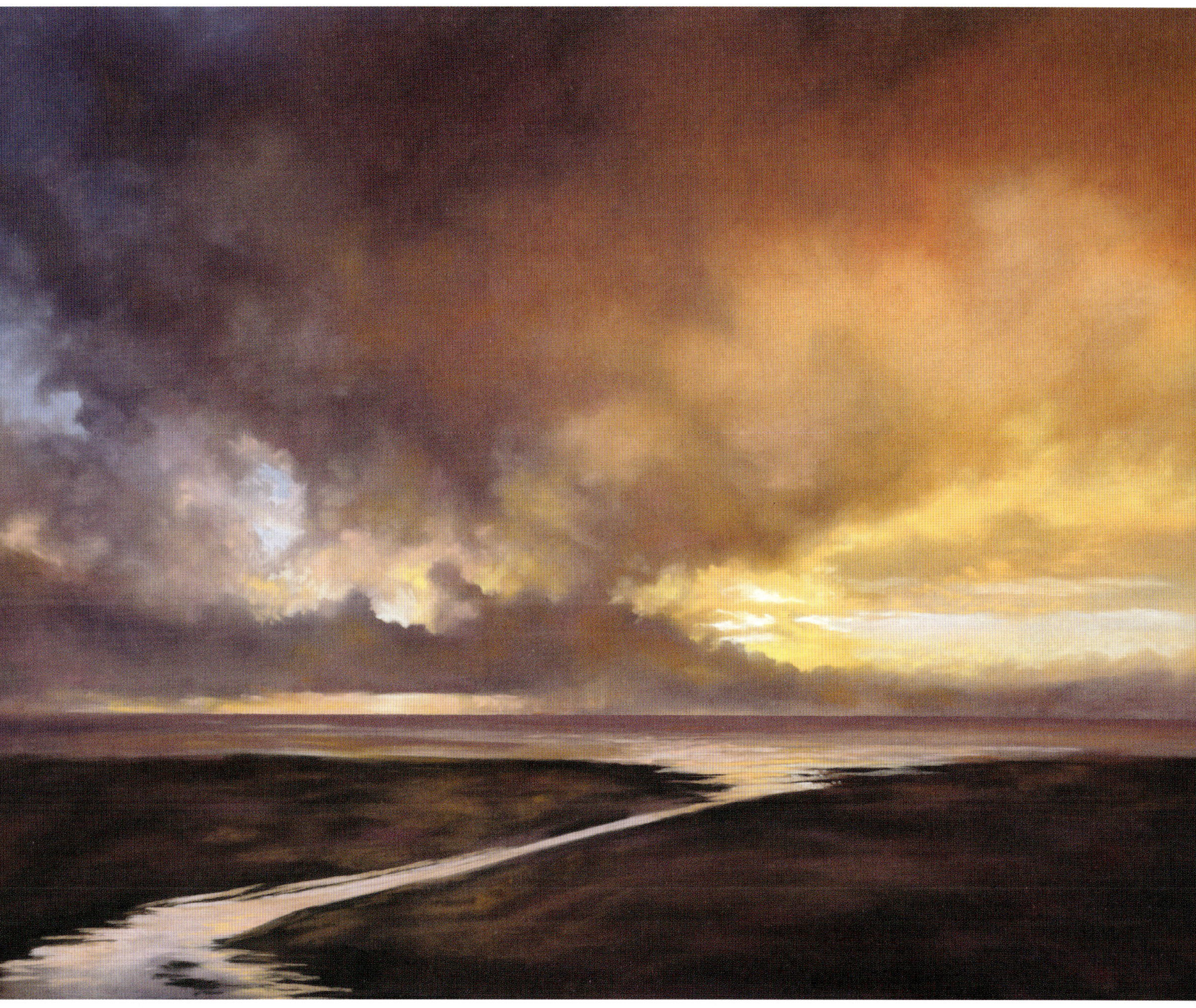

Fixative and storing work

There is a role for fixing work if there is very little tooth on the paper or you are using something like charcoal on cartridge paper. Fixative will then help the image remain on this kind of surface, where one inadvertent gesture or accident can remove the image.

When working on Pastelmat, I don't use any fixative, as in my experience it can darken or change colours. It can also leave spray marks spattered and dotted over the work. The pastels on this paper are not going anywhere in a hurry. The tooth is very strong and the layers will stay. It is not going to fall off or shed lots of particles. In short, no fixing please – and don't go anywhere near it with hairspray either!

I recommend using glassine paper to cover work to store it, or framing it with a floating mount.

Stormy Sunset, Ayrshire
95 x 65cm (37½ x 25½in)

ALL ABOUT PRESSURE

The third of my 'three Ps' is the importance of pressure. Unless otherwise specified, all layers of pastel colour should be built up using thin layers, which are then blended together with your fingers or the colour shaper tool. The pressure you use affects the colours (see 'Blending' below), and will also depend on the direction and movement of the marks you create. It's important not to over-blend areas and instead use varying pressure to form different textures across the surface.

Applying pastel

It's easy to be heavy-handed with pastels, but a light pressure, using the side of the pastel, needs to be used when working with the layering technique. By working this way, you ensure the tooth of the paper doesn't fill too quickly. This will allow you to build subtlety and variety while also allowing you to add final details.

Blending

As we progress with each piece, we will add further layers of pastel using the same delicate pressure on the pastels. The blending of these layers will become gradually more considered. At each blending stage, it's important to focus again on pressure – but this time it's the pressure of your fingers.

You have total control over how the pastels blend with each other purely by applying less or more finger pressure. You can create a difference in the colour in different sections of your work, even when these areas have had the same amount of pastel applied to them:

Less pressure With only light pressure used, underlying layers will be undisturbed, leaving the surface colours dominant and obscuring those underneath. Your mark making will remain, creating movement and texture.

More pressure When pressing harder, the colours underneath will rise more to the surface and interact with the colours you're putting on top – and the less dominant those surface colours with be. Any mark-making will also blur and soften, and can disappear entirely.

Shaping and detail

The final stages involve adding pastel using a heavy pressure to add detail or dominate the colours underneath, and to bring sharp edges and contrast. We use a shaper tool to keep and enhance definition. These final touches need very little blending – indeed, the last marks you make often don't need any blending at all.

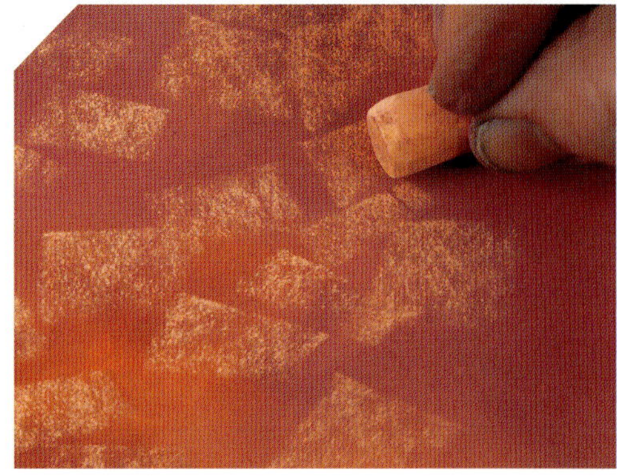

Application: light pressure

Apply your pastels lightly, so that the underlying layers are visible. You can always add more colour later – but build it up gradually.

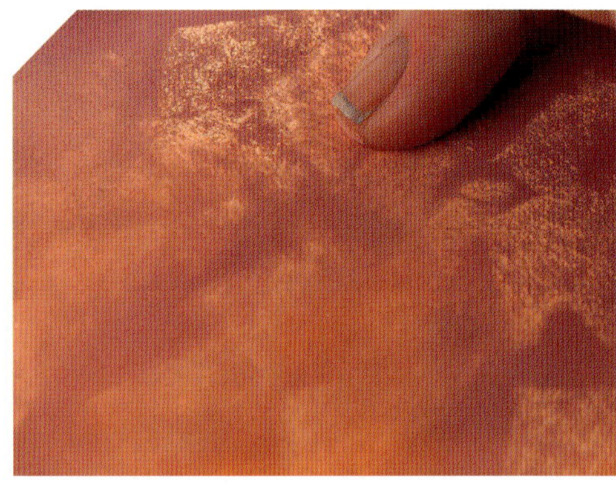

Blending: light pressure

Using a very light touch ensures that the marks made above are blended in subtly, but an overall sense of movement and surface colour is retained.

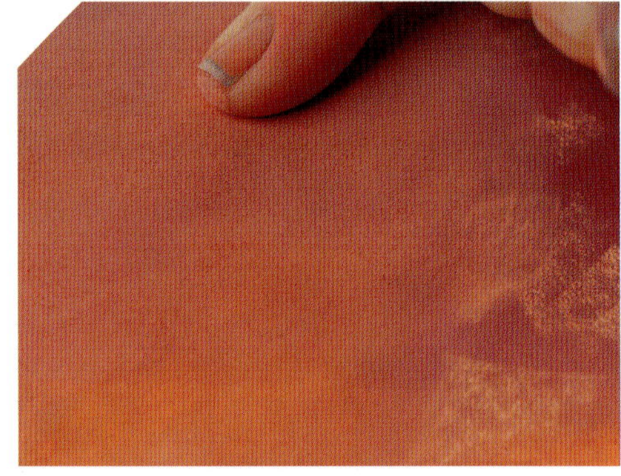

Blending: heavy pressure

Using a lot of pressure to blend pushes the surface pastel layer down into the tooth of the paper, interacting more with the underlying layers. The result is a flatter finish, and the layers of colour interact to a greater extent.

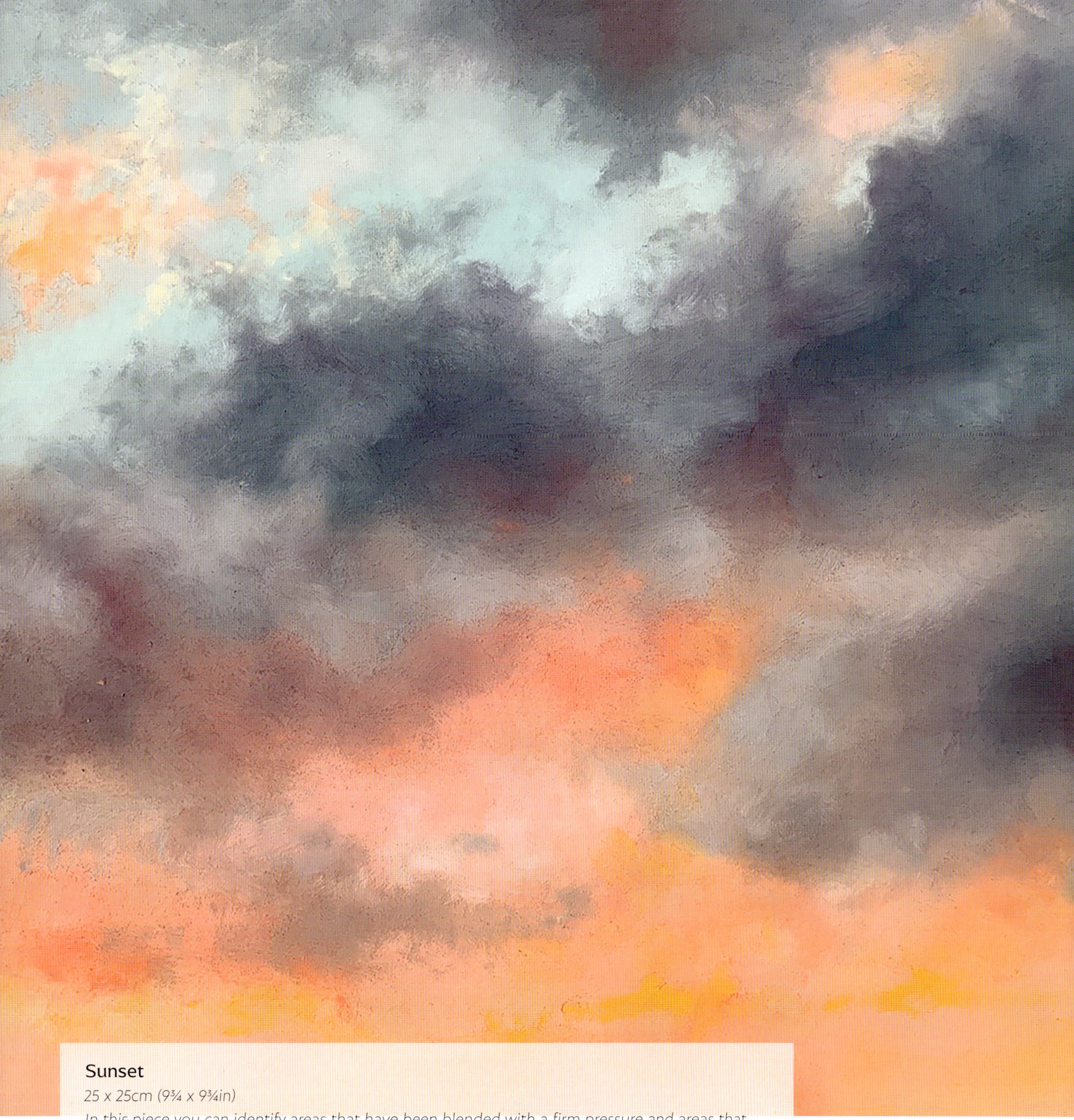

Sunset

25 x 25cm (9¾ x 9¾in)

In this piece you can identify areas that have been blended with a firm pressure and areas that have been blended with a light pressure. For example, the more detailed cloud areas towards the top have been worked in very lightly, using a shaper tool to retain the details and sharp edges. The cloud areas underneath these details have been blended more firmly to spread and diffuse the colours and mark making.

Bear in mind that the vivid colour sections in the lower part of this piece, although lacking detail, have also been blended lightly, in order to retain the richness of the colour in these areas.

HANDLING PASTELS

Although the first few layers will be blended, as you build the pastel on the surface of the paper, it becomes important to understand and investigate the different marks you can create with the pastel, and what each type of mark is useful for. These are the key ways that I handle pastels to achieve my skies, but feel free to develop and add your own as you explore.

On these pages, I explain the variations of mark-making and the different ways you can handle a pastel. The techniques are demonstrated on plain white paper so the mark-making is clear, but in most instances, apart from the flat technique, these marks will be used to build up layers on top of previous colours and blends.

Flat

Most of the layers in your artwork will be built up using the flat side of the pastel. We use broad strokes of the pastel applied with minimal pressure – you should be able to see the paper or other pastel layers through your mark-making.

Before the first blend, the sweeping gestures and long strokes made with this technique make up the majority of the marks we make. As we add more layers, this changes to a shorter mark – the block, which we look at opposite.

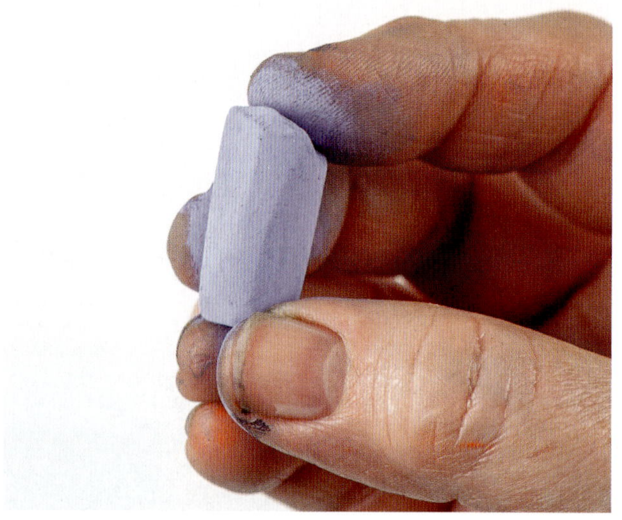

Pinch the ends of the pastel between finger and thumb, and brace it with your middle finger.

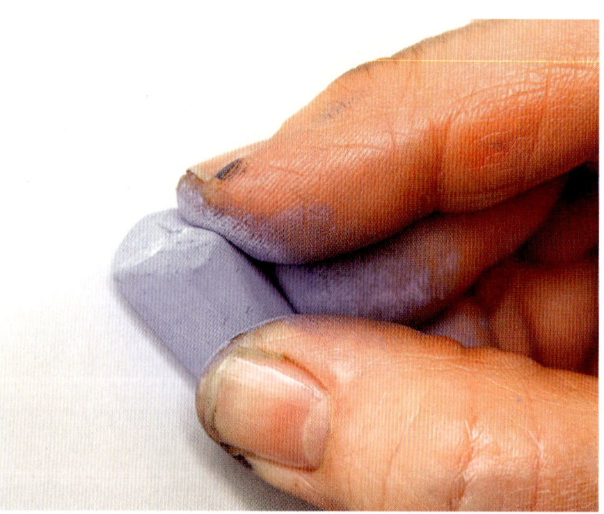

1 Place the whole side of the pastel flat against the surface.

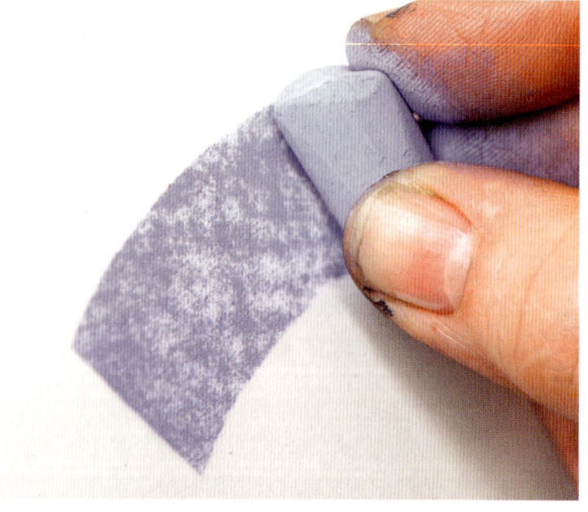

2 In a smooth action, pivot from the elbow to draw the flat of the pastel across the surface.

The block

This is what I call the short, almost square, mark we will use to build up pastel colours on top of our initial layers. Blocking is a technique that creates dynamic marks by applying the pastel using different directions while it is being held flat, as shown.

When blended, these marks begin to create an interesting mottled surface to build detail on to – as well as developing movement in the sky.

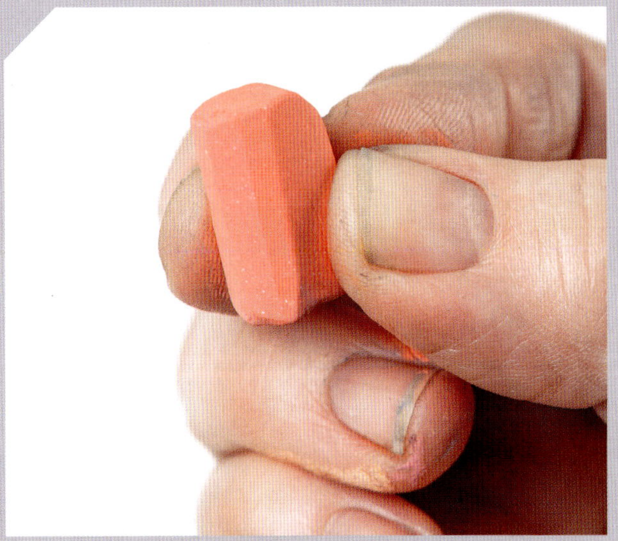

Use three fingers to pinch the pastel, slightly more loosely than in the flat technique.

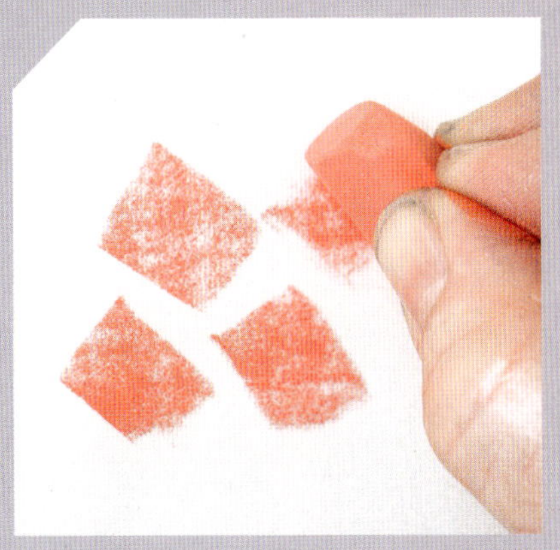 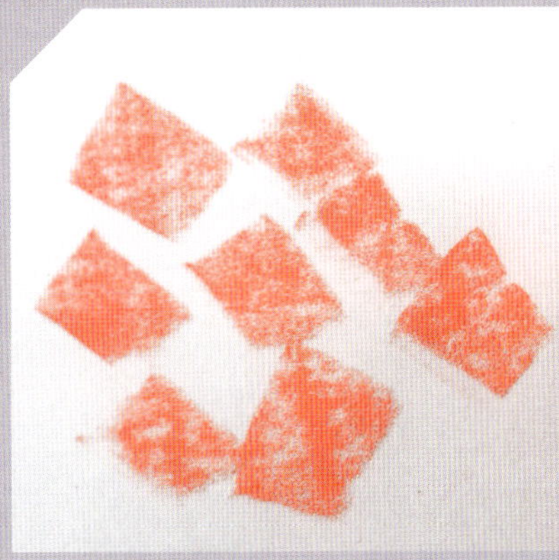 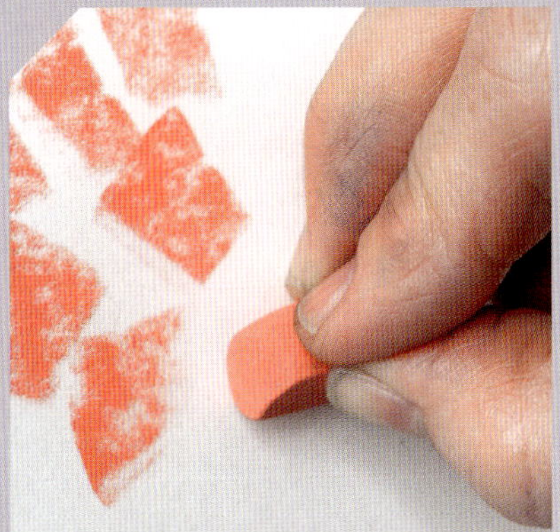

Move from your wrist to make lots of separate short, choppy marks. Be careful with your pressure and keep it light – it's easy to get carried away when making dynamic marks.

The slice

As you add detail, you often need to get a thinner line – for example with fingers of thin cloud. This is best done by rolling the pastel onto the long edge and slicing across the work – usually horizontally. We will use many of these gestural marks to add dynamic detail to windy skies and sharp edges of cloud.

This technique isn't easy to do with a new and round pastel, but as we tend to use the slice at a later stage in the work, this is rarely a problem – by this point, even new pastels will have formed flat edges.

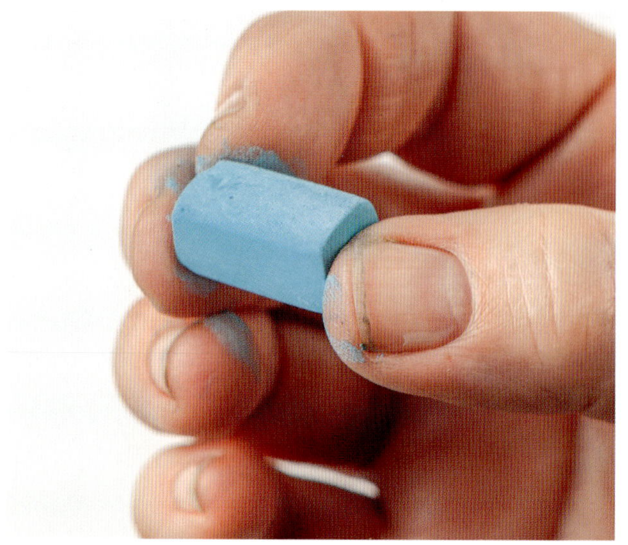

Hold the pastel at both ends, unbraced.

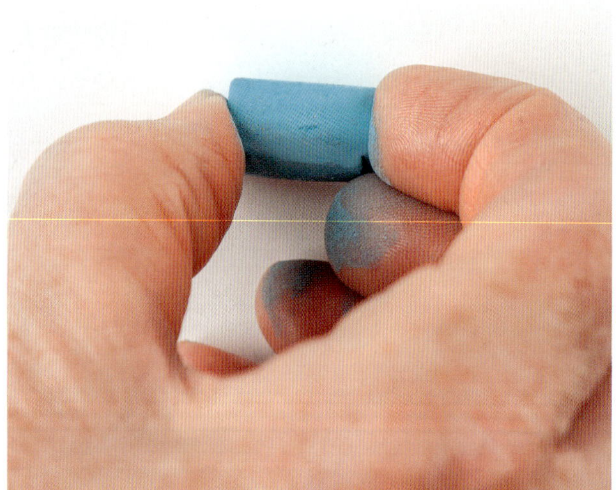

1 Place the side of the pastel flat against the surface.

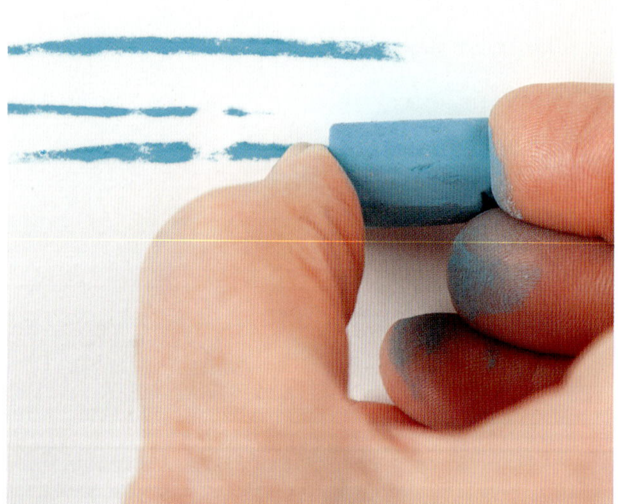

2 Pressing firmly, draw the whole pastel sideways to create a strong, fine line. You might like to think of this as a long 'flick'; vary the pressure, lifting the pastel away towards the end to create a slight fade in and out at the beginning and end.

The nibble

This mark is also produced by rolling the pastel onto the long edge, but rather than slicing quickly, we use slower and more controlled motions. While moving the pastel horizontally, we also move it up and down very slightly and erratically. This creates a 'nibbled' look to your line and is ideal for thinner clouds, as well as other interesting details like distant waves or the texture of the landscape.

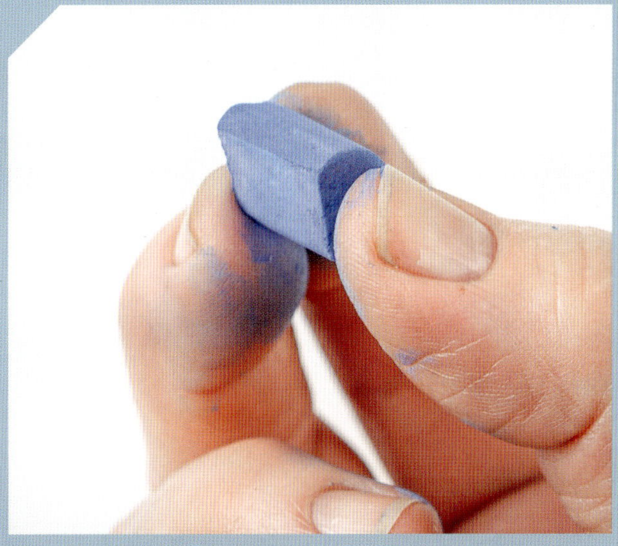

Just like the slice (see opposite), hold the pastel at both ends, unbraced. The difference is that you use two fingers to hold it, to give you a little more control.

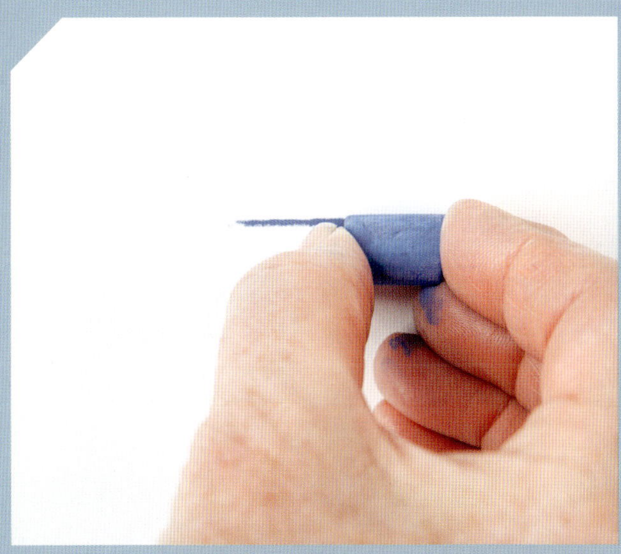

1 Place the side of the pastel flat against the surface and draw it sideways, just as for the slice.

2 Without lifting the pastel away, pause and move it up and down slightly, then continue with the sideways movement.

Twist, rock and roll

It is important to develop some of your own moves when working with the pastel. Twisting, rolling and rocking the pastel as you work generates exciting and energetic marks and can be useful for adding texture and movement.

I recommend you explore this technique on a spare piece of paper before using it in a piece. This will allow you to get a feel for how you can move the pastel across the surface, and the shape of the marks it will leave behind.

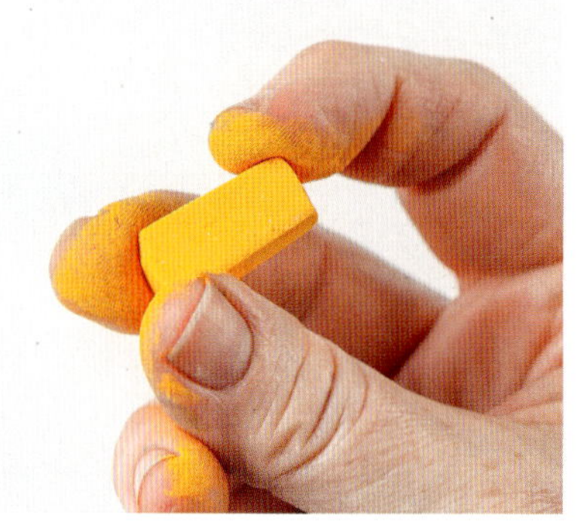
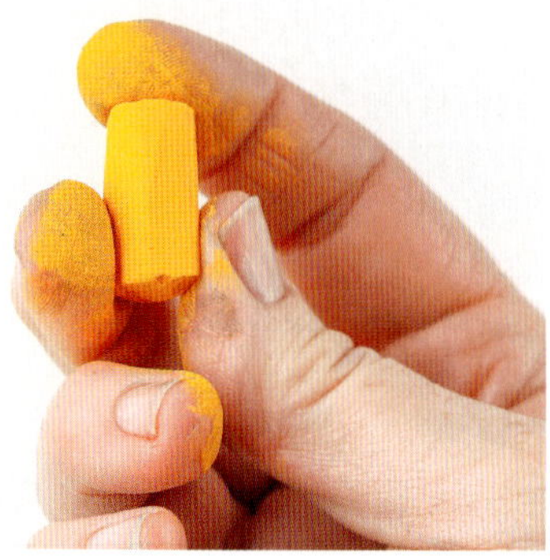
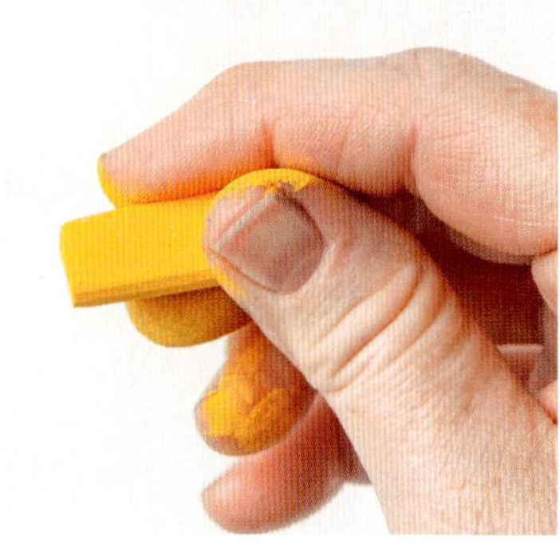
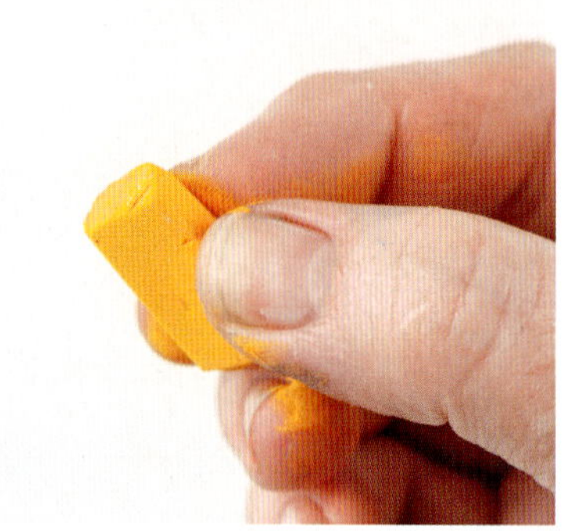

Here, the key is flexibility. Your fingers need to hold the pastel securely enough that it doesn't slip, but not too firmly, so that you can still roll it around in your fingers.

Place the pastel on the surface and then begin to make your marks. Move the pastel continuously as you work, shifting and changing the part that makes contact with the paper.

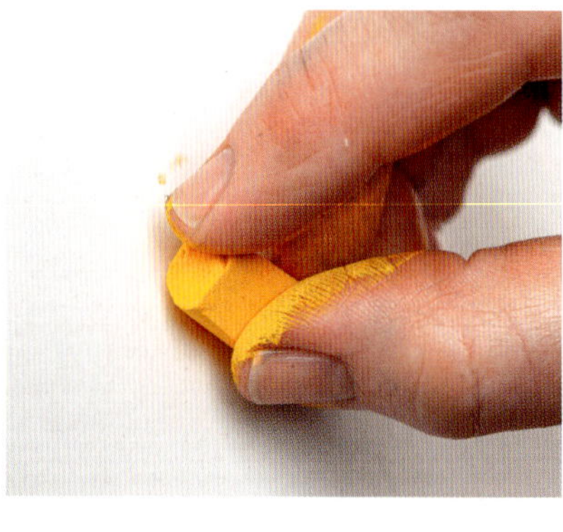
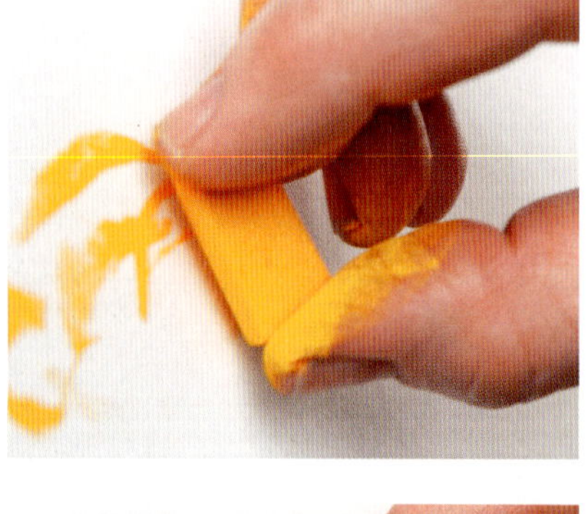
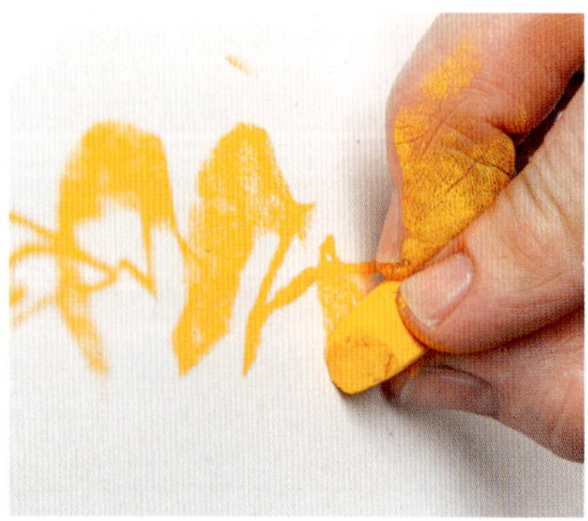
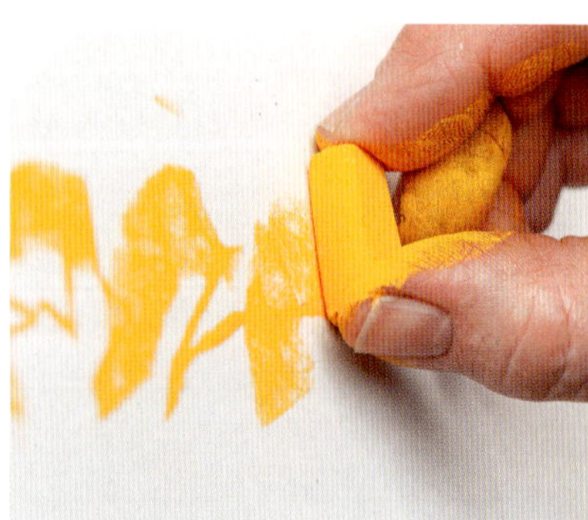

The tip and tilt

Final stages of working with pastel always involve using the tip of the pastel. This means we are working over previous layers and often not blending. Using the tip covers and controls the colours that have gone before, filling the remaining tooth of the paper.

Marks made using the tip can involve dots, dashes and small circular movements. This technique produces detailed marks, and isn't possible without using high quality pastels: the cheaper ones just won't adhere to the surface by the final stages.

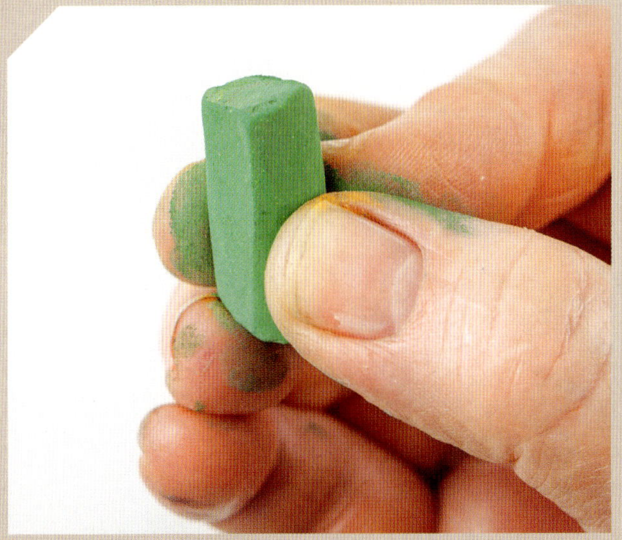

Hold the pastel as you would a stub of a pencil; nice and firmly between three fingers.

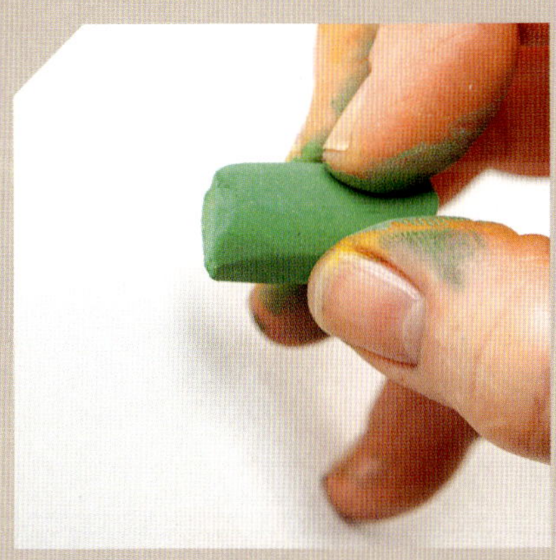

1 For extra control, you can use your little finger to brace your hand against the surface.

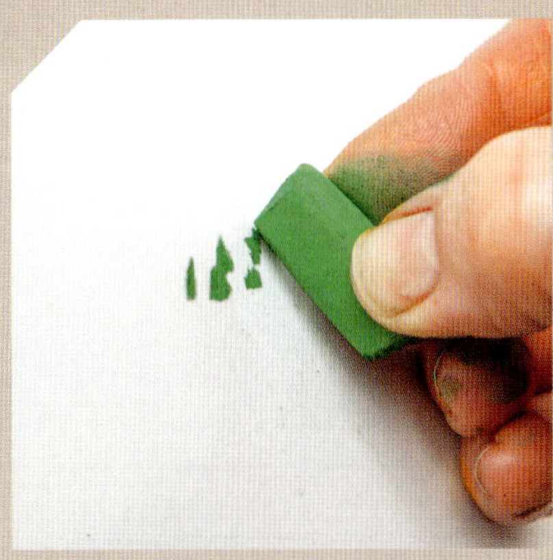

2 Lower the tip of the pastel onto the surface. Use the tip to make small, detailed and controlled marks.

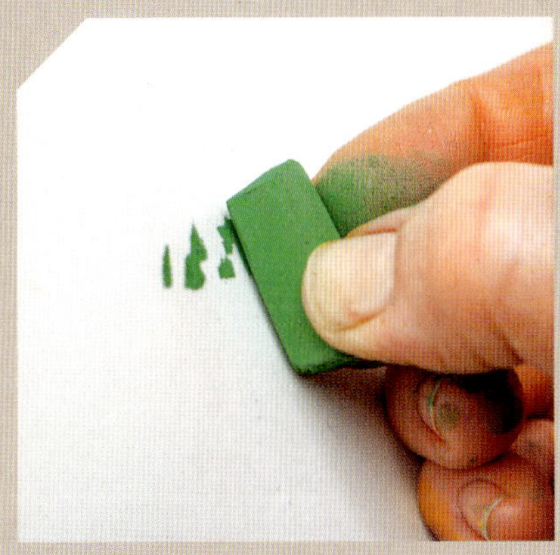

3 If needed, you can also tilt the flat of the pastel towards the surface, but keep the pressure mostly on the tip.

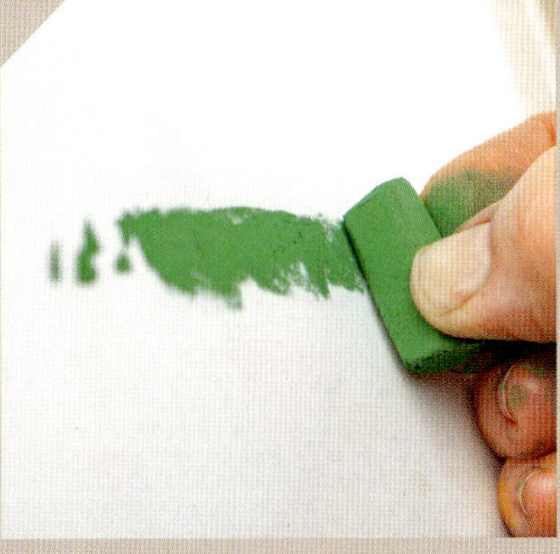

4 As you draw, you'll end up with a clear top to the mark, which tapers away as shown. This is useful for things like creating horizons and hills against the sky.

First layers *This speckling is what you're looking for with your first layers. The pastel is being picked up by the tooth of the pastel paper.*

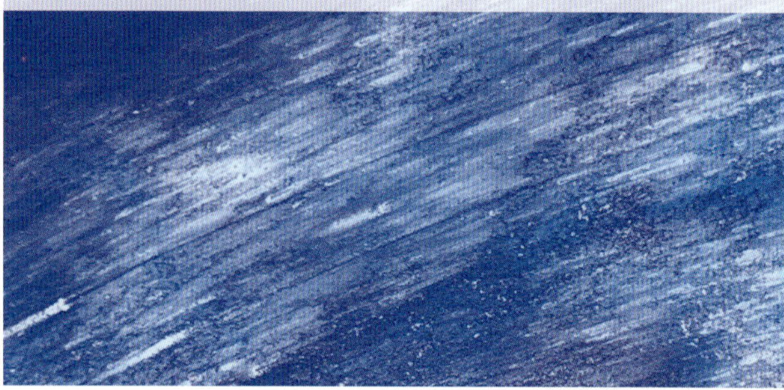

Ready to blend *As you continue to build up layers, the tooth will gradually fill, until the pastels start to smear when applied, as shown.*

The first blend

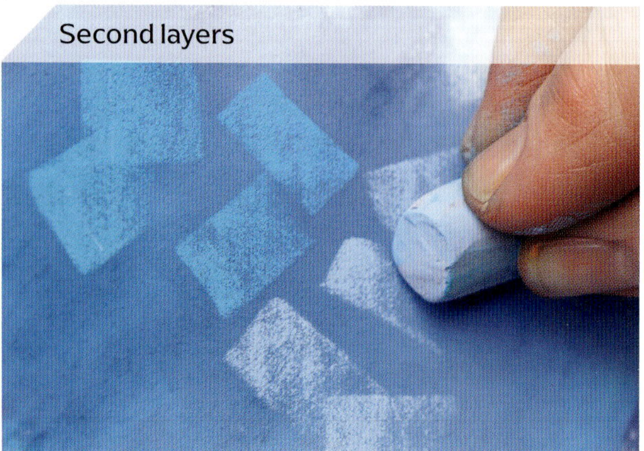

Second layers

BLENDING: STAGES FOR DEPTH

To create the depth and breadth of marks and colours in the work we will use many (many!) layers. Each stage of building a layer in the artwork has two parts: the first is the application of a number of pastel colours, the second is the blend.

There are a number of things to bear in mind to ensure you get the best results. It is very easy to get carried away and over-blend. This will move pastel colours beyond where you applied them, which leads to both colour and mark-making becoming muted and murky.

The following explains the general process you will learn to use. It doesn't mean that there won't be additional stages at times – and stages can sometimes be repeated a number of times to achieve the correct results before moving on. Nevertheless, these pages show how the depth of a particular area is built up through the repetition of careful layering and blending.

Stage 1: The first layers and blend We start by making multiple thin layers of pastel, applying them using broad and sweeping gestures and minimal pressure with the pastel. The first blend is done with a firm pressure, plenty of energy and lots of movement across the surface. Use broad movements of three or four fingers, or sometimes the side of hand or base of thumb. We usually blend in a circular motion, but always respond to the movement seen in the clouds.

A common question at this stage is 'when should I start to blend?' The answer is not too complicated: If you can still see the paper through the pastels, it probably needs more colour to be applied. Other than this, just give it a try once you have applied some pastel. The pastel should feel firm but begin to mix together on the surface. If it doesn't start to blend, add another layer of the same colours then try again.

Stage 2: The second layers and blend The surface is now ready for us to place dynamic, blocky marks of pastel (see page 19) in order to build on top of the first blend. Using two fingers or fewer, make smaller gestures, with more careful control of where the pastel is moved. Applying less pressure with your fingers ensures that the mark-making of the pastel is retained to some extent. At this stage we are aiming to create an 'interesting' surface, with plenty of movement, on to which we can then add the next layer.

Stage 3: The third layers and blend This stage involves adding more pastels carefully to key areas to build further movement. We are bringing focus to particular areas, and working towards adding the darkest and lightest colours in the piece. At this stage, pastels may be applied using different mark-making techniques rather than just flat or blocking – for example, the slice. (see page 20). Usually this stage involves using just your little finger to blend, and careful control with minimal pressure. A shaper may be used at this stage too.

Stage 4: The shaper layer For this stage, pastel is added using the tip of the pastel, or more precise movements like the nibble (see page 21) – and it is usually applied only in key areas. The shaper is moved across details with minimal pressure to blend and pull pastel into areas. This creates focus and detail where needed. Complementary colours and highlights are added here, and touches of white may be added too, if appropriate.

Stage 5: Finishing touches At this stage we check that we are happy with the colour and composition – paying attention to balance, texture, movement and the focal point (or points). See page 111 for tips on how to avoid over-working a piece.

*At all times, bear in mind
the three Ps: pastels,
paper and pressure.*

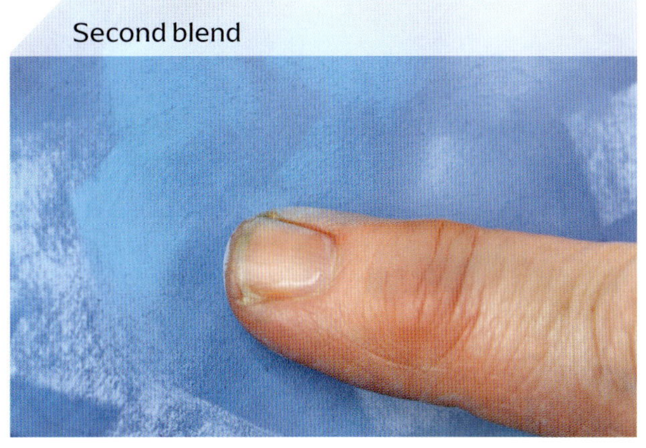

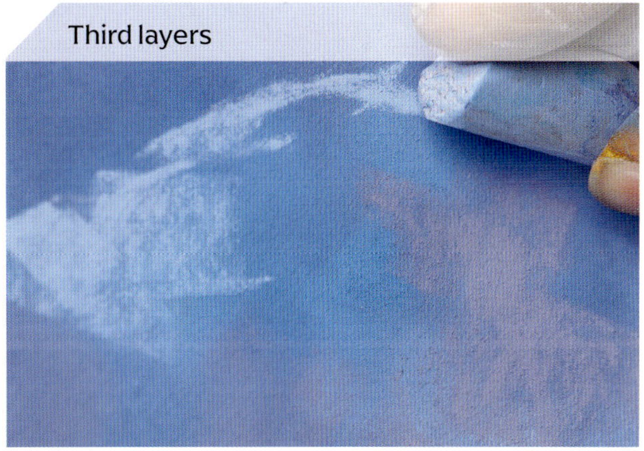

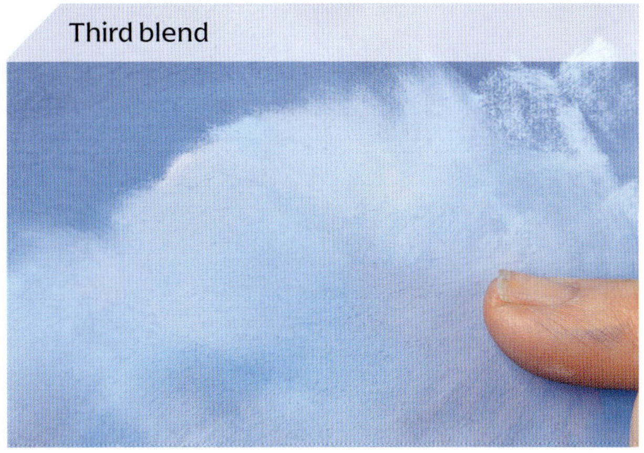

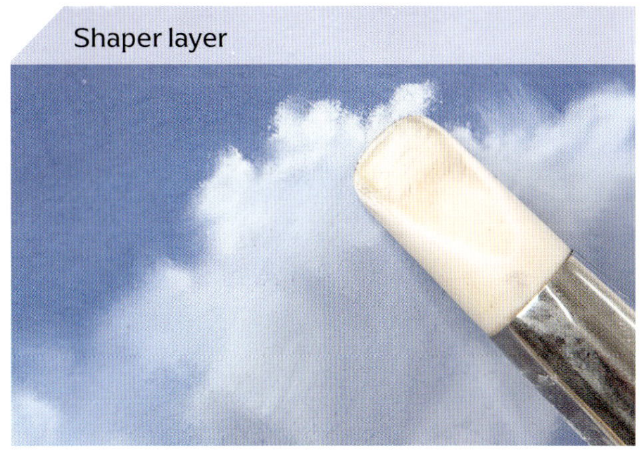

OTHER ESSENTIALS

With the key materials and techniques in hand, you're nearly ready to tackle the projects – but you'll need the following few extras, too.

Old bristle brush (A) Useful to dust off any errors or things I want to change in a piece, these should be firm and allow you to brush briskly and precisely over the surface to remove any layers and return an area back to the tooth. Although the paper will still look tinted, you can then work back over it.

Colour shaper tools (B) These tools make it possible to create sharp edges and subtle details. They look much like a brush but have a silicon tip in place of bristles. Available in a variety of shapes and sizes, colour shapers are vital for creating contrasting sharpness and definition. No matter how tiny your fingers are, they will always slightly blur what you are working on when you blend.

Carbon or pastel pencils (C) These can add textural detail to a piece. I recommend Wolff's carbon pencils because they combine the precision of graphite with the colour depth of charcoal, giving you a sharp yet dark mark. I recommend buying a set of four with a variety of softnesses, from B to 6B. There are many brands on pastel pencil on the market. I recommend buying a basic set of twelve from a well-known maker, as it can be handy to have when and if needed.

Framers' tape (D) I recommend taping all the way around your work. This secures it to the board and ensures that you don't catch the edge of the paper when applying pastel in sweeping gestures. Use framers' tape. It's more sticky than masking tape, but peels away better and can be left longer without leaving a residue around the edge of the work. Good quality framers' tape is PH-neutral and so is safe for archival use.

Board (E) I recommend work on a drawing board at a fairly steep slant so that you can see your work clearly without any distorted perspective. Secondly, working at an angle helps to ensure pastel dust will not gather too much on the surface. This isn't usually much of an issue as we are using high quality materials so there will only be a limited amount of dust to worry about.

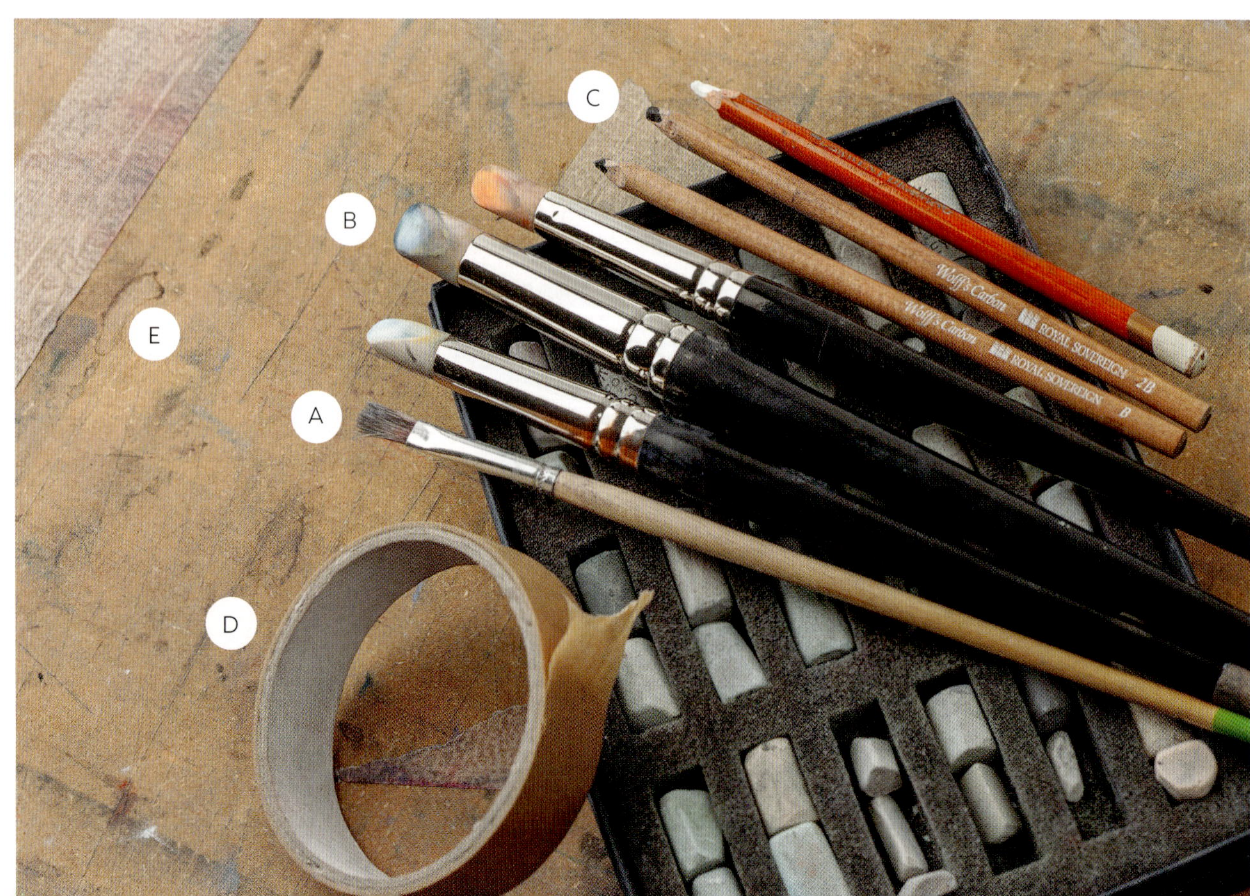

Choosing a colour shaper

I favour a brand of colour shaper tool made by Royal Sovereign; their colour shapers come in soft, medium and hard, which refers to how resistant the silicon tip is to pressure. The one I use most is a size 10, flat chisel and (most importantly) soft tip. When choosing a shaper:

- Pay for quality. Don't buy cheap multipack colour shapers from your local discount store. They'll be too hard or sharp-edged.

- A colour shaper is different from a blending stump, those strange paper-wrapped tools lurking, unused and grubby, at the bottom of every artist's tool box.

- Be sparing. Shaper work is best used sparingly and not across the entire art work. It can bring focus and key details to areas, but can make the piece feel too busy if used everywhere.

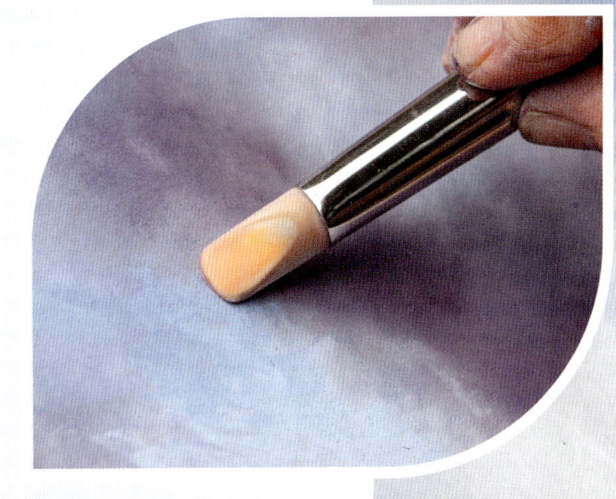

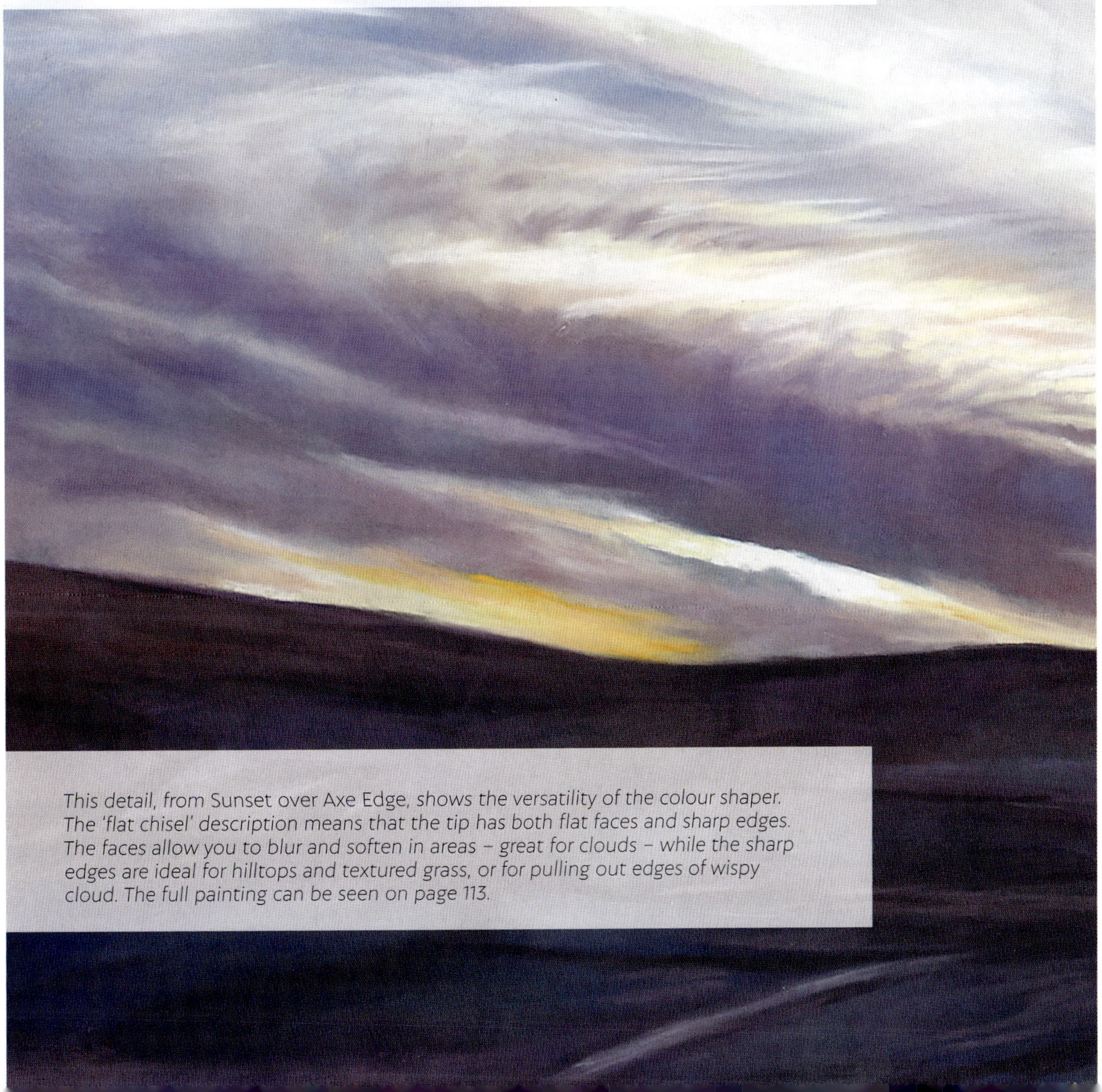

This detail, from Sunset over Axe Edge, shows the versatility of the colour shaper. The 'flat chisel' description means that the tip has both flat faces and sharp edges. The faces allow you to blur and soften in areas – great for clouds – while the sharp edges are ideal for hilltops and textured grass, or for pulling out edges of wispy cloud. The full painting can be seen on page 113.

Pastels and colour

NLIKE WET MEDIA LIKE PAINT, pastels cannot be mixed on a palette prior to being applied to the picture. Pastels are instead applied in layers and mixed directly on the paper, and combine to create different tints or hues either through blending or visually as layers interact (see 'All about pressure' on page 16).

Combining colours through layering will aid you in evoking movement and a more dynamic feel to your sky paintings. My rule of three, explained overleaf, will help you to develop this way of working with colour but it is useful, before we start, to refresh our understanding of basic colour theory.

COLOUR BASICS

Because colour theory has an immediate practical application in pastel work, here is a refresher in colour theory basics and related terms:

Hue The specific nature of a colour – the 'blueness' of a blue, for example, and what distinguishes a navy blue from a duck egg blue. Each pastel code refers to a specific colour, which often (but not always) suggests the hue. BV9, for example, is a blue-violet pastel.

Tones, tints and shades Colours of similar hue but differing in lightness are tones of that hue. Tints are lighter tones; shades are darker tones. The number in the Unison pastel codes will help you to identify nearby tones – BV8 is a lighter tint than BV9, while BV10 is a darker shade.

Warm and cool colours Red-tinged or yellow-tinged colours appear to come forward, or advance, in a picture. They create a vivid, energetic feel and are referred to as warm colours. Green-tinged or blue-tinged colours retreat in a picture and can create a calm mood. They are referred to as cool colours.

Complementary colours Colours that sit opposite each other on the colour wheel (see right): yellow and purple, for example. Complementary pairs always work well together, to create vibrant but balanced work.

Harmonious colours Colours close to each other on the wheel – such as red, orange and yellow – will also work well together.

Tertiary colours The varied colours created by mixing two-thirds of one primary colour (red, yellow or blue) with one-third of another primary colour; or mixing even amounts of a primary colour with a secondary (green, orange or purple).

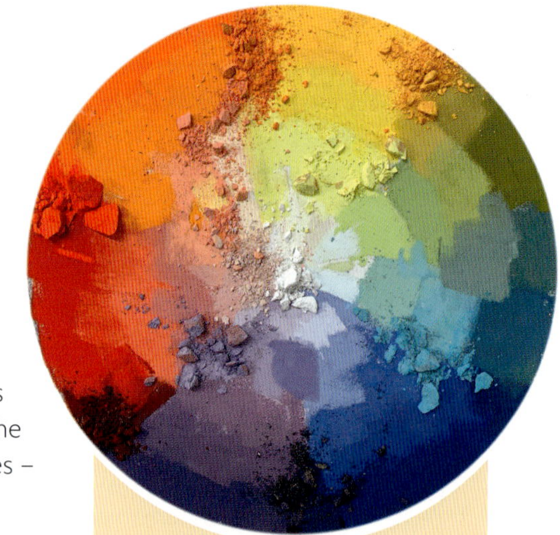

Colour wheel

A colour wheel, like that shown above, is always useful to have nearby as a reference or resource when creating art. You can find lots of examples of colour wheels online to look at – I recommend you find one with a variety of tints and shades, rather than just single colours around a wheel.

Choosing the right colours

This is an important skill that will develop with time and practice. It is important to build on your basic knowledge of the colour wheel and develop an understanding of how pastel colours interact with each other – what works and doesn't work. For example, this combination of complementary purples and yellows work very well together. This kind of knowledge will come with practice and experience.

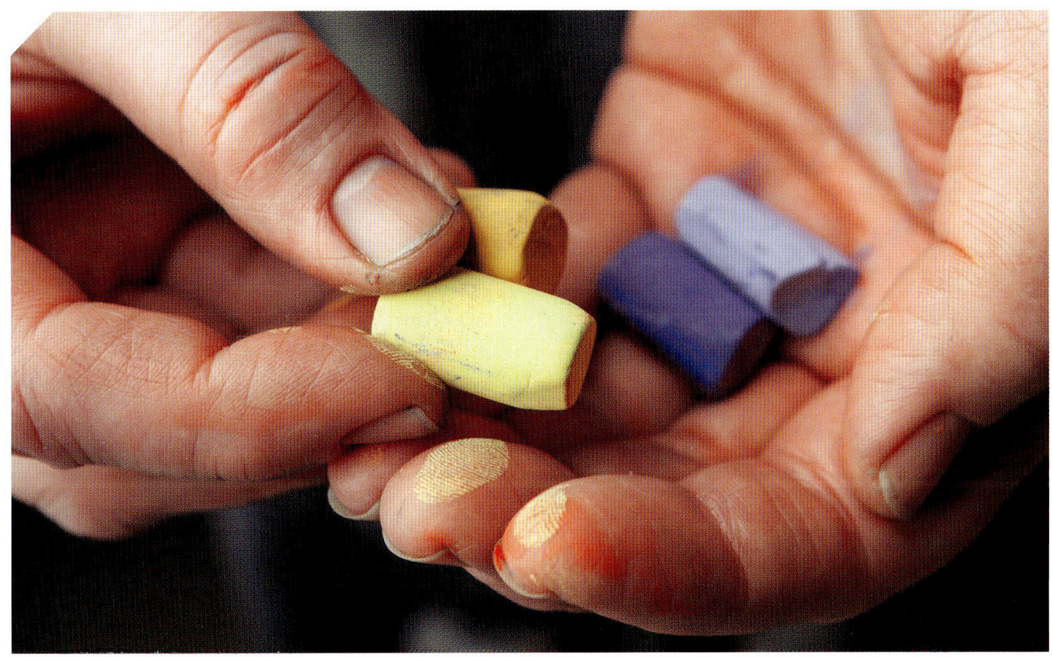

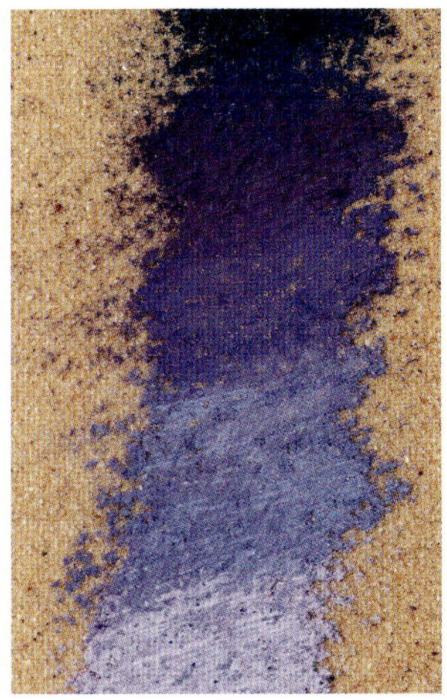
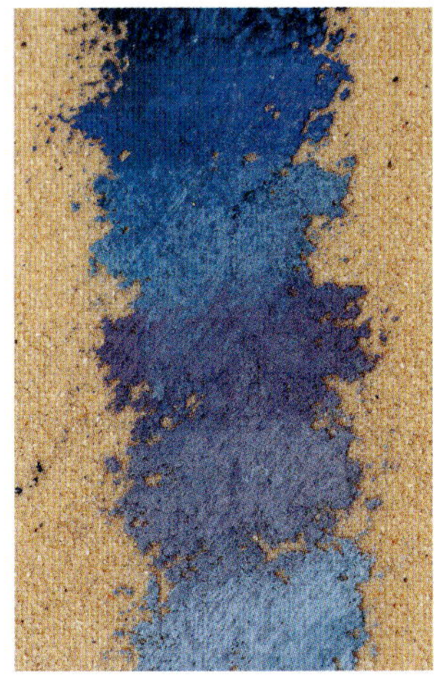

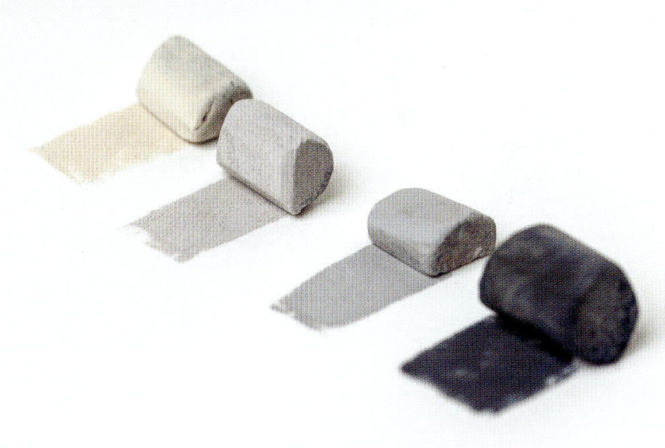

Hues and colour temperature

While both groups of pastel marks above are broadly blue in hue, the left-hand group are mostly warm purple-blue hues, while the right-hand group are mostly cool turquoise-blue hues.

Tones

It's easy to understand tones in black and white! Here's a range of grey-hued pastels, from the lightest tint on the left to the darkest shade on the right, showing the range of tone.

THE RULE OF THREE

While a cloud may appear one shade, as you look closer you will see subtle variations of tint and shade within its surface – and it is this that reflects what we would see in nature. Our task is not to find one pastel to match the exact shade of grey we see in our cloud, but instead to create the hue on the surface of the paper through a combination of three or four different pastels. This will create a richer, more subtle result.

For each area on which you are working, use a group of at least three pastel hues in slightly different tones. This is my 'rule of three', which you will be asked to select and apply throughout the projects later in the book.

We do this so we can produce an expansive and seemingly endless range of subtle tints and shades within each area – that same diverse sweep of colours that you can observe in the clouds themselves as they move across the sky.

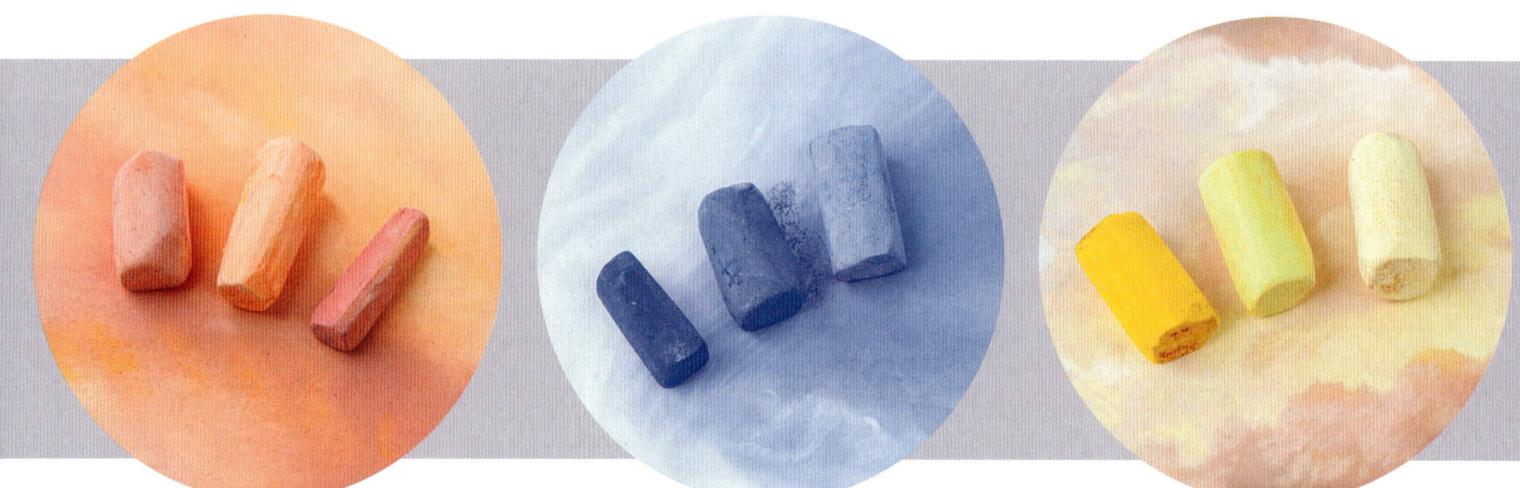

Choosing groups of three

To be effective, the three colours you choose need to be closely matched hues. The small differences between each will allow us to produce subtle tints and shades within each cloud or sky area.

If you are unsure which three will be right for an area, apply them together to some scrap paper and blend to see if they work.

Example sets of three

Above left: The pastels R6, R18 and R12 make up this triad and are ideal for building depth and richness in sunset clouds.

Above middle: BV11, BV10 and BV8 are wonderful for showing the subtle variations in hue that occur in a brilliant blue sky.

Above right: Y12, A10 and A12 are perfect for adding luminosity and strength to the brightest part of a sunset.

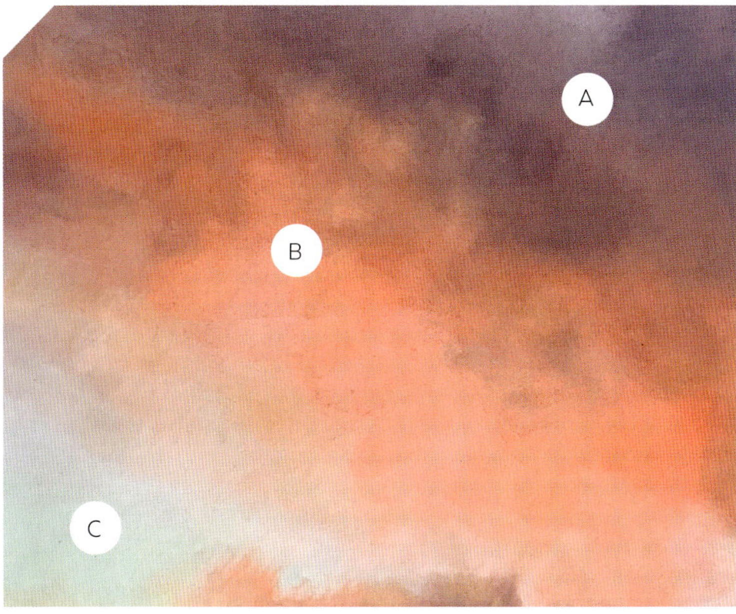

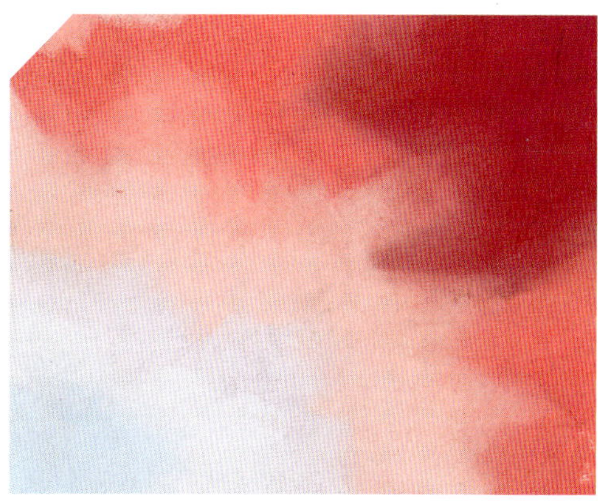

Avoid flat results

Using single colours creates flat, blank areas with no variety, as shown above.

Using groups of three pastels means we can build delicate harmonious variations that create three-dimensional depth, detail and movement within the clouds themselves.

The rule of three in action

Rather than create solid areas, by using the rule of three, we can build delicate variations that create three-dimensional depth, detail and movement within the clouds.

For example, in the darker section of this cloud, marked 'A', I used one set of three for that area: BV3, BV5 and A36. These three colours could all be described as dark in the context of the cloud as a whole, but they are three subtly differing hues – a dark lilac, a purple, and a warm dark. The same is true in other areas of the cloud, such as those marked 'B', where I used R6, R18 and R12 or 'C', where I used LT8, A10 and A12. The tones are all relative. In the example above left, none of the pastels used were objectively dark; just lighter or darker relative to one another within each group of three.

Note that you don't have to stop at three pastels – you can use more to add further variety and interest. In 'C', for example, I also used a touch of BV1.

The example above right was worked with just a single pastel in each of the light, medium and dark areas. You can see that the example above left shows much greater subtlety and more evocative 3D effects, which in turn creates more realistic clouds.

Layering and the rule of three

Using at least three tones in each area creates interest – as shown in this pre-blended example. Can you identify the three different hues I've used in each area?

It's the repeated layering and blending of those three pastels in a particular areas that creates the depth and richness.

As always, the 'three Ps' – pastels, paper and pressure – are crucial to success.

CHOOSING A PALETTE

Colour theory underpins how I build colour in my work. When selecting colours for a piece, I start by choosing a palette that is within a harmonious range – that is, selecting from across roughly a quarter of the colour wheel. Using different tones of three or four harmonious colours will enable you to create a richer and more intense depth and breadth of colour within your work.

I add colours of various tints and shades within this range, some lighter and some darker. But the crucial point is that because they are harmonious, when I do my first and most energetic blend, I won't create a ghastly colour by accident – like an unwanted green in a sunset.

Next, I add neutral colours, like greys and browns to my colour combination – although I need to bear in mind the underlying base of these colours. For example, green- or blue-tinted grey shades. Or red-tinted browns.

After the first blend, I expand my palette and work towards adding complementary colours and further depth of tints and shades.

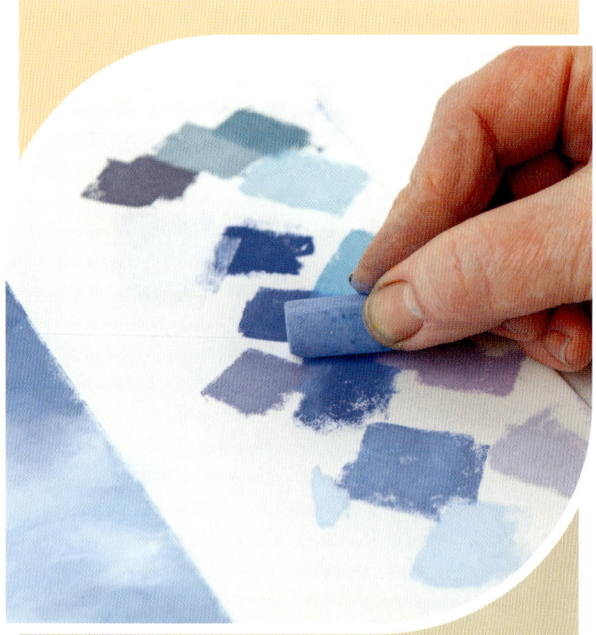

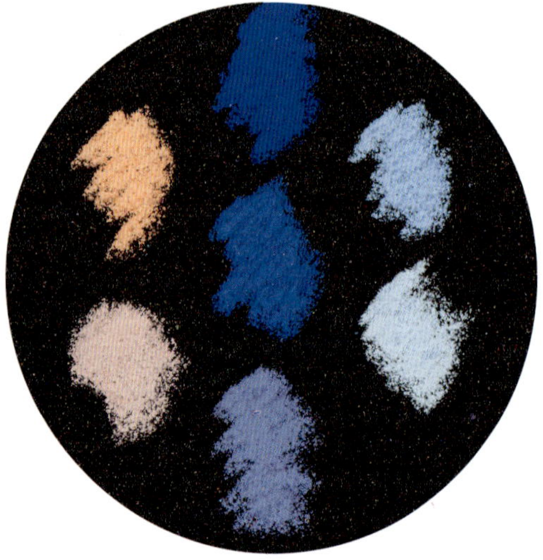

Testing colours

It's key to know how a colour is going to appear alongside others on your paintings, or you could introduce a clashing, discordant hue.

I use masking tape to mark out an area on the paper to the right of my painting. Here, I can apply small touches to test out colours before I add them to the painting, ensuring everything works in harmony.

It is also useful for making sure you're got just the right tone. As you have removed the labels, it's sometimes hard to distinguish similar tones from one another.

You can, of course, test on a scrap of paper, or keep close reference on which pastels you're using, but this method is both quick and convenient, and means you don't have to turn away while you're in the flow.

Starting and expanding your palette

The three closely related blues in the centre are an example of a core group of colours (chosen with the rule of three in mind) when you are selecting a palette for a picture with lots of blue sky. They are all closely related and will work well for the empty sky areas. However, you need to expand this palette and add more colours for clouds. The two additions on the right are lighter tints within the blue quadrant of a colour wheel, which are harmonious, and so these can be added. Those on the left, however, have a distinctly orange hue and therefore clash with the core palette, creating brown when mixed.

These sorts of combination should be avoided at the initial stage. You would need to select colours with a more purple hue to ensure you remained within harmonious reach of blue.

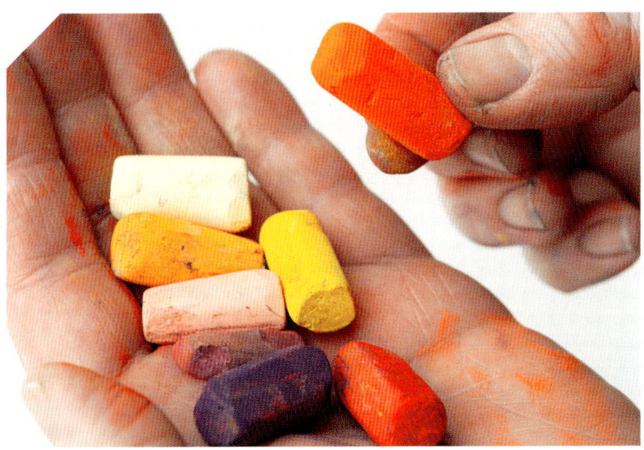

A basic sunset palette

The majority of these colours are drawn from roughly a quarter of the colour wheel: around the reds and purples, in various tints and shades.

To this I have added a harmonious orange and a complementary yellow (opposite a warm purple, not a cool blue purple) to give me a good starting point for a sunset.

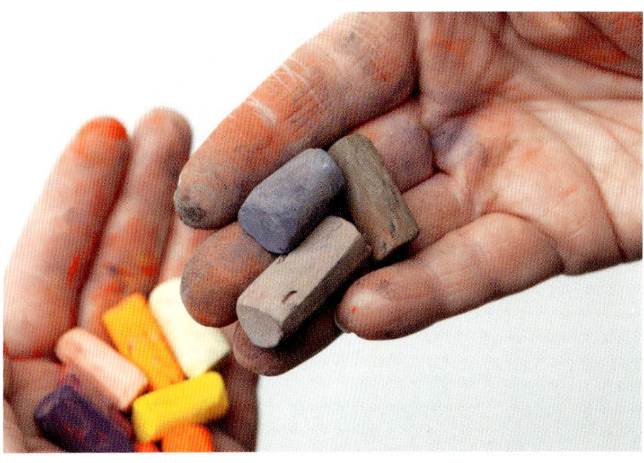

Expanding the palette

The neutral hues I'm adding to this palette are all warm, red-tinged browns and greys. This ensures that the palette as a whole is harmonious, even when adding the landscape.

Detail from Summer Sunset over Ladybower

To capture the dramatic sunset in this piece, I have used colours that range from strong orange into dark blue. This means organizing your palette into two distinct sections – one for the warm orange colours used in the lower part of the sky and one for the cool dark colours used towards the top. I selected warm brown shades for the landscape areas, and some bridging colours (see overleaf) to allow me to move from one area to the other – in this case a strong pink shade and purples.

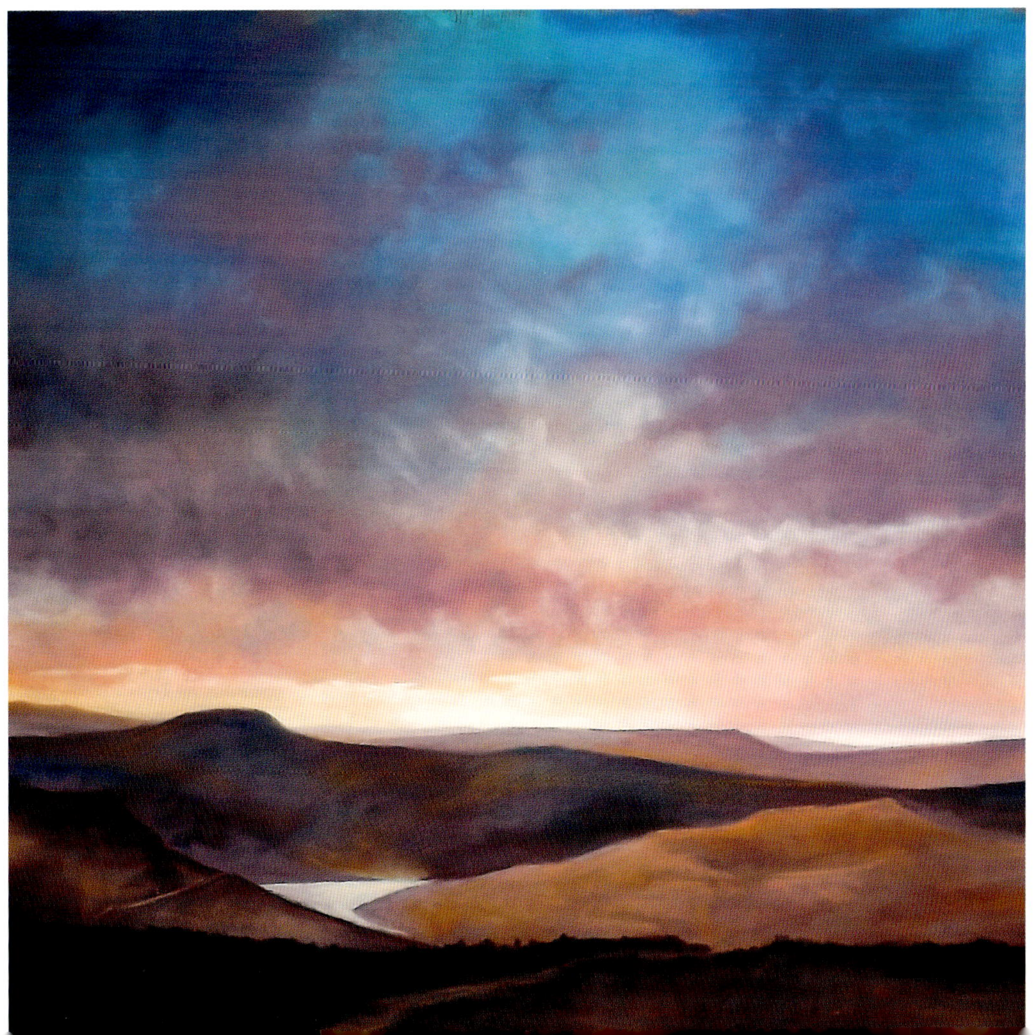

BRIDGING COLOURS

As part of the layering process, we need to mix pastels on the surface, but there are times when you need an intermediary colour that will form a bridge between two different areas that can't otherwise come together, because the colours aren't harmonious – which means they'll mix into a muddy, unpleasant brown, grey or green.

For example, blue-grey and orange mix to make a nasty shade of brown (see below left). When working from an orange sunset into a grey-blue cloud, you will therefore need a bridging colour to sit between them. In this case a pale pink or a pale lilac will work well. Either of these colours will mix with both the blue/grey and the orange, and keep the two apart.

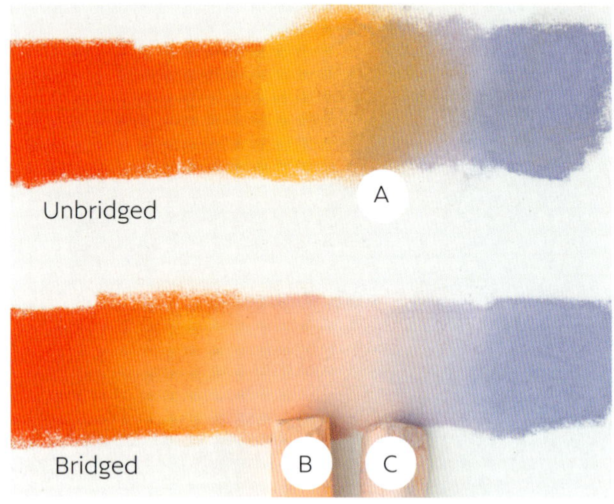

Here, I have blended red through from blue-violet to orange. In the unbridged example at the top, a muddy area (A) appears between the blue and orange as these colours mix and form an unpleasant brown colour.

At the bottom, you can see the how the neutral bridging colours (B and C) provide a buffer, allowing the adjacent colours to blend cleanly into each other, creating a harmonious 'bridge' between the two primaries.

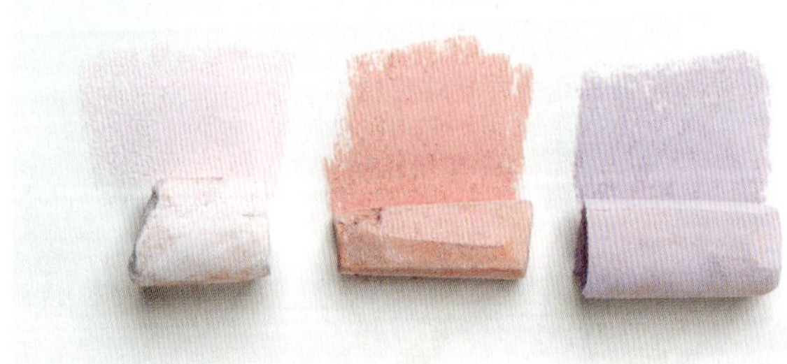

Example bridging colours
Subtle tertiary colours, like these three pastels – LT5, R18 and A4 – tend to be the best bridging colours, as they allow for subtle transitions between primary or secondary hues. The specific bridging colours you need to use depend on the overall palette of your artwork.

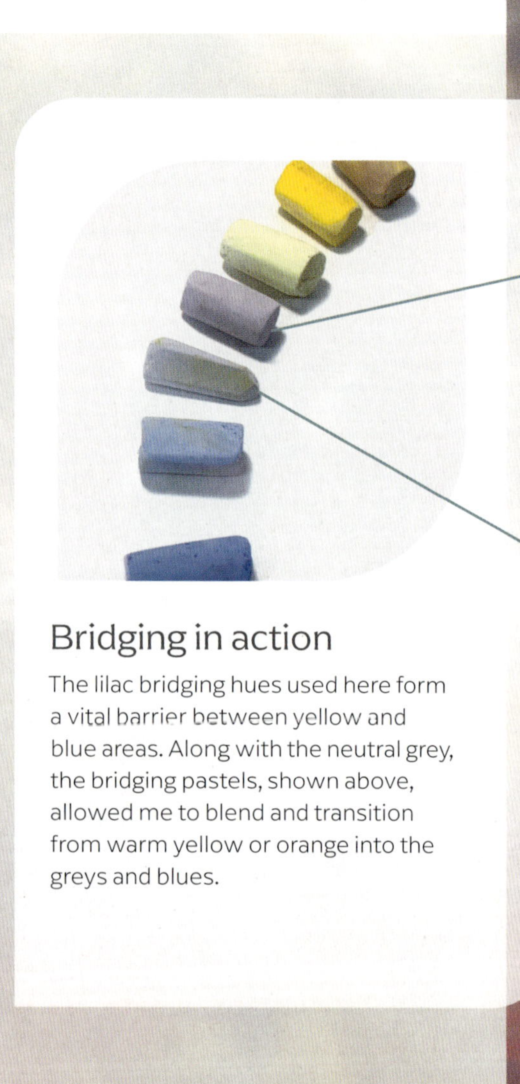

Bridging in action

The lilac bridging hues used here form a vital barrier between yellow and blue areas. Along with the neutral grey, the bridging pastels, shown above, allowed me to blend and transition from warm yellow or orange into the greys and blues.

Autumn Light
45 x 45cm (17¾ x 17¾in)

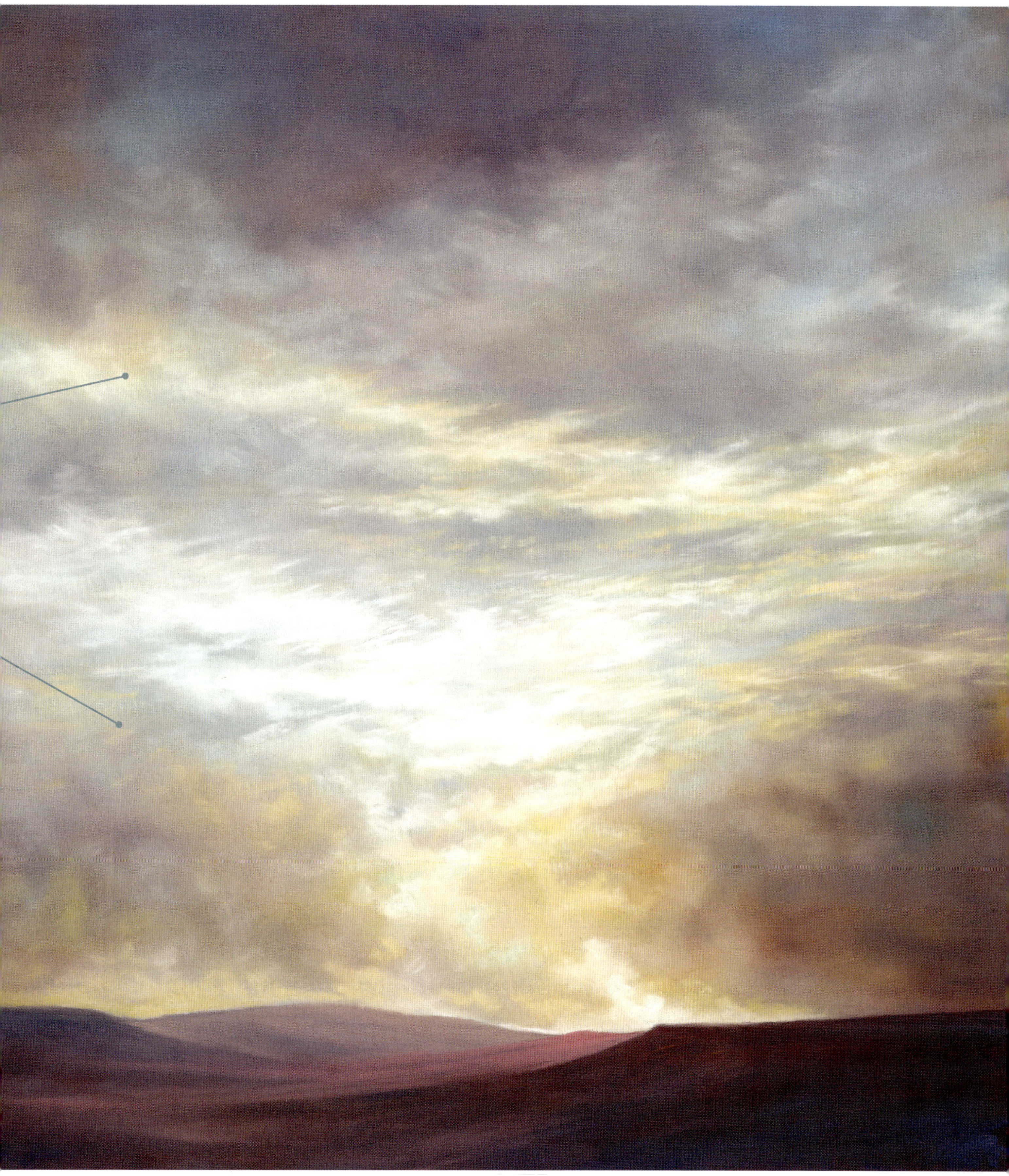

Painting skies

T O RECREATE DRAMATIC SKYSCAPES IN pastel, we bring together a number of different elements. Skies are transient and change quickly, so quick sketches and photographs are useful to record shapes, colours and light. The resulting artwork, however, is not a simple copy of these photographs. Memory and experience of the sky is combined with the reference to create an edited, focused piece that captures the mood as well as the components.

While you cannot draw on your memory of the particular skies that I use for the projects, you will likely have seen other similar skies or have taken your own photographs of comparable clouds. Think back to these skies as you work.

Prepared paper and test strip

The area for the painting has been marked out, and I've also used masking tape to reserve a space on the right for testing colours.

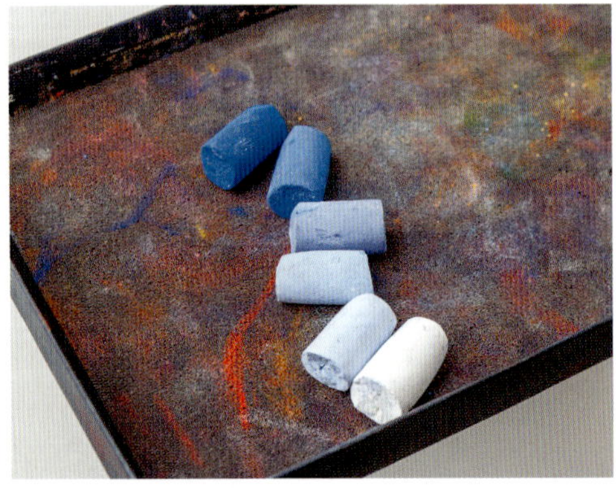

Organized colour palette

Keep the pastels you need for each stage in tone order; from dark to light.

BEFORE YOU BEGIN

The projects progress from the simplest, which lets you learn my methods with a more limited palette, through to more complex paintings. You are, of course, welcome to approach them in any order you choose.

Each project is broken into stages, so you can see how the repeated layers (see pages 24–25) build up and are refined into the finished artwork. There's no need to replicate each stage exactly: just make sure that you have covered the important points at each stage before moving on.

There are some key points that come up in every tutorial so I have outlined them here rather than repeat them each time.

Basic materials The pastels you need are listed with each project. You will also need a sheet of paper at least 40 x 40cm (15¾ x 15¾in) – I recommend Clairefontaine Pastelmat, in white – and a colour shaper. Useful but non-essential extras are grey, brown and ochre pastel pencils; and carbon pencils (see page 26) for finishing details.

Prepare your paper Tape your paper all the way around (using framer tape ideally). Add an additional strip of tape down one side for a colour swatch and checking area.

Organize your palette At the start of each stage, I recommend laying out and grouping all the colours you might use. This will help you to visualize which colours go together and link in a harmonious way – and later you can add bridging colours or complementary colours.

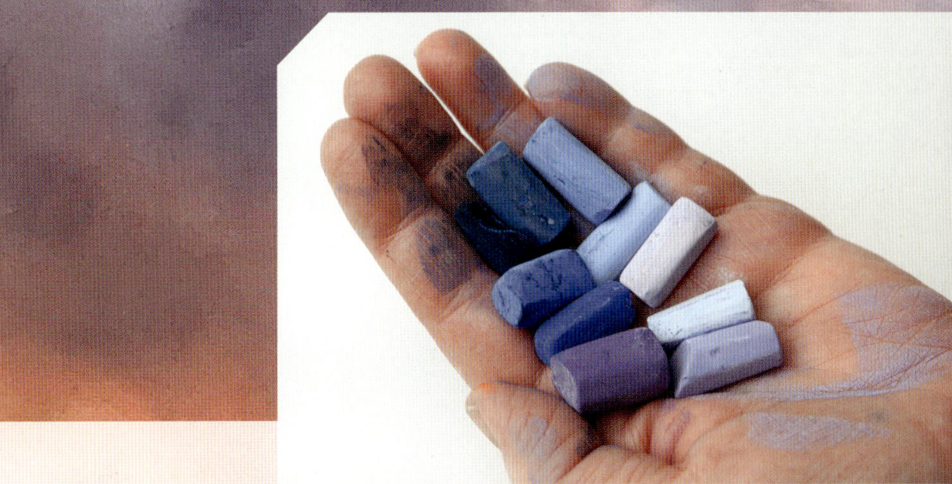

Pastel-painting advice

Artistic interpretation Parts that work in a photograph don't necessarily translate well into a painting. Edit and select: leave elements out, adjust composition and colour balance, and enhance (or create) a distinct focal point. We are not beholden to the photograph and should make artistic choices to develop the expressive and beautiful results we want.

Go straight in In more complex skies, a few initial marks in pastel pencil can help to position key areas – but that is all. Drawing out fine details is a wasted exercise as the sweeping layers of pastel quickly cover any drawing. If you feel more comfortable doing more work to plan the layout, feel free, but don't rely on it: it will vanish quickly.

Blending Whichever blending stage you are at, pay attention to keeping within a colour area when blending. Don't move into another area unless you are making a conscious effort to mingle two areas together. This helps to keep colours from becoming muddied.

Keep it clean Clean your fingers between blending different areas of colour – it's so important. A quick wipe on your apron will suffice. You don't need to scrub them clean, just remove surface dust so colour doesn't transfer to where you don't want it.

Handling the shaper tool The shaper is best used to add subtle or sharp details to your focal areas, not when you are blending large areas. Don't press hard, let the weight of the shaper itself drift over the surface. Be erratic with your mark-making and how you handle it. Avoid regular and repeated up and down movements along things like cloud edges.

Use your fingertips Applying small amounts of colour directly works well for adding an extra touch of strong colour where needed.

Pressure Above all, remember the importance of pressure, which controls both how much pastel you apply to the surface, and the colour you create using your fingers or a shaper tool.

Help the flow
I find it helpful to hold all the colours I'm using in a stage in my hand – it's much quicker than dipping in and out of a box, and allows for quicker comparisons, too.

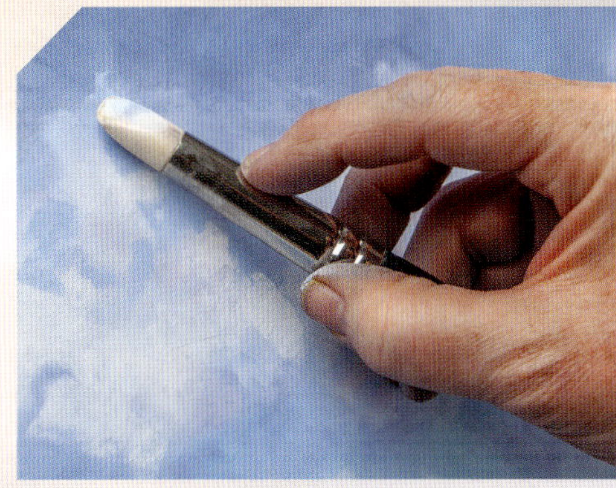

Holding the shaper
When working on clouds, don't point it like a pen; hold it beneath your palm so its parallel to the surface.

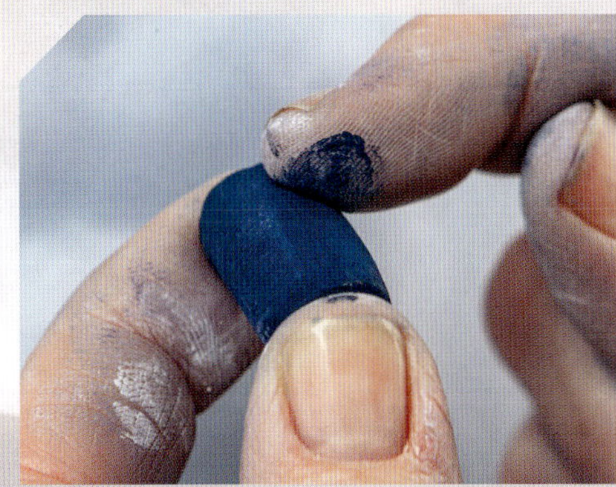

Applying pastel to your fingers
Just rub your finger on the pastel to 'load it' with colour.

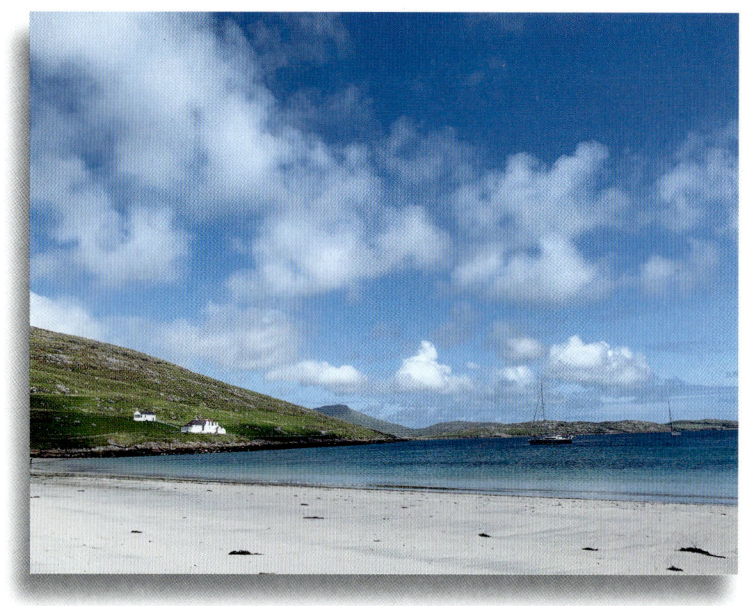

Blue Sky, White Clouds

This first tutorial will teach you to create the kind of clouds and sky we might see on a pleasant summer day – white clouds bubbling across the blue, with the wind creating wispy threads amongst the crisp cumulus edges. We will use a limited, harmonious palette so that you can learn the layering technique without having to cope with complicated colour mixing. We only apply white at the very end, for the brightest, cleanest highlights.

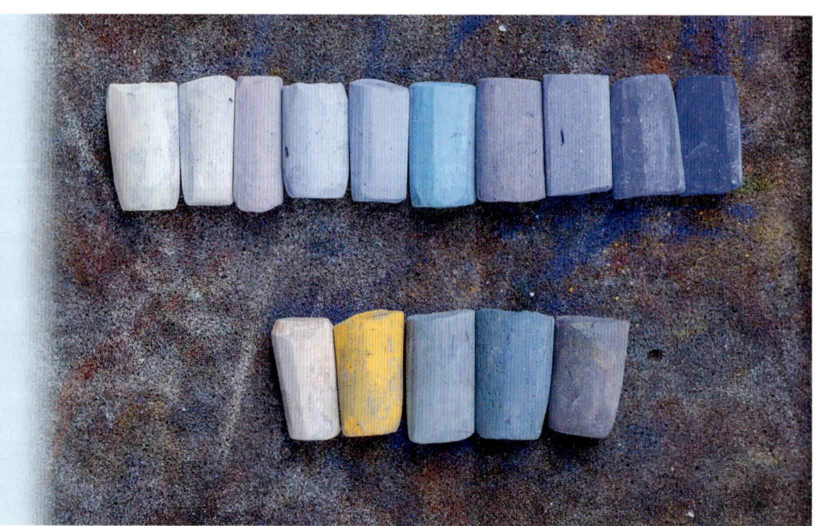

SELECT YOUR PALETTE

We need a good quality soft white, plus three to four shades each of grey and blue; plus a lilac. I chose:

Sky LT1, LT12, BV3, BV4, BV8, BV9, BV10, BV12, BG10

Land BV16, A52, G33, Y16, LT5

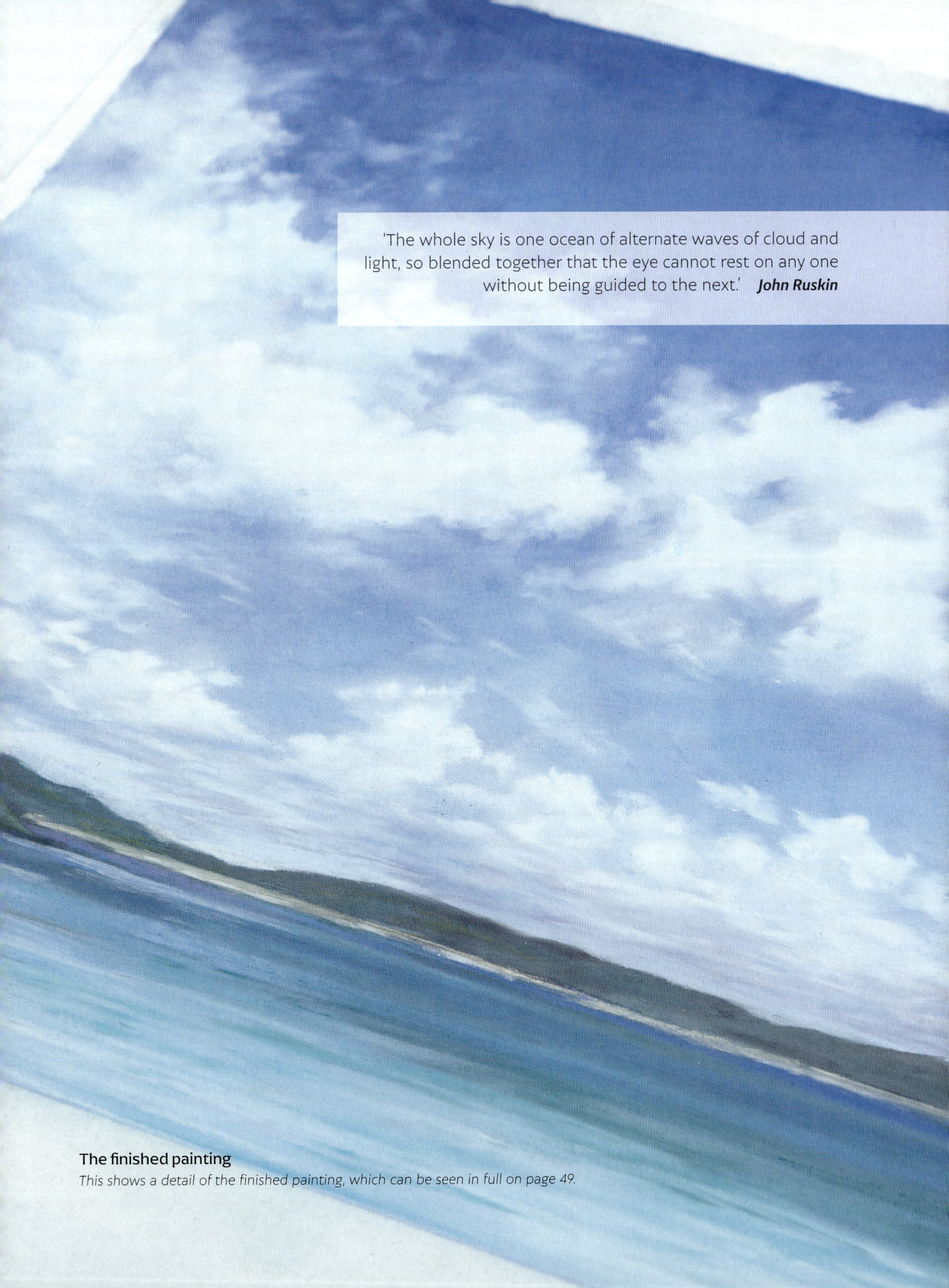

The finished painting
This shows a detail of the finished painting, which can be seen in full on page 49.

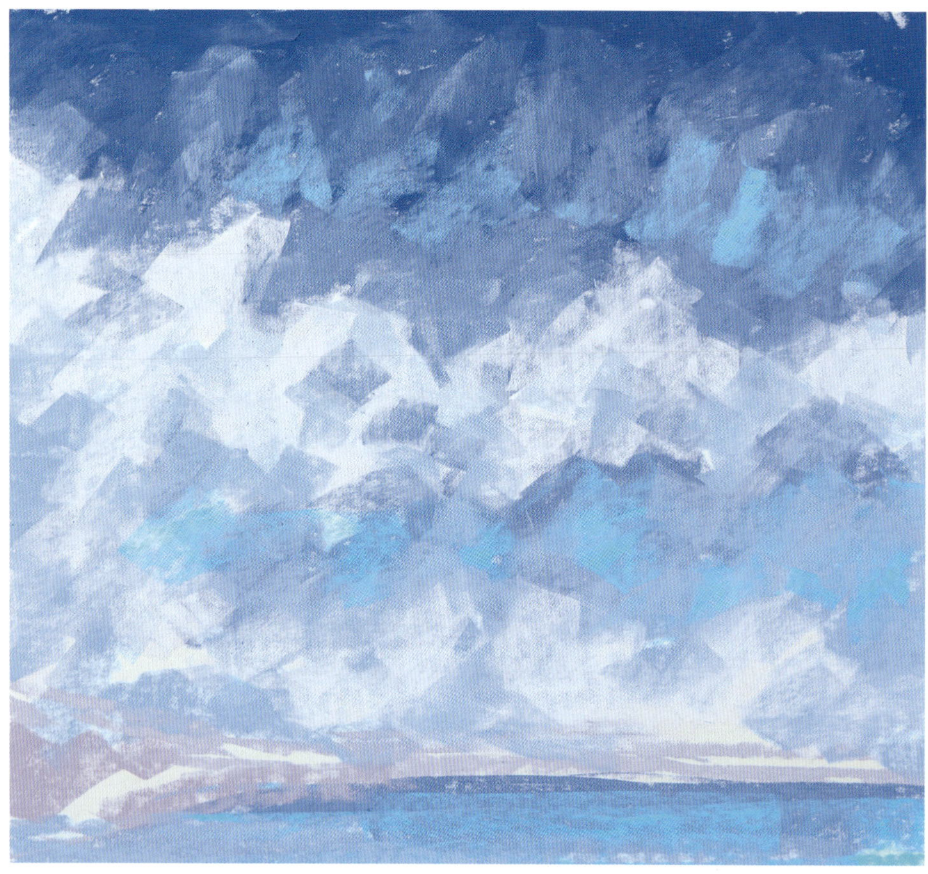

The painting at the end of stage 1 – initial marks.

STAGE 1

Mark-making

- For the pale area of cloud, use three harmonious pale greys (no white) in broad sweeping strokes. Echo the direction of the clouds. Overlap colours as you go. Use slightly darker shades towards the lower part of the clouds. Add a tint of lilac towards the bottom.

- Add darker blue at the top of the blue sky area down towards a mid blue, then paler blue in the lower areas.

- Add a sweep of basic dark tones for the sea to the horizon. Blend this with horizontal movements.

- Blend in the sky. Use circular movements and good pressure. Keep fingers clean between areas.

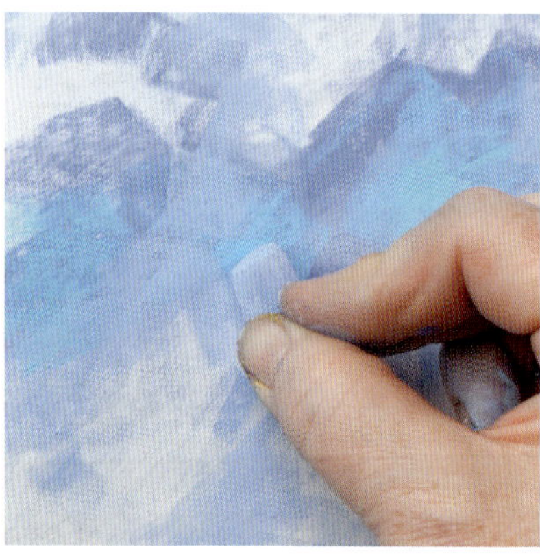

Flat technique

All of the marks at this stage are made using the flat technique on page 18.

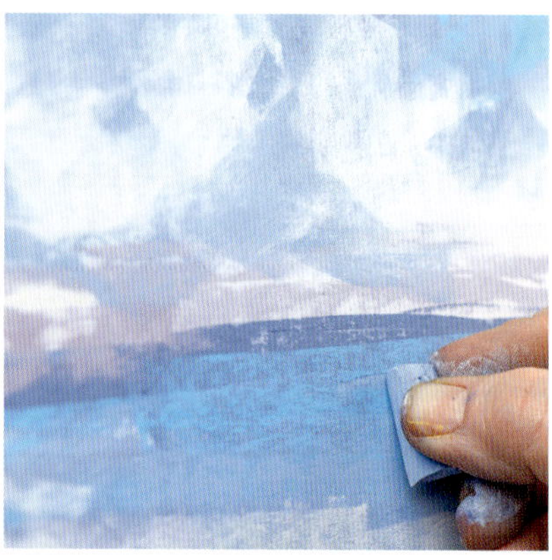

Sea

The colours used in the sea are the same as those in the sky – the difference is simply that the sea is painted with horizontal strokes, rather than the variety of choppy marks used in the sky.

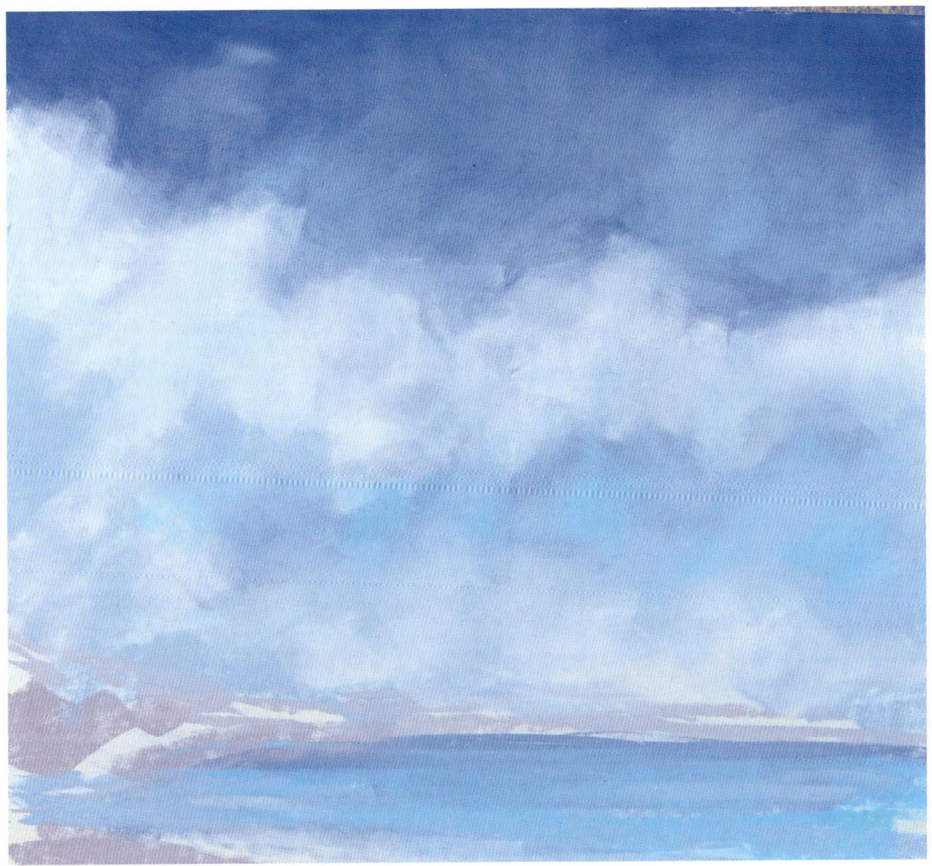

The painting at the end of stage 1 – initial blend.

Blending

- To avoid the sky becoming one big blur, it's important to blend broad areas independently first, then blend the transitional areas. Start with the paler areas, and then progressively darker areas. There's no need to clean your hands thoroughly between each area, but do wipe off the excess on your apron.

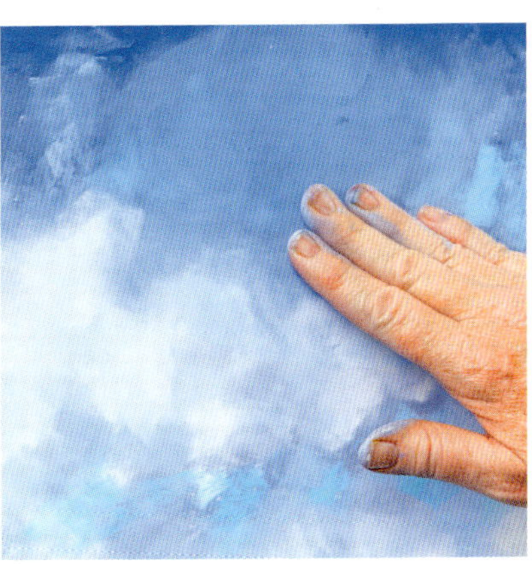

Blending sky

When blending in the sky, use three fingers and a circular movement, starting at the centre of each area and working outwards.

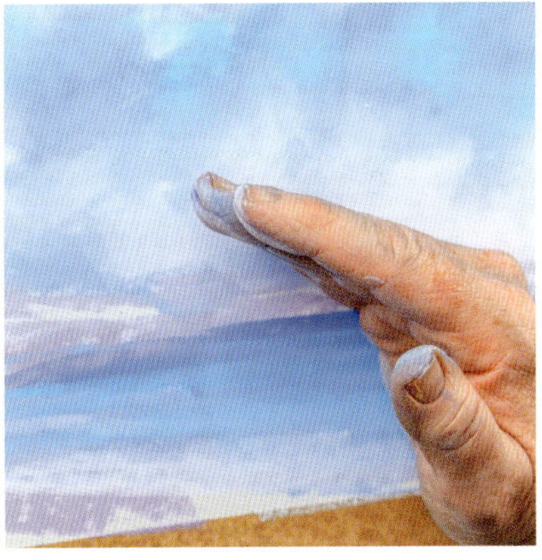

Blending sea

When blending the sea, rather than using your fingers, you can use the edge of your palm below your little finger, and horizontal movements. Don't blend the sky into the sea.

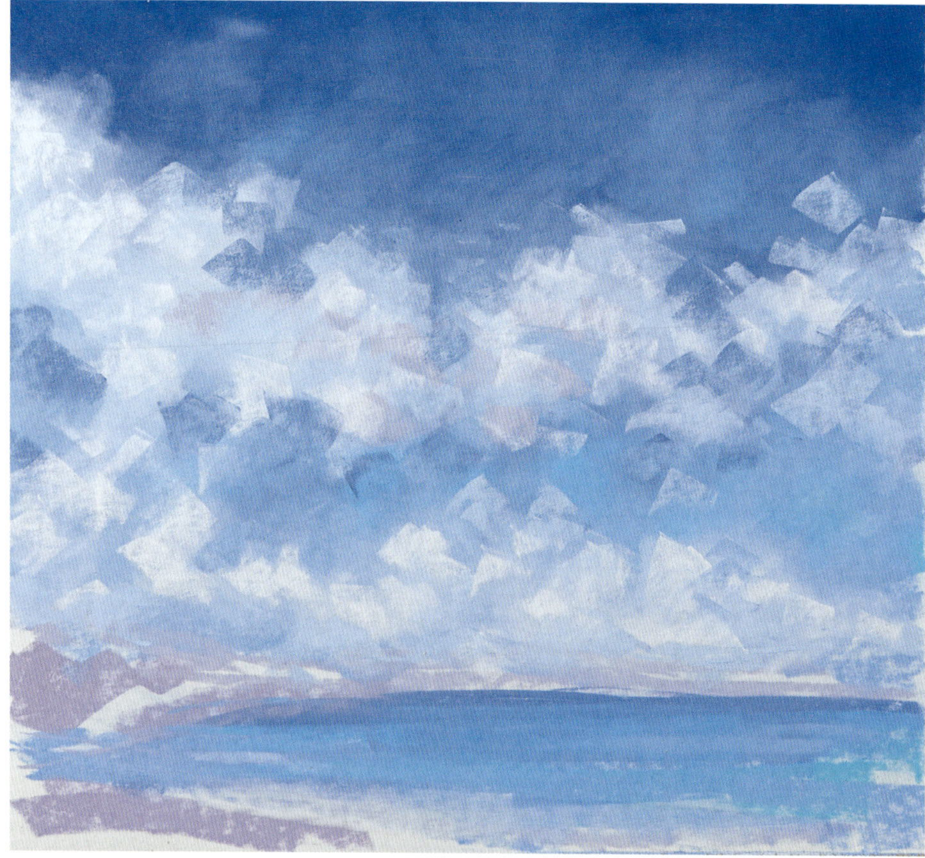

The painting at the end of stage 2 – blocky marks.

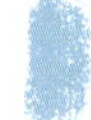 # STAGE 2

Mark-making

- Add blocky marks to the cloud to build more dark areas, then blend them lightly. Do the same for the lighter areas. Vary the direction of these marks, thinking about direction in the clouds.

- Repeat as needed across all the clouds. Aim to create an interesting mottled surface. Apply some artistic licence – you're not copying the photograph, but interpreting it.

Next layers

Remember the rule of three (see page 30) when adding the next layer to each area – use a light, mid and dark tone for each area you are working on. Apply the pastel with the block technique on page 19, and use this stage to cut into the broad areas; reshaping the clouds areas.

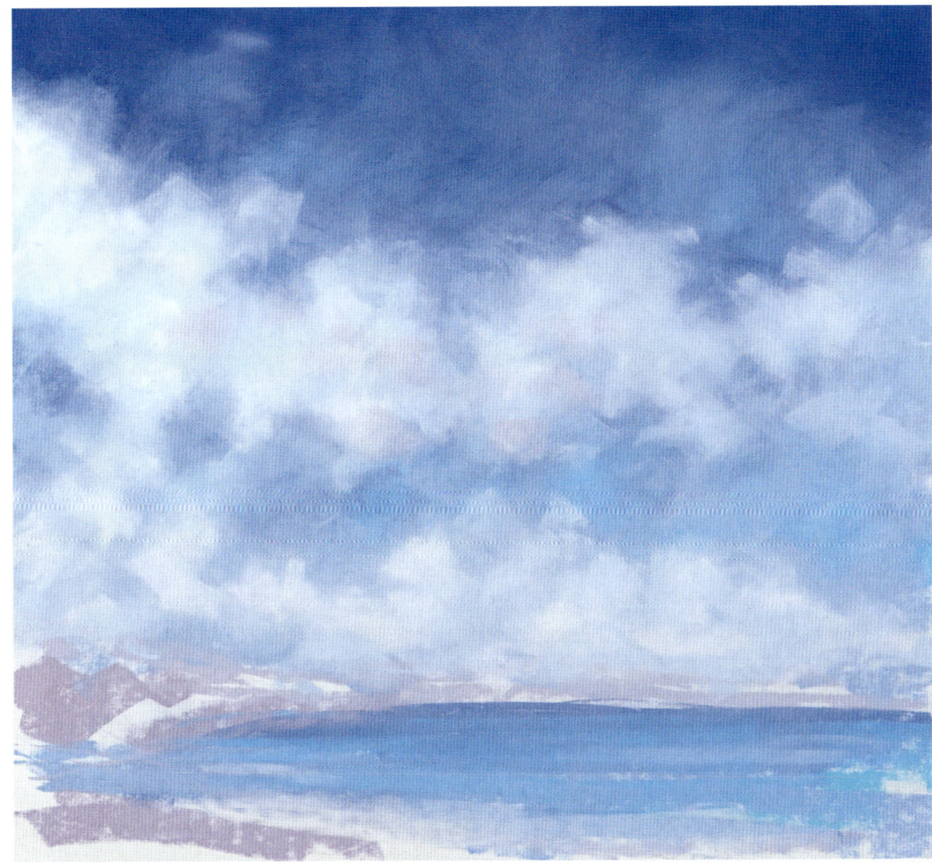

The painting at the end of stage 2 – blended.

Blending

- When blending, use one or two fingers with a gentle pressure. We want to retain a little impression of blockiness: overworking things will flatten the colour and reduce the dynamism.

- Build up multiple mark-making layers with the block technique, but keep your pressure light: don't add so much pastel that it will interfere when you are applying detail on top later.

- Push the pale pastel into the blue of the sky a little, and layer and repeat multiple times if necessary. We're aiming to create a diffuse, interesting, mottled cloud surface to build upon.

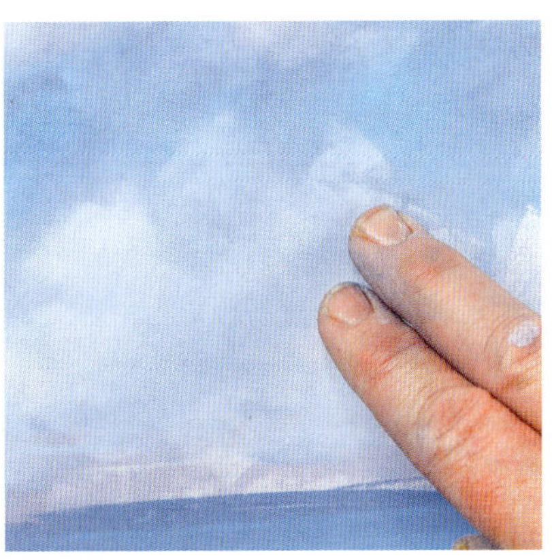

Gentle blending
Smaller movements ensure more control than earlier

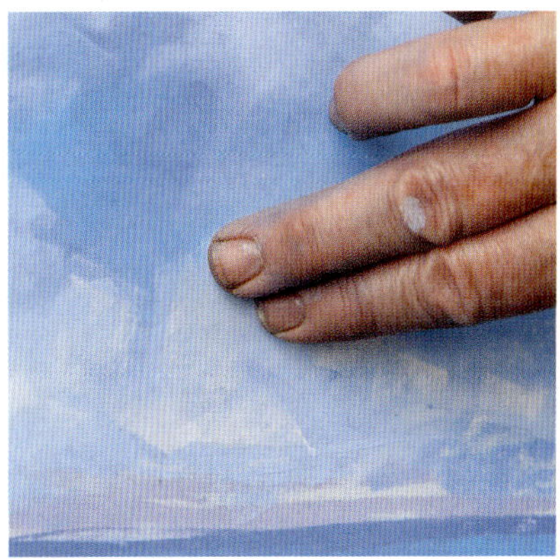

Pushing
Directional blending allows you to control the shape; simply by pushing the pigment on the surface around.

Stay aware of the colours – avoid spreading the darker tones too far into the paler areas.

STAGE 3

Unlike the previous stages, where we applied and blended across the whole painting, here we work more gradually, in more discrete areas. This allows you to refine and judge the work as you progress.

Don't focus on particular details at this stage; just try to develop dynamic cloud shapes that flow. Use darker shades of blue at the top of the sky, and lighter at the bottom.

- With pale pastels chosen using the rule of three, tip and roll using the angles and edges to create movement in the paler cloud area.

- Blend with energy but not too much pressure – and be careful not to push the light too far in to the blue.

- Now focus on the edges where the cloud meets the blue. Allow these two areas to intermingle slightly.

- Next, add paler areas to parts of the solid cloud area to build up the sense of a three-dimensional effect.

- Use the rule of three: pale grey, pale lilac and a pale blue, to add movement to clouds lower down. Work over all the clouds, adding dabs of colour – some lighter, some darker – to each area to develop the three-dimensional feel.

- Using your fingers will make it hard to retain the shapes of the clouds. Switch to a colour shaper for this stage.

- Blend lightly and use sweeping movement with the shaper. Use fingers to soften areas where it feels too 'busy'.

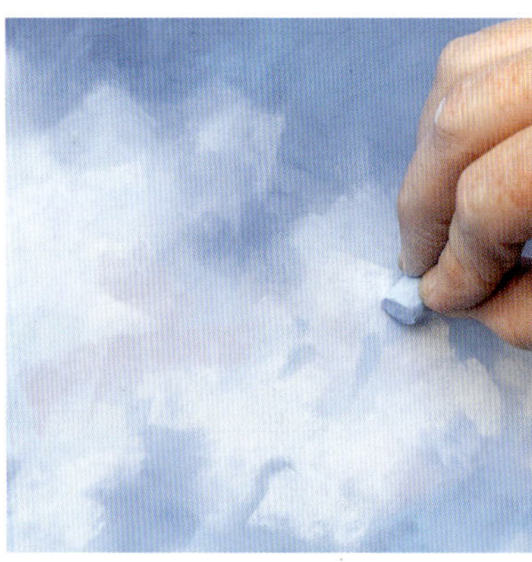

Variety of marks is key

Twist, rock and roll: by using the pastels at different angles, you will be applying more pastel to the surface, building up the depth of colour.

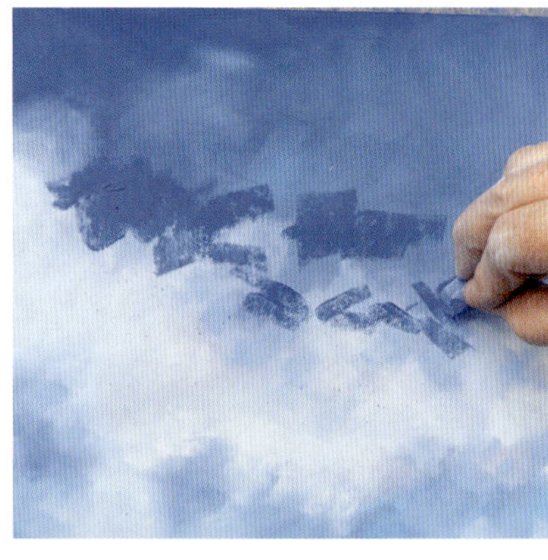

Re-establish tone

Adding darker blues to the edge of the cloud where it meets the sky will sharpen the cloud shapes in places.

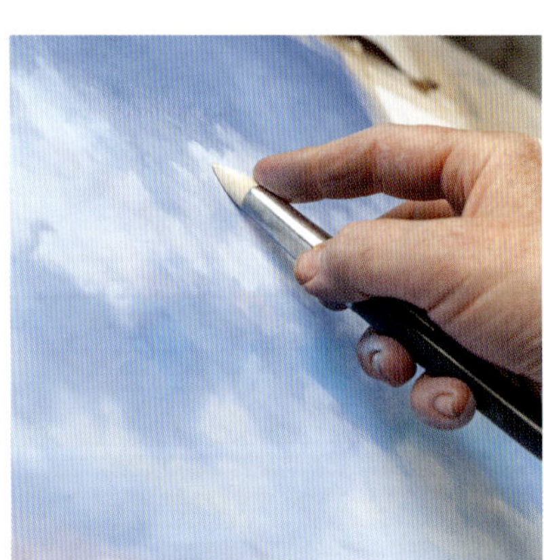

Holding the shaper

The whole flat face of the shaper should be in full contact with the surface, so hold it as shown.

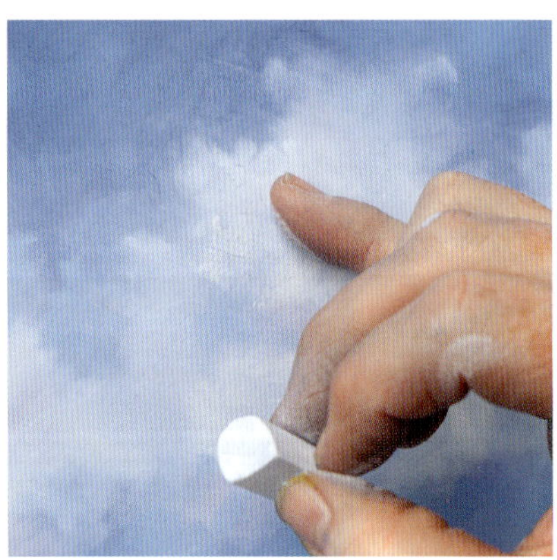

Refining

Consider the marks as you go. Even during the blending stage you can add additional touches of pastel, then blend them in.

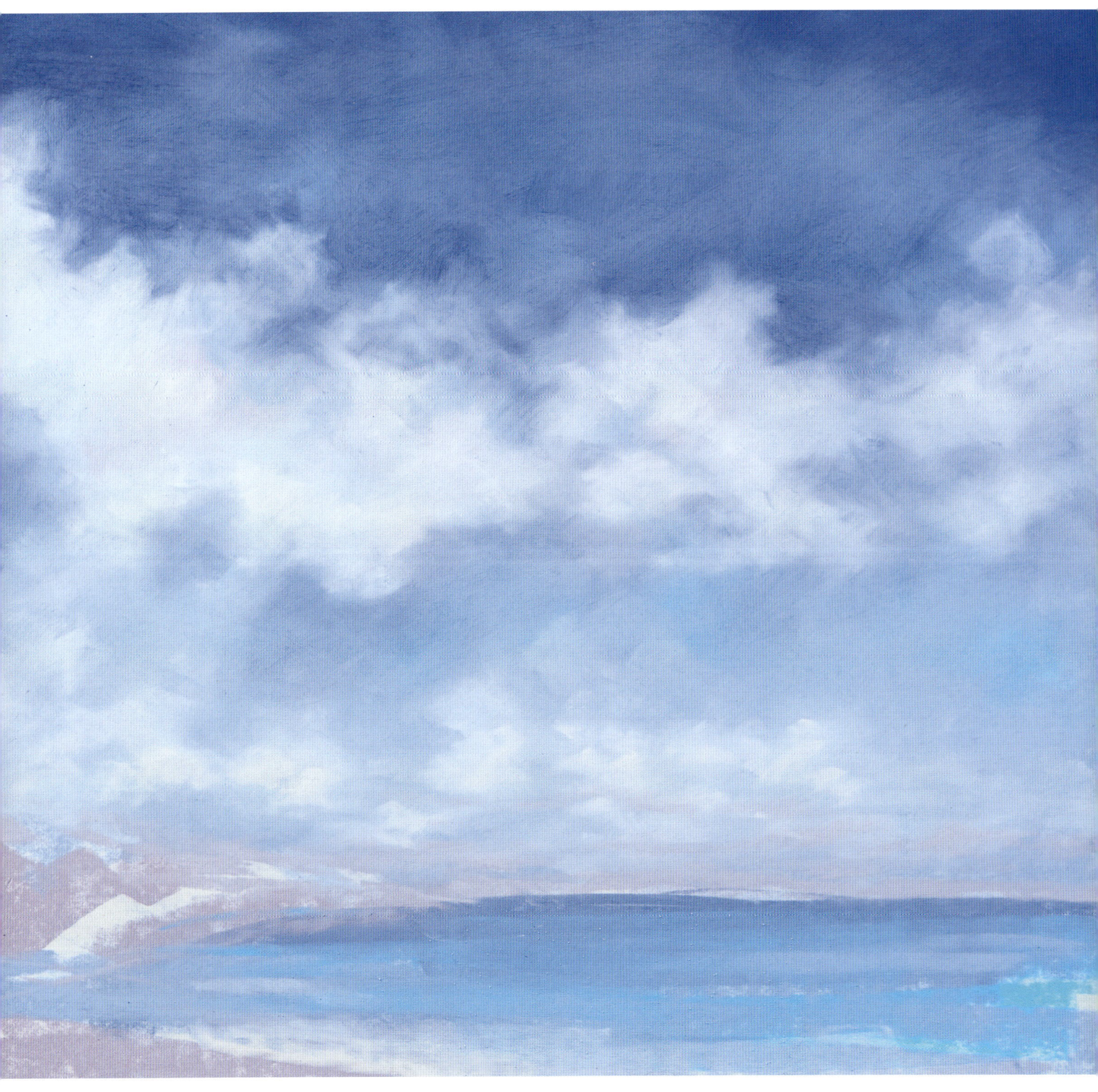

The painting at the end of stage 3.

This stage concentrates on picking out the focal areas, in order to lead the eye through the composition. It also refines the sea and the land.

- The first focal area is slightly above and to the right of the centre (A); the second slightly below and to the left (B); and the third is on the right-hand side of the sea (C). This leads the eye through the composition.

- Assess and re-assess the focal areas against the whole painting as you work, to ensure that you are considering the composition as a whole.

- Be disciplined: it's easy to begin working too far out from the focal areas, which then dilutes the impact. Keep the work most refined in the focal areas, and leave other parts less developed.

- Add white pastel to the edges of the cloud using the tip to apply dots, dashes, swirls. Be careful to be erratic: to avoid repeated patterns: apply the marks semi-randomly to create a naturalistic edge of the surface.

- Use a shaper tool to move along the edges of the clouds carefully; lightly controlling how they push up against the blue.

- The shaper is perfect for softening in detailed marks without losing them completely – as shown at (D), for example. Nevertheless, remember to keep the blending minimal. The moment you work over the white with a shaper tool, it lowers the brilliance of the white slightly.

- Use the shaper to pull threads of white out in the blue where needed. Push the light into the blue and pull the blue into the light as needed.

- Use the side and also different angles of the pastel to get different marks. Soften the marks with the shaper but don't over-work it. Use the shaper tool to push the pale edges clouds back over the blue sky.

- Move on to the sea and land after you have refined the sky. Use the same colours in the sea as the sky, building up the tone through layering; and use harmonious but differing colours for the land.

- Add darker tints to the lower part of the clouds, particularly along the horizon.

Reserve detail for focal cloud areas

Use finer mark-making techniques and the brightest tints to apply delicate dots and dashes using the tip. Use minimal, if any, blending to ensure you keep some sharper marks.

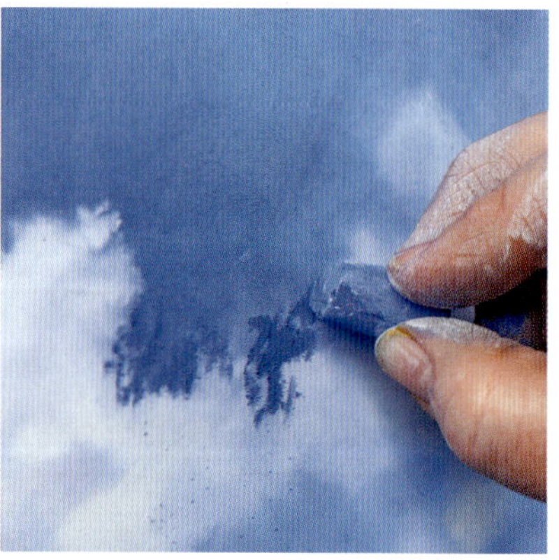

Control the contrast

High contrasts in tone draw the eye, so to help push the white forward in the focal areas, you can cut into the light cloud areas with darker-toned blues. Push this towards the light edges, then re-apply white on top to add detail.

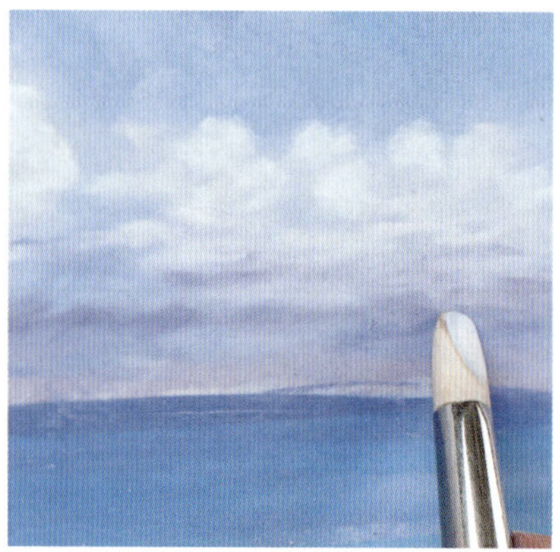

Blending the sky at the horizon

Use the shaper with broader, near-horizontal marks to blend the sky near the horizon. This will help to create a sense of distance.

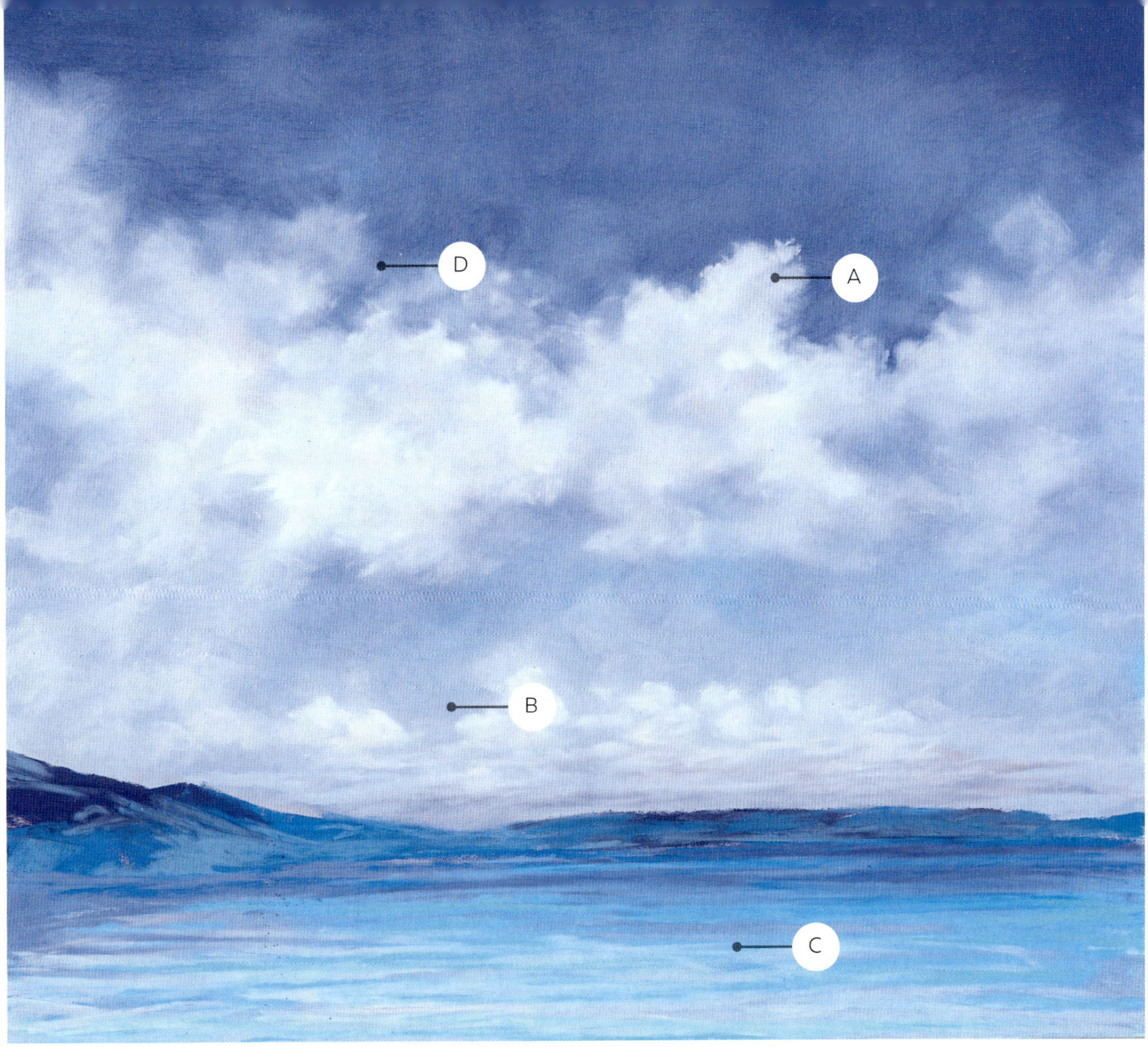

The painting at the end of stage 4.

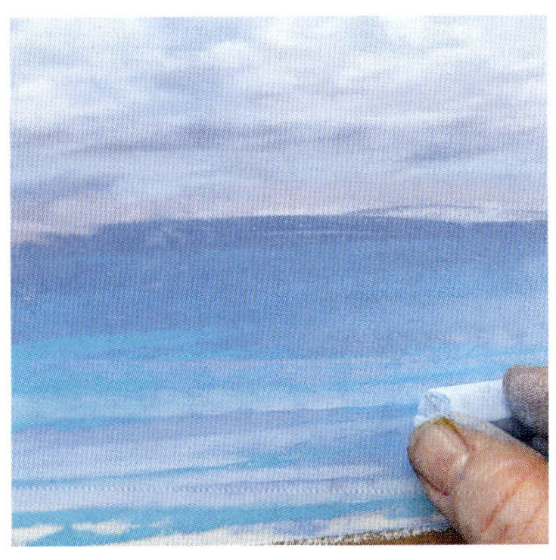

Sea

The sea is darkest at the horizon, where it meets the sky, and gets gradually lighter in tone as it approaches the viewer. Use slicing marks to apply the colours.

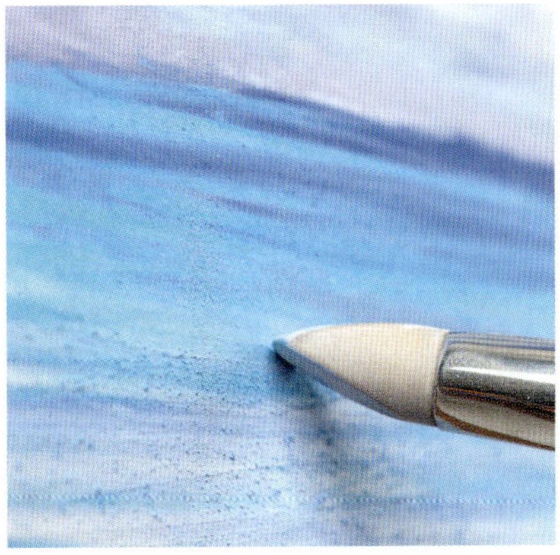

Blending the sea at the horizon

Use the side of your hand to blend the bulk of the sea with broad horizontal strokes, then switch to the shaper for more control in the critical area near the horizon.

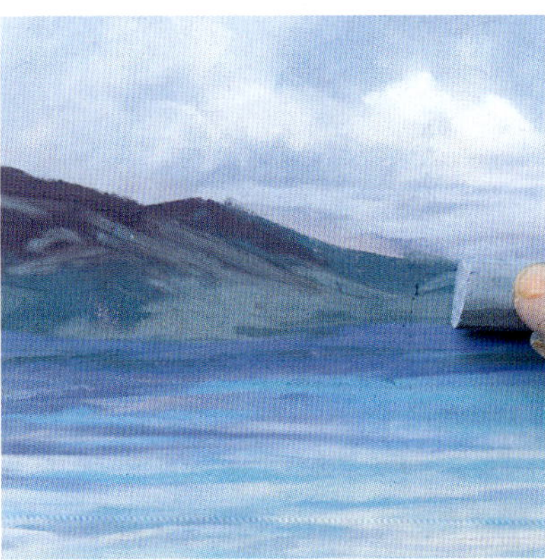

Land mass

Apply the pastel boldly, taking it up to and then over the sky. Use smaller marks to hint at the topography and detail, but don't overdo things.

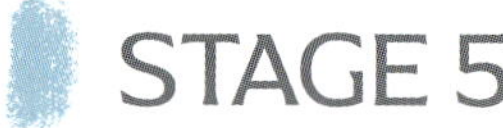

STAGE 5

This stage brings the work to completion. Be careful not to over-work things –
you might like to read page 111 for some more thoughts on how to decide a work
is finished.

- Reuse your pale shades to work them in along and away from the edge of the
  clouds to create wispy edges (see page 112 for tips on this) and add to the cloud
  shapes. Blend with the shaper and use it carefully at the edges to push the light
  along to create the effect.

- Add more white to the central area and blend down towards the horizon.

- Aim to create a zigzag of lighter clouds in central areas to draw in the viewer.

- When you are happy with the sky, think about the land and the horizon. Add
  layers of land colours – ochre and purple/lilac/grey/brown. Blend lightly in
  sweeping gestures from side to side, leaving a bit of texture. Use some paler
  shades towards the foreground, applying the pastel with choppy block marks
  and use minimal blending.

- Get a dark pastel and firmly draw in your horizon, blending down into the land.
  Use your shaper to control the edge and blend.

- Use the slice and nibble techniques to make marks in the water. Use the tip of
  the shaper to slice and blend these.

- Finally, take a look at the whole picture. Re-touch white to the clouds and light
  in the sea in the focal areas (see page 47). Add unifying marks or colours, then
  soften areas away from the focal areas using your finger.

Unifying marks

*Small additional marks, made across all the clouds with the
nibbling technique (see page 21), will help to add a sense of
diagonal movement to the sky, and a feeling of the clouds
moving and changing.*

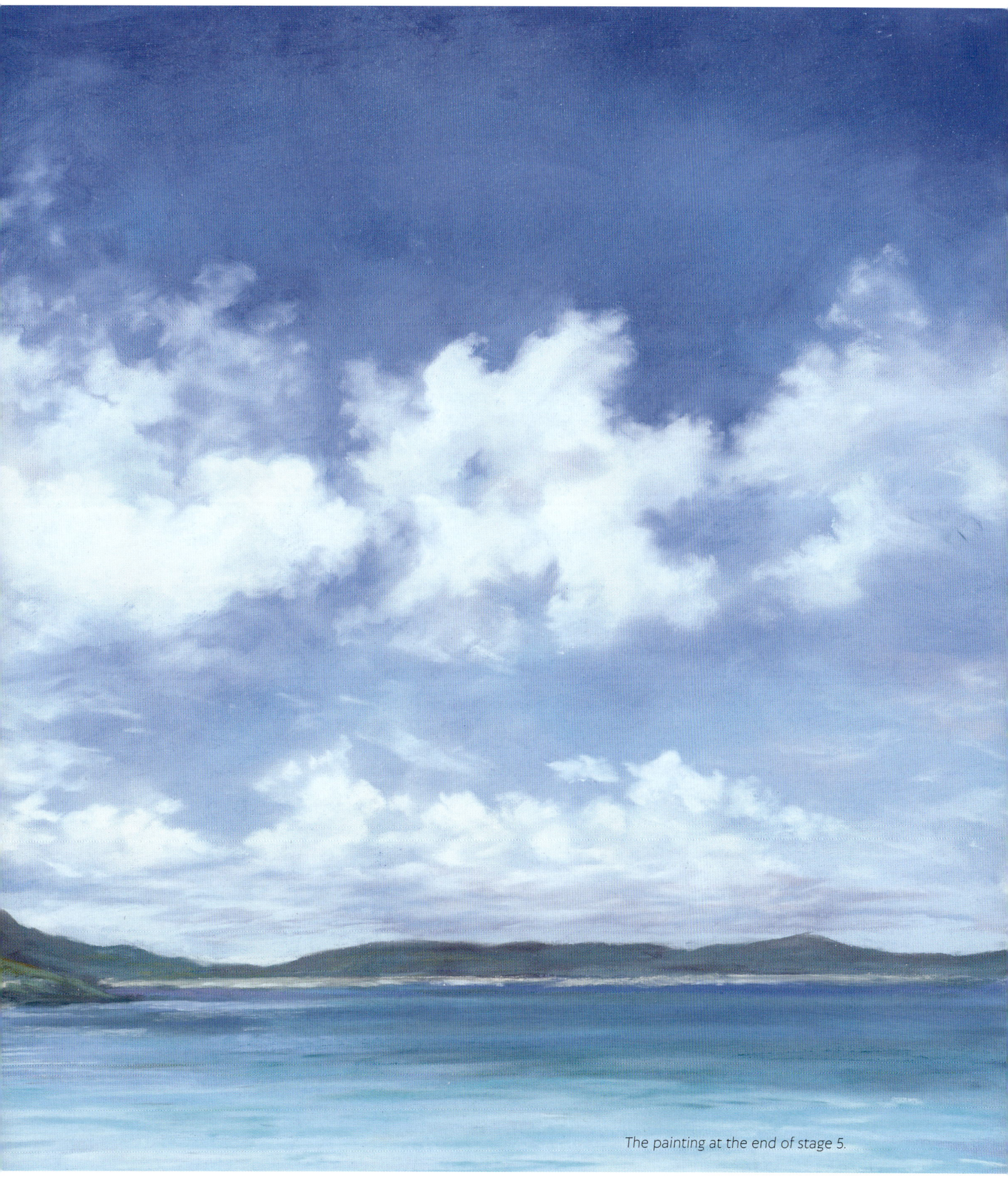

The painting at the end of stage 5.

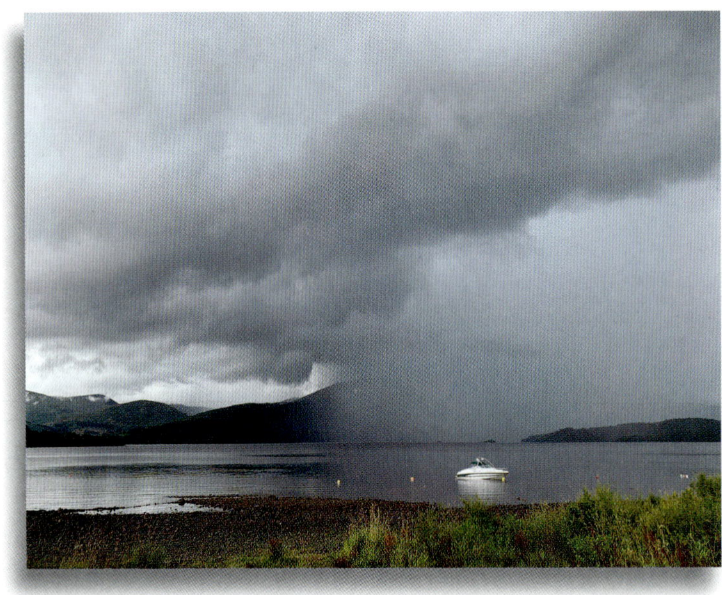

Cloudburst

This tutorial will take you through how to create a cloudburst of rain sweeping down past the mountains and along the distant shore of Loch Lomond in Scotland. The techniques you learn here will allow you to explore all kinds of rain effects, from subtle distant showers through to more dramatic weather. We will investigate how grey clouds can be exciting and evocative, as well as exploring movement in clouds through mark-making and layers.

This is a harder piece to balance compositionally because of the dominant cloudburst. Using the right amount of light and detail in the mountain horizons, as well as texture in the bottom left of the loch shore will help.

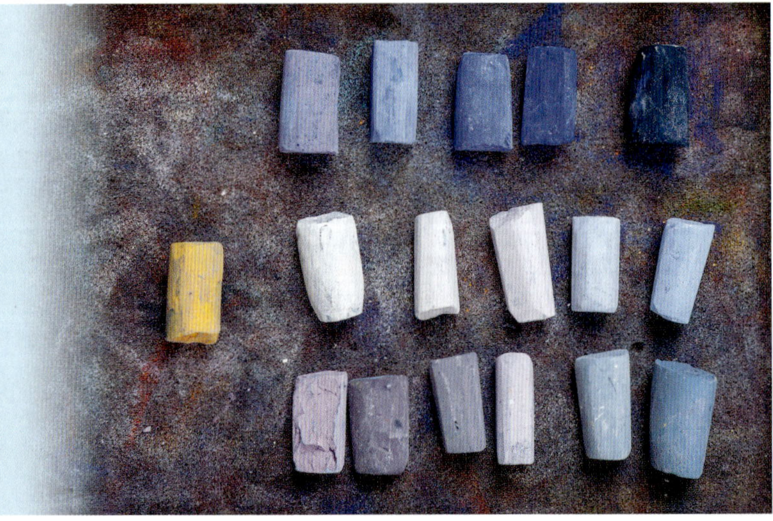

SELECT YOUR PALETTE

A range of greys from very pale through to very dark. Test them by making colour swatches to check they are not green- or brown-tinted greys. We need blue- or purple-tinted greys. I chose:

Greys LT12, BV8, BV9, BV10, BV12, BV3, BV4, BV5, BV16, G33, A52, D23

Other colours LT1, Y16

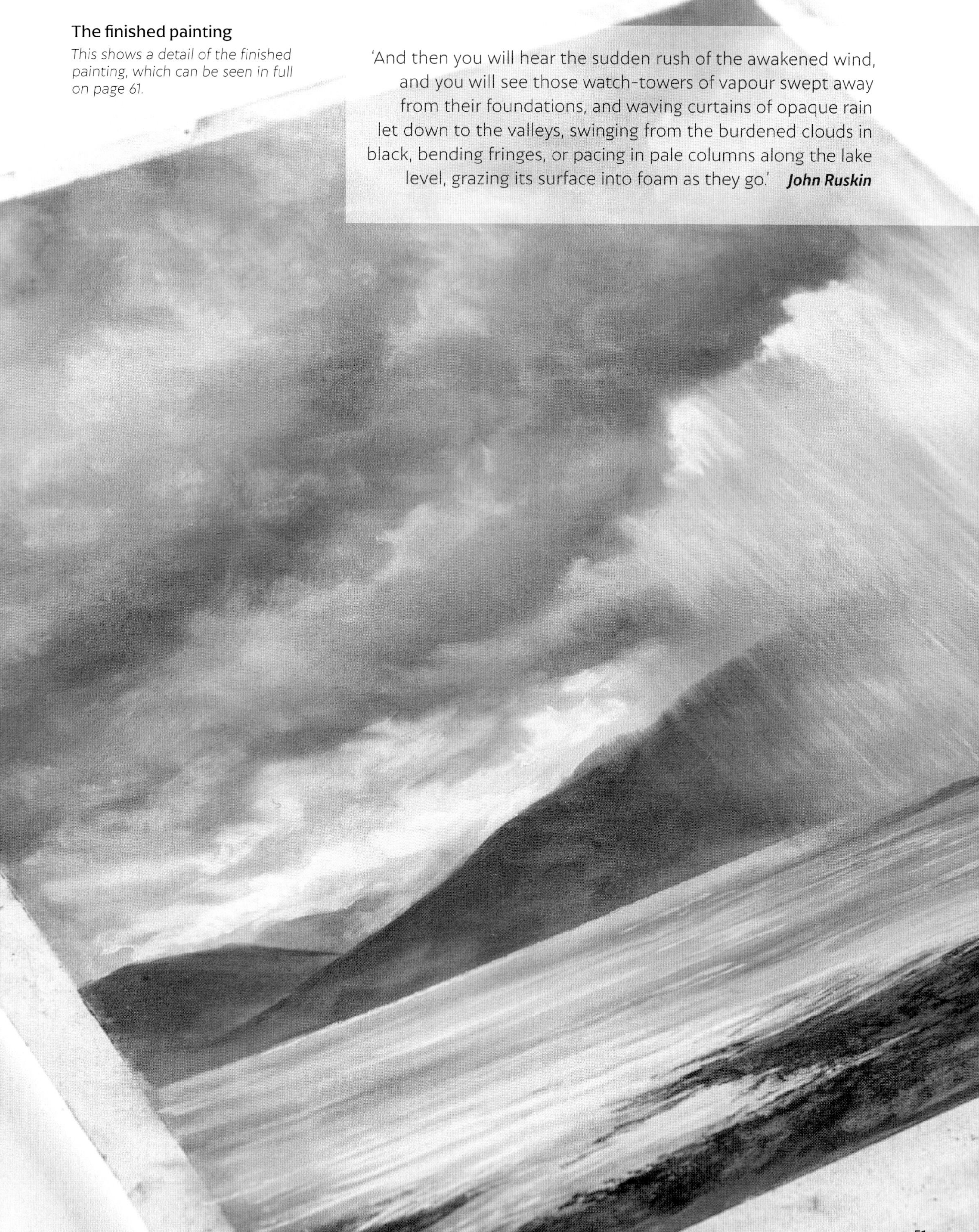

'And then you will hear the sudden rush of the awakened wind, and you will see those watch-towers of vapour swept away from their foundations, and waving curtains of opaque rain let down to the valleys, swinging from the burdened clouds in black, bending fringes, or pacing in pale columns along the lake level, grazing its surface into foam as they go.' **John Ruskin**

STAGE 1

Mark-making

- Refer to the photograph (on page 50) and work out the structure of the cloud. Try to break it down into light, mid and dark areas.

- Use three shades of mid-grey tones to build the first cloud layer.

- In addition to the darker grey for the darker areas, add small amounts of dark blue and dark purple in the dark areas – use this very sparingly.

- Add lighter grey to the paler areas to establish a sense of tonal contrast between different areas.

- Use dark grey and purple for the land, and apply the pastel with less dynamic, more horizontal marks.

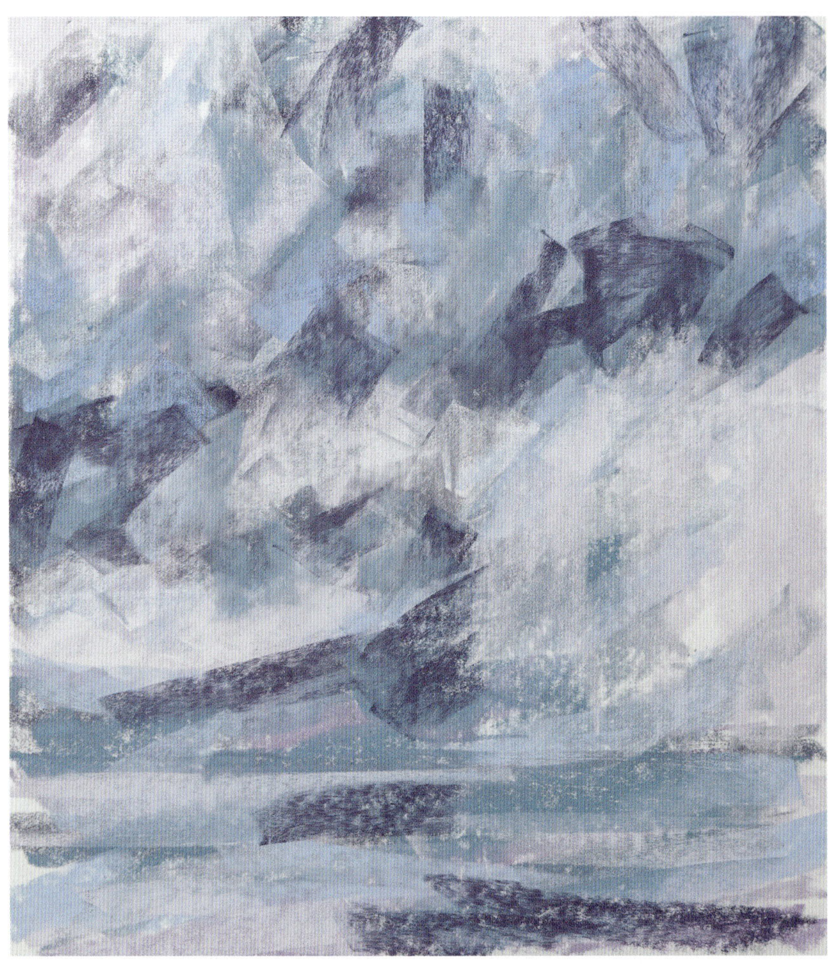

The painting at the end of stage 1 – initial marks.

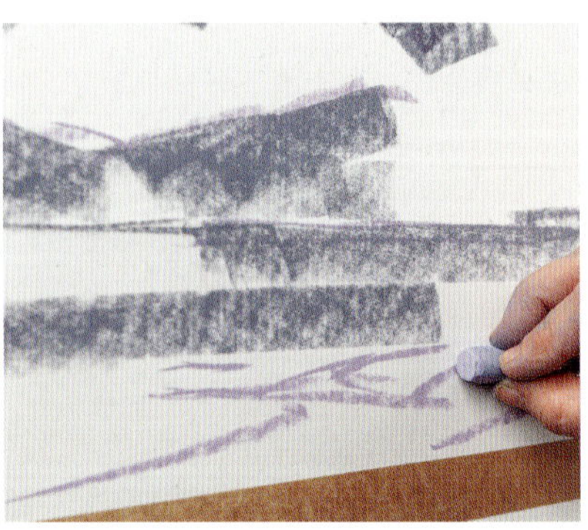

Sketching

Use slicing marks to sketch in the land. You don't need any detail – just enough to establish the main shapes and help you avoid working over it.

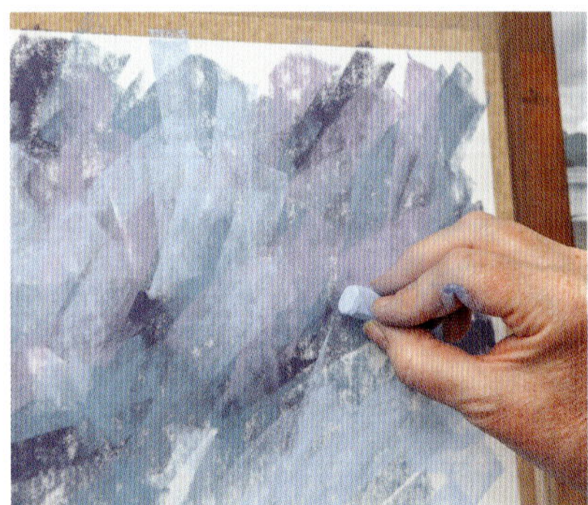

First cloud layer

Block in the sky with sweeping gestures and the pastel held flat. Think about the direction and structure of the clouds as you work.

Blending

- To get the correct intensity of colour, there has to be plenty of pastel on the surface before you start to blend.

- Blend vigorously, but don't spread the colour beyond where you want it to be. Work gradually in small circles in the sky, and overlap areas as you go, but keep some distinction between them.

- The touches of blue and purple should give more depth of tone to the grey, but not overwhelm them.

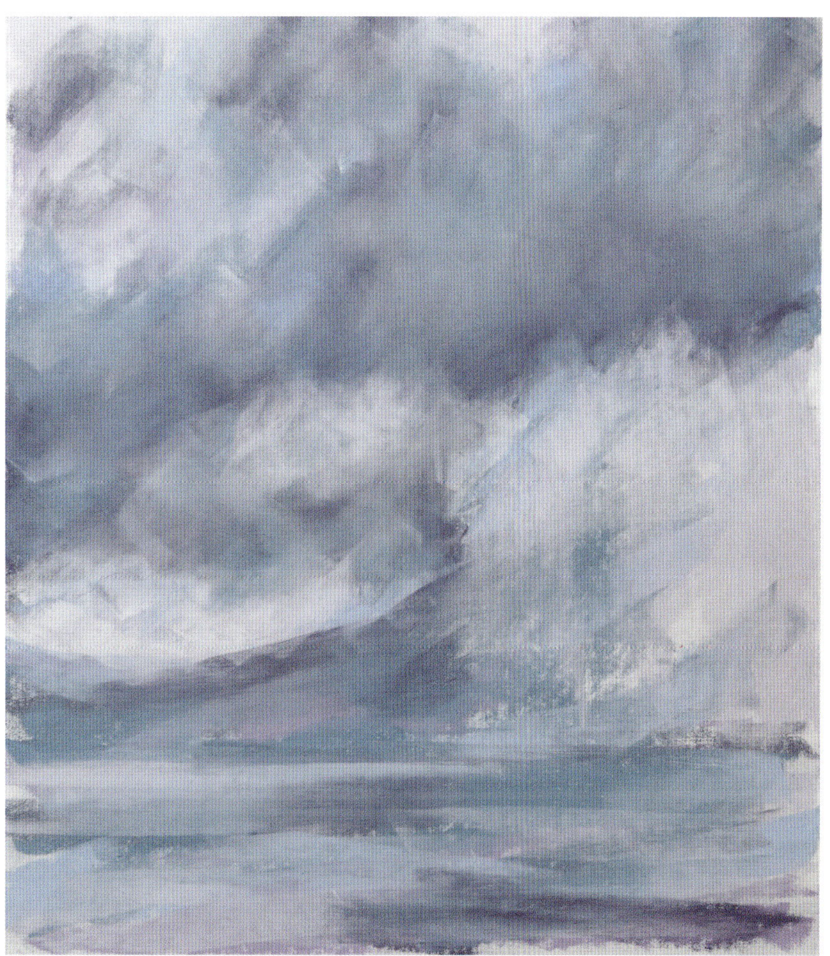

The painting at the end of stage 1 – blended.

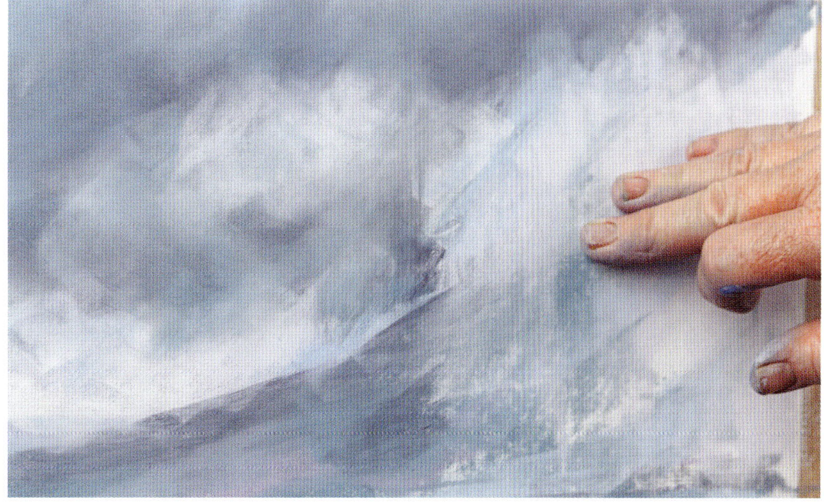

Blending the hills and rain

Use more directional strokes to blend the hills in; this helps to keep the hill line visible. Apply a pale colour to where the cloudburst is going to be.

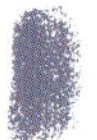
STAGE 2

This stage requires repeated mark-making and blending to build up the required depth of tone.

Mark-making

- Apply the rule of three: use three shades of darks to add smaller block marks over the clouds. Mix and layer as you go and change the direction of the blocking to create dynamic movement.

- Do the same with the set of three lighter tones, pushing and pulling the pastels to create the impression of movement.

- Repeat as necessary until the surface is ready to blend.

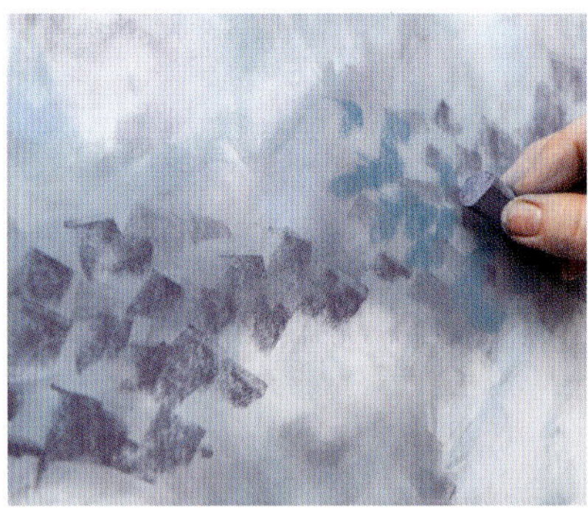

Diagonal dynamics
Establish a broad diagonal direction for the cloud by building up areas of dark and light with your dark blocks.

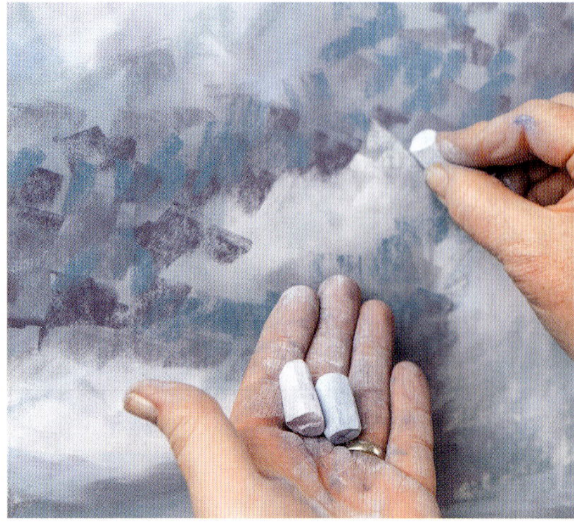

Lights
Storm clouds aren't as dark as you might think – in the context of the land, they're still quite light in tone. For this reason, it's important to ensure you have enough light tones in place.

Blending

- Start by blending the dark areas, then move on to the lighter ones.

- Blend with minimal pressure so you don't lose the block marks entirely.

- Vary your movements, pushing and pulling with your fingertips, to create movement. Try criss-cross and circling motions.

- After first blending, assess, then add new marks to areas that need strength, and repeat the blending.

- The area on the right-hand side will be falling rain, so blend it in with repeated downwards strokes to establish the direction.

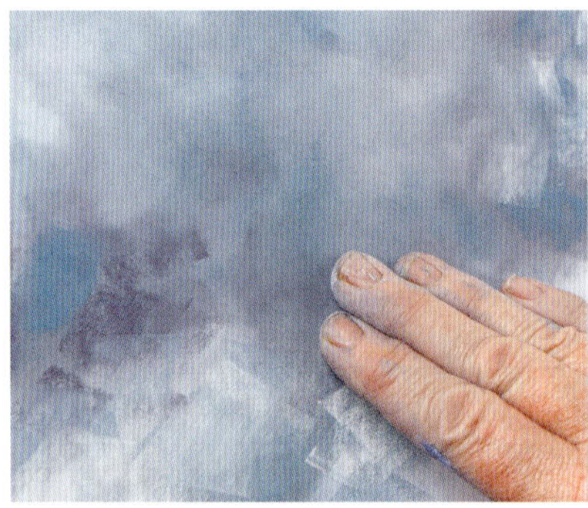

Selectively blend the darks
As you add more layers and blend, you'll start to see patterns and interesting marks emerge. Don't be tempted to over-blend these.

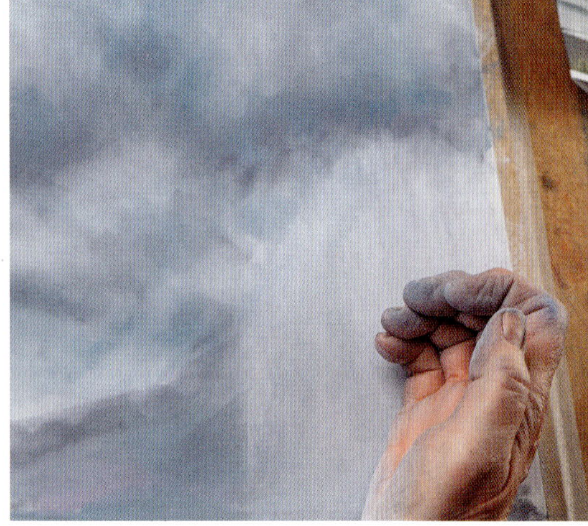

Cloudbust foundations
You need enough pigment applied here that the side of your hand moves smoothly across the surface without catching. If it drags, you need more layers.

Work repeatedly downwards, not back and forth; lift your hand away at the end of the stroke and start again from the top.

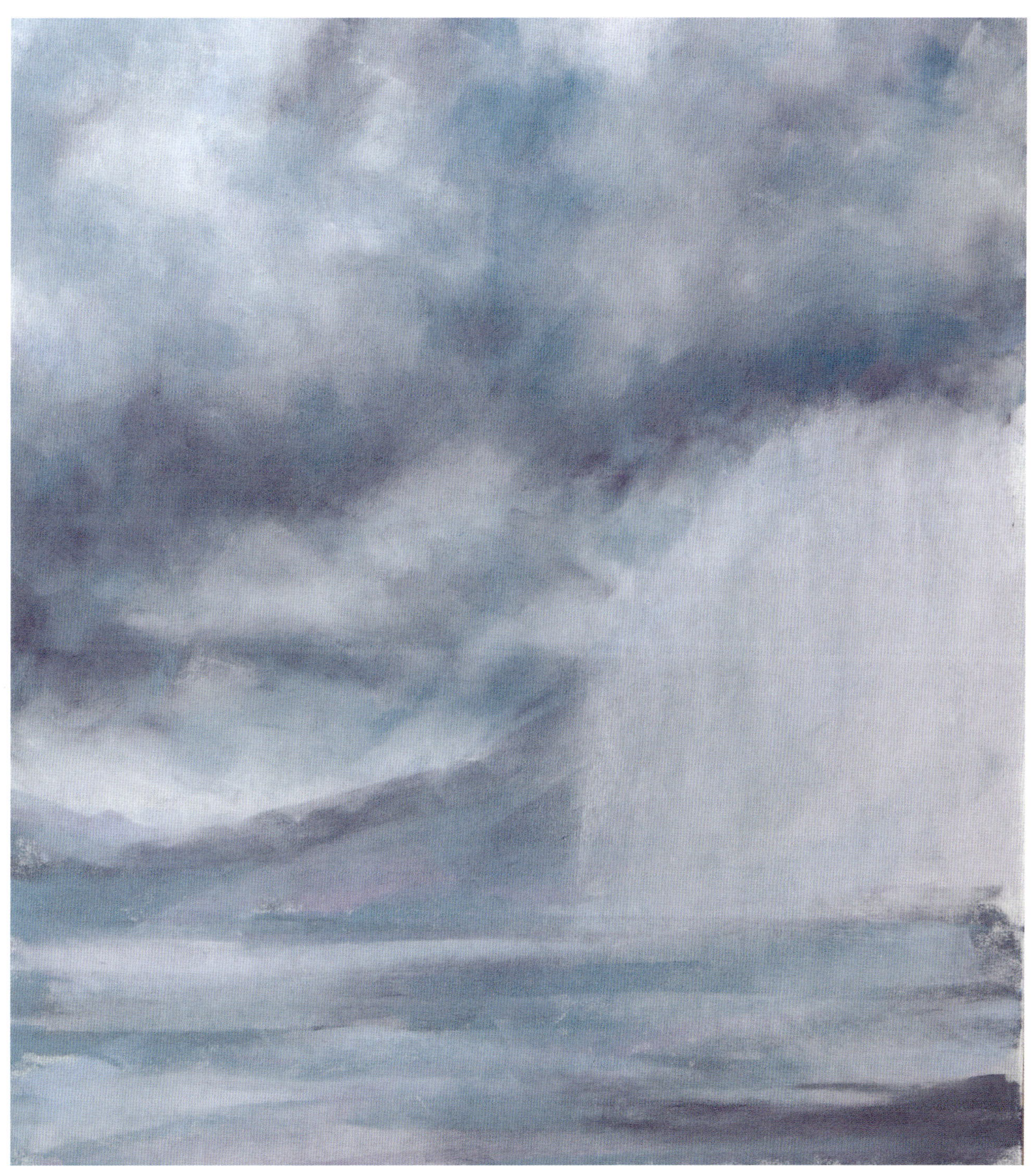

The painting at the end of stage 2.

STAGE 3

We need to think about edges, structure and movement. We are going to focus on the boundaries between different cloud areas to ensure that the painting doesn't become completely shapeless – we want to have a contrast between the soft edges of the rainfall and the distinct areas of the cloud bank.

- Use smaller rock and rolling marks to work along the edges of the clouds.

- Use pale shades to add marks to the other side edge.

- Blending lightly with your little finger, push the pastel to form edges. Push from both the light and the dark sides. Merge where needed.

- Aim to create an overall sense of movement across the clouds at a diagonal angle (A and B).

- Assess the amount of movement and ensure the clouds are creating the right structures. Push, swirl and pull as needed, and add more pastel as required.

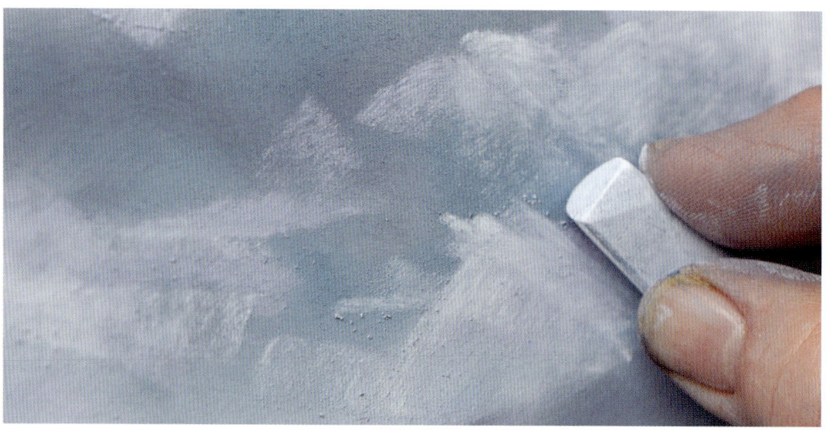

Darks and lights

Apply the darks, blend them in, then add lights over the top. This gives the correct depth to the tone.

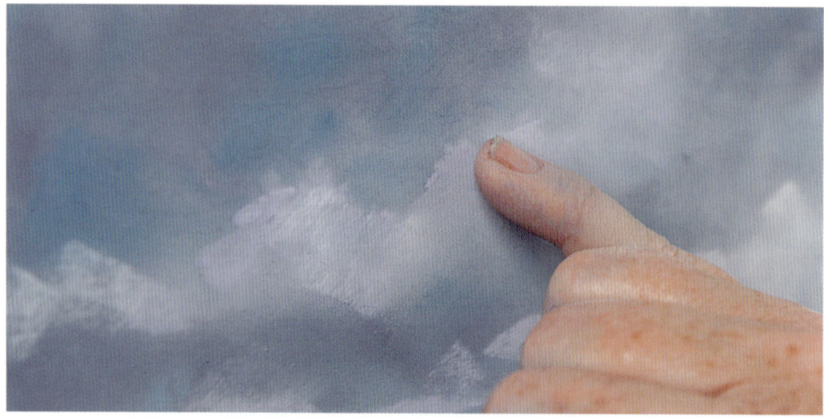

Building structure

It's easy to think of clouds as soft, shapeless forms – particularly the heavy banks of rainclouds. Pay attention to the shapes on the reference photograph, and don't overblend your marks.

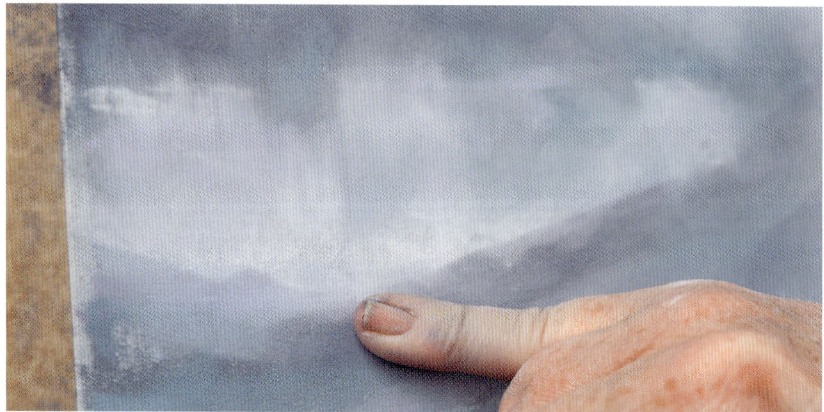

Small streaks

The smaller, more distant rainfall on the left should be added in the same way as the main cloudburst, by applying enough pigment to ensure that there is a lack of 'grip' when you blend downwards. Use a single finger for this small area.

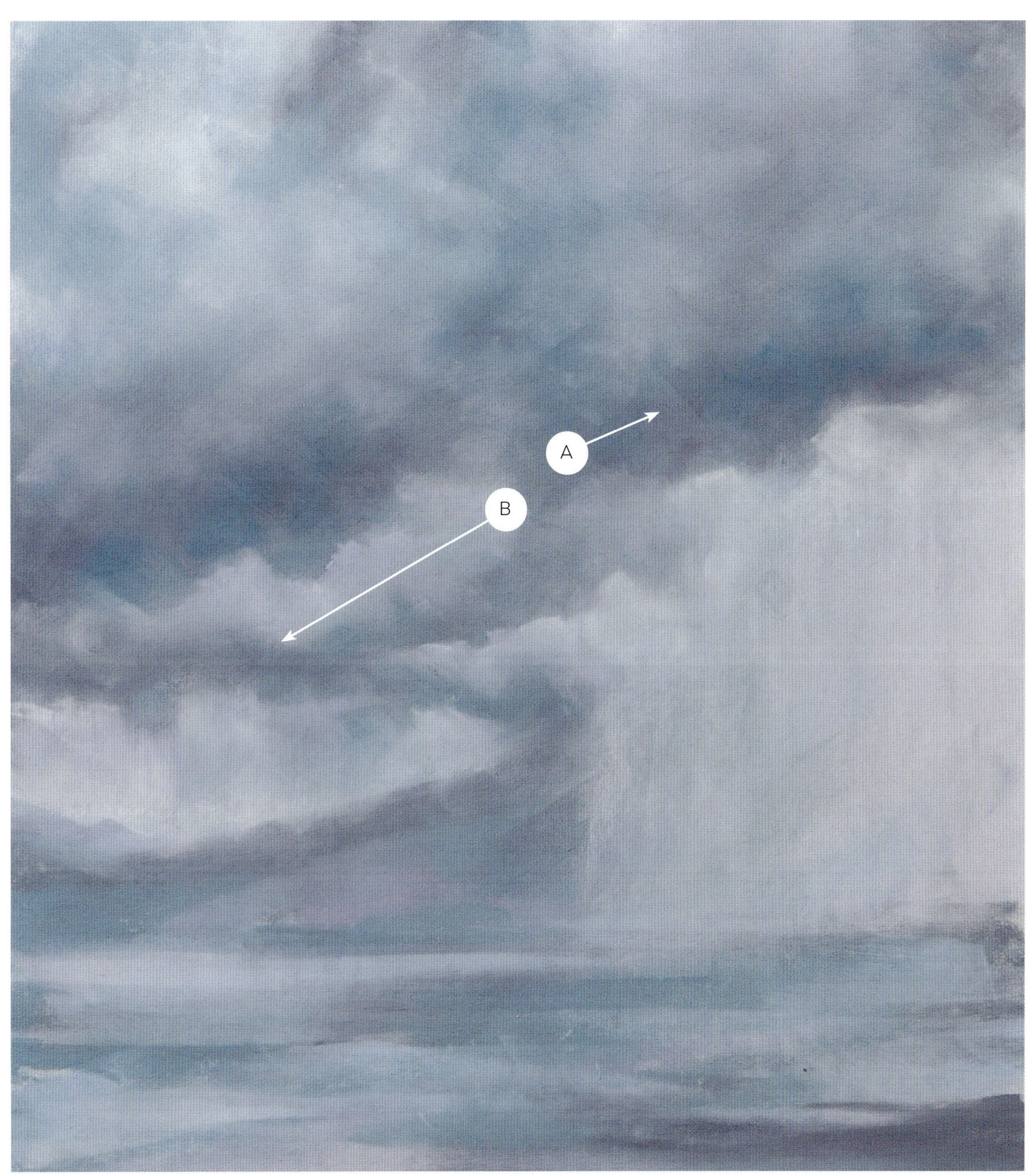

The painting at the end of stage 3.

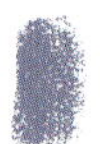

STAGE 4

It is time to add the very lightest and very darkest shades. Consider the balance of dark and light areas. Use artistic licence where needed to bring balance to the composition.

- Before we add the light, add a hint more colour in those dark clouds. For the dark, rub your finger on the darkest grey pastel and tap the surface to apply dark fingerprints where needed. Build the marks with blue and purple in the same way, and blend gently with swirling movements.

- Use the tip of the light (not white) pastels to add some detail to the focal area above the horizon, tipping and tilting the pastel as you work. Nibble into dark areas to create fingers of cloud.

- Add a hint of lilac to the area above the horizon. Add white, using the tip with firm pressure. Blend these sharper marks lightly with the shaper to ensure they retain their impact.

- Once happy with the sky behind the mountain, tip and tilt your dark pastel along the edge of the mountain to create sharp details. Blend with your little finger for the edge. Add mottling using blocking then gently blend in, using the shaper at the edge.

- Add horizontal nibbling marks with light grey for highlights on the loch, then pull and soften them with the shaper.

- Strengthen the horizon line with light blue and white, using masking tape to give a sharp edge.

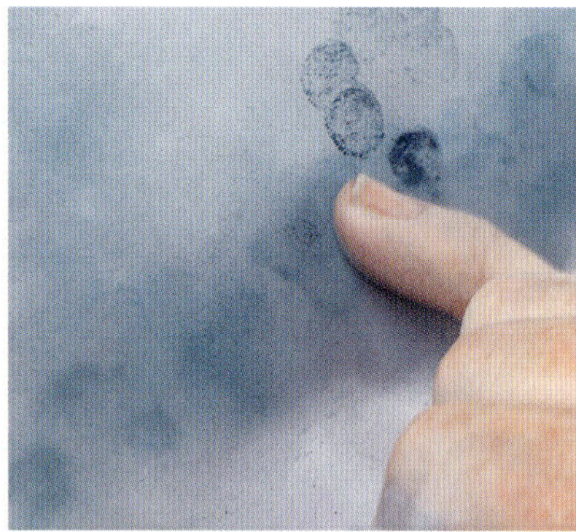

Fingerprints
Applied with a dabbing motion, fingerprint marks will blend away (right) to give a bubbly, swollen appearance to the cloud.

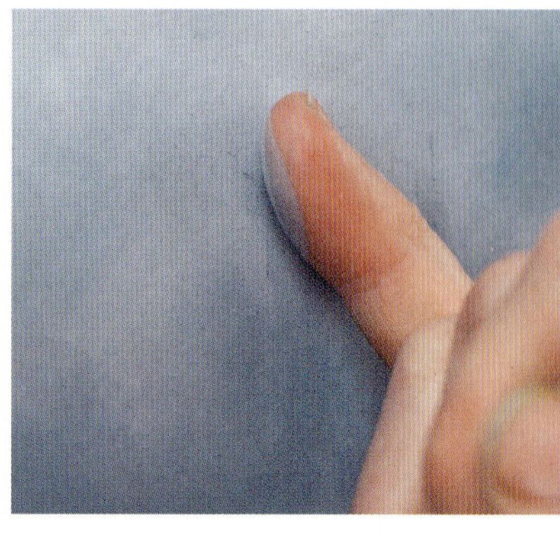

Pushing pigment
The depth of pigment applied in earlier stages means that we can manipulate the tones on the surface. You can use your finger to push dark areas into light and help with shaping.

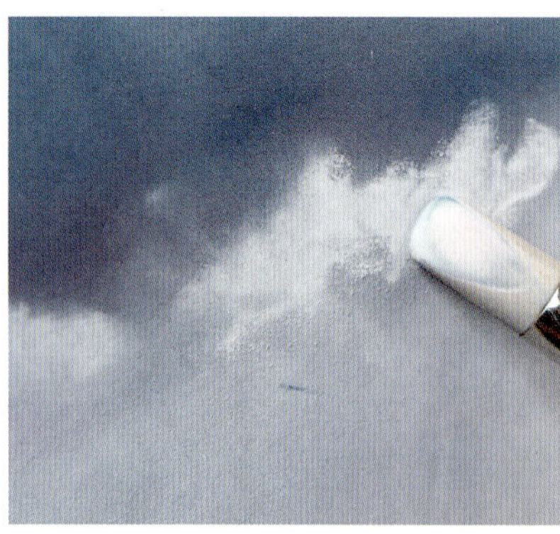

Bright marks above the rain
Using the colour shaper will soften in these marks while keeping the contrast in tone.

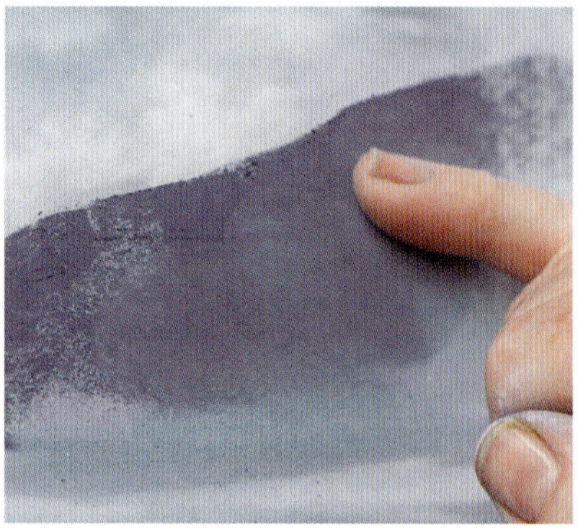

Mountain
Soft blends at the right-hand side and base give depth to the rain, and provide contrast between the crisp ridge line and mist-shrouded base.

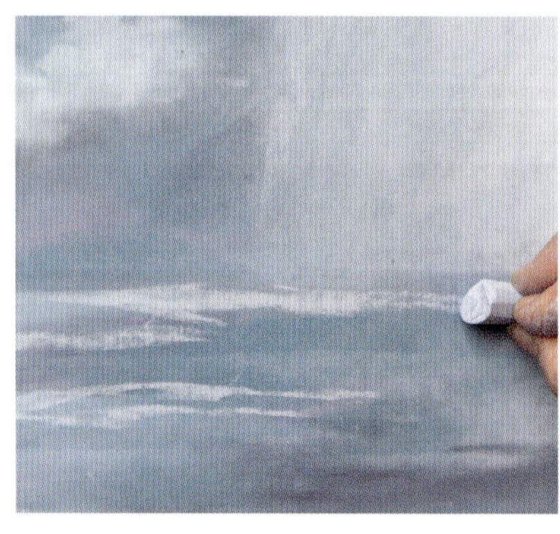

Nibbling
These marks can be used both for creating more distant brighter clouds on the left and, unblended, for light on the water.

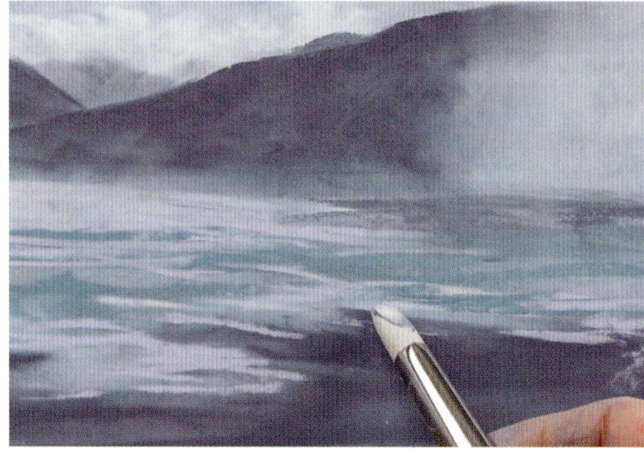

Water detail
Use horizontal strokes with the shaper to slightly blend the ripples. There is more advice on adding the horizon on page 124 if you'd like some tips.

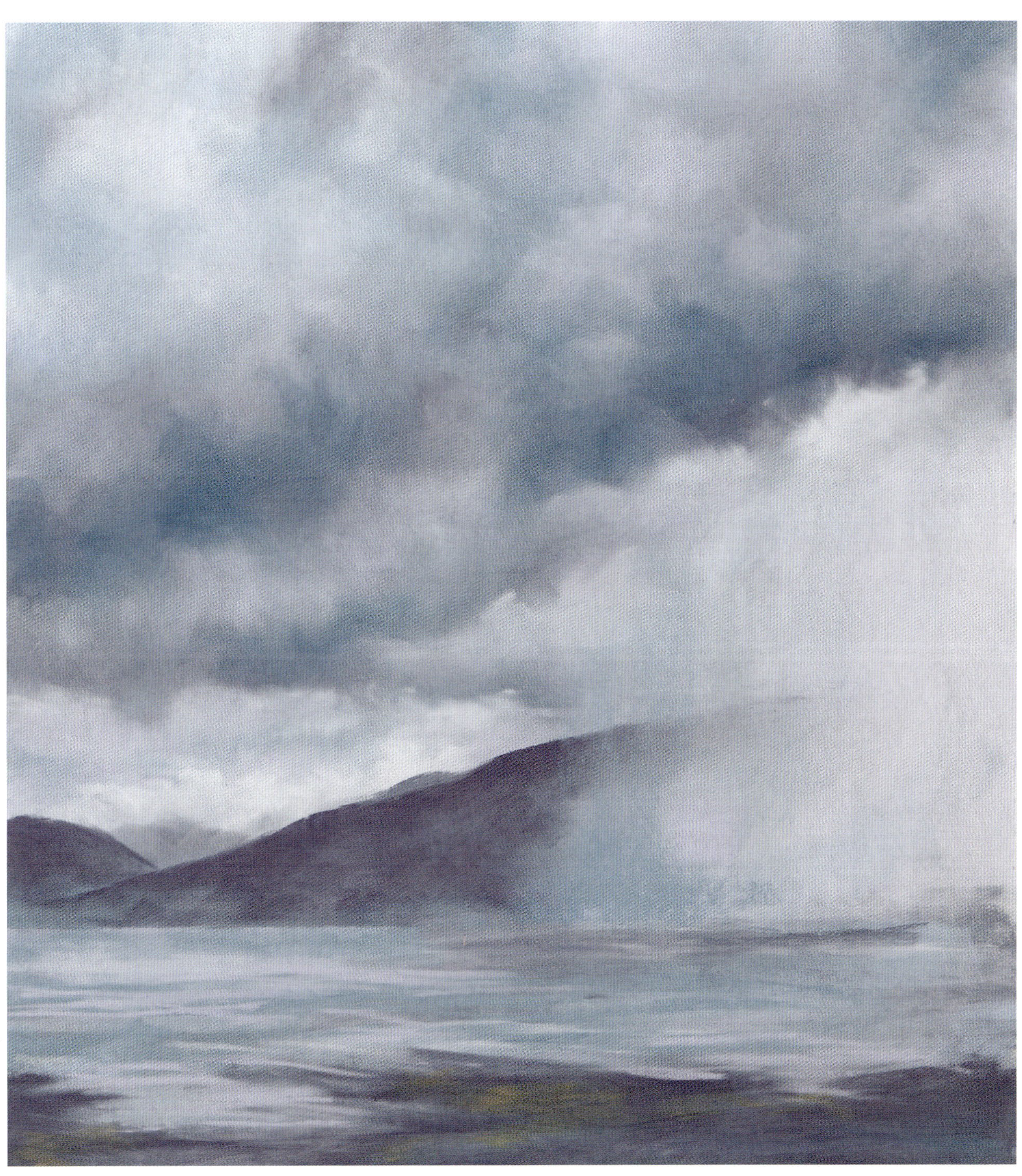

The painting at the end of stage 4.

STAGE 5

It's now time to add the final details, but it's critical to add them sympathetically and ensure they feel like part of the picture. Generally speaking, you should aim to enhance what's already there, rather than adding new details at this stage.

- Develop the rainfall with a trio of light tones: mid grey, light grey and pure white, blending the colours in with the side or heel of your hand.

- Add a layer of white pastel at the base of the dark cloud with firm pressure. Pull this down as shown to the right, then add and soften further as needed.

- Finish the rain effect by putting in the foreground island with the same colour as the mountain.

- Assess the balance of dark and light across the clouds and whether you need more light or white areas. Add as you deem necessary.

- Assess dark areas and hints of colour – if necessary, add them with your fingers, not direct pastel marks.

- Add more texture as desired to the foreground; including grasses and bright highlights on the water. If you wish, you can use pastel pencils or Wolff's carbon pencils for these details.

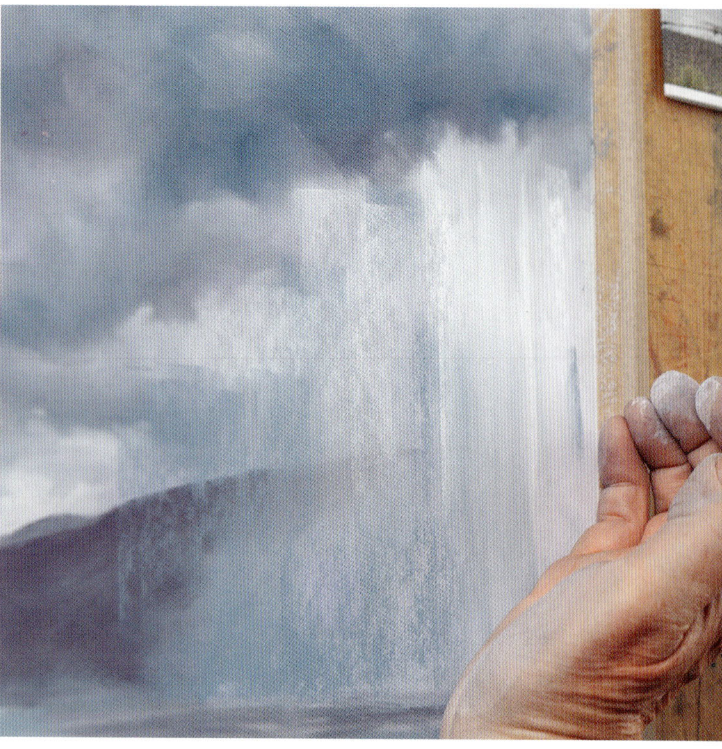

Rainfall

Apply the pastels in straight, broad marks from top to bottom; and blend in the same way. Don't ever work back upwards, and clean your hand between each blending stroke you make.

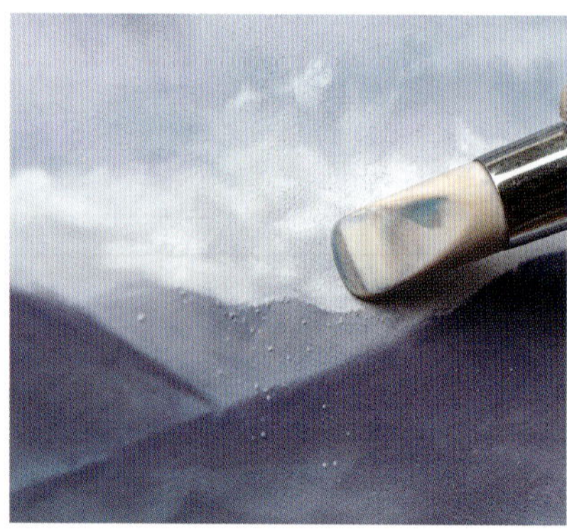

Bright horizons

Brightness is important here, as it gives necessary contrast with the dark cloud that dominates the painting.

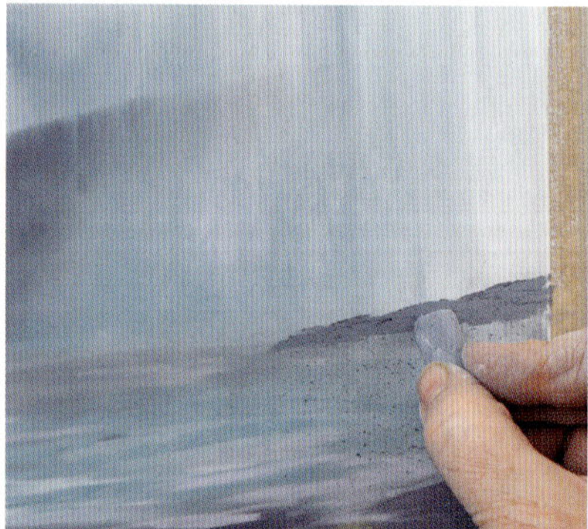

Foreground island

An exception to the usual rule of 'no new areas' in the later stages, this island is crucial to throwing the rainfall back into the painting. It can only be placed at this late stage.

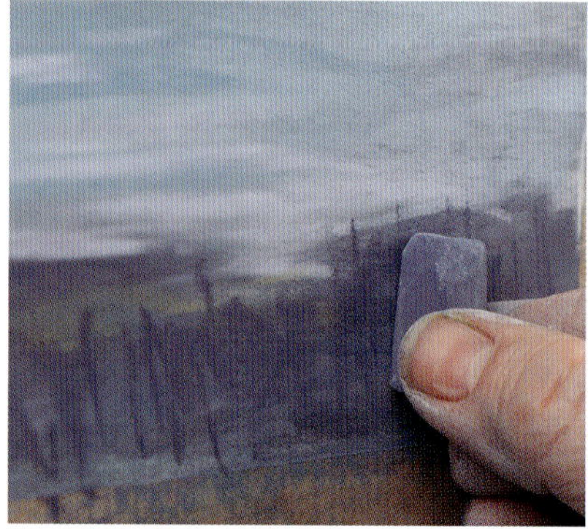

Grasses

Some vertical slice marks, made with the same moody purple as the land masses, create detail and weight in the lower corner. The addition of contrasting ochre pebbles adds detail and interest, too.

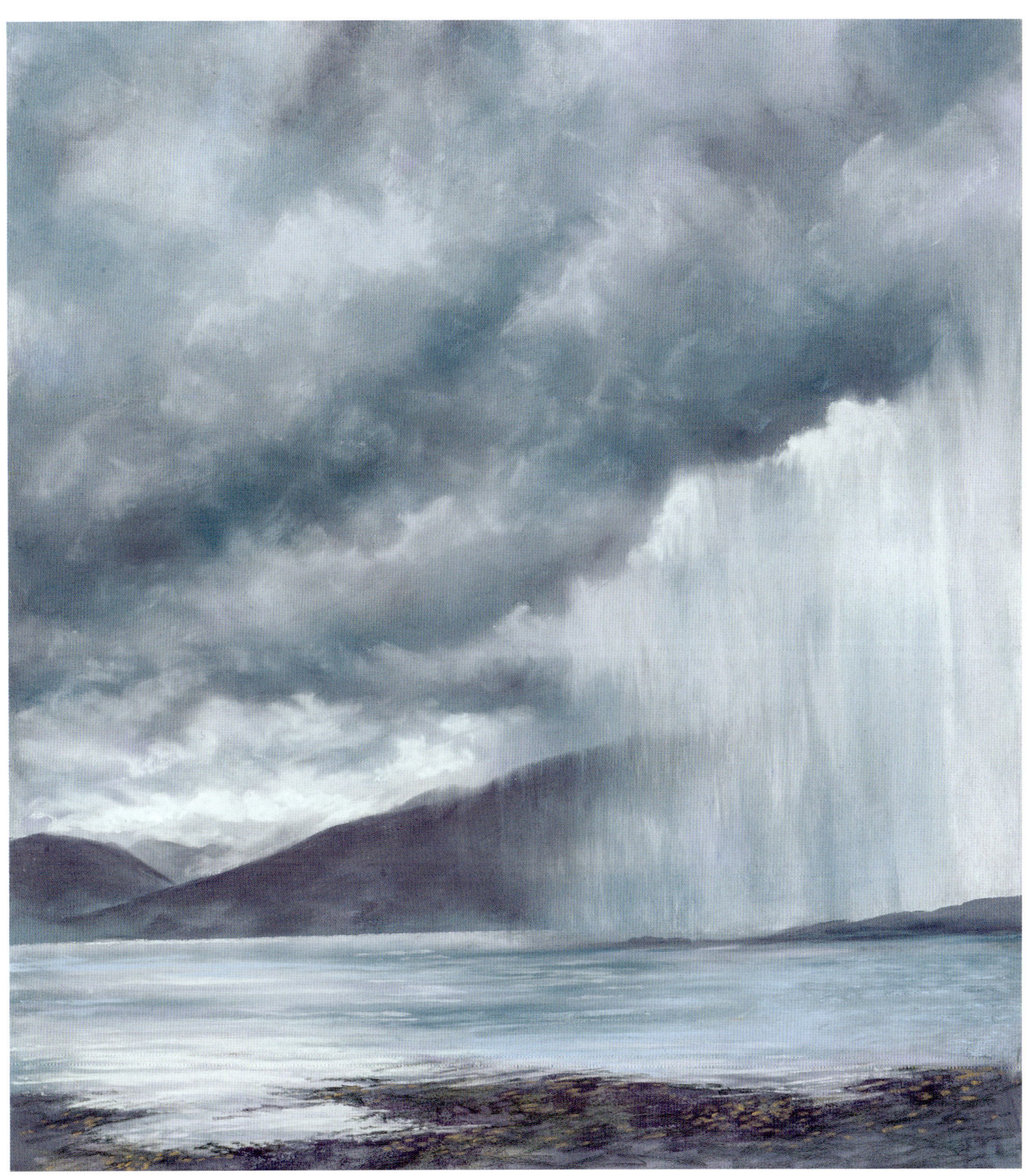

The painting at the end of stage 5.

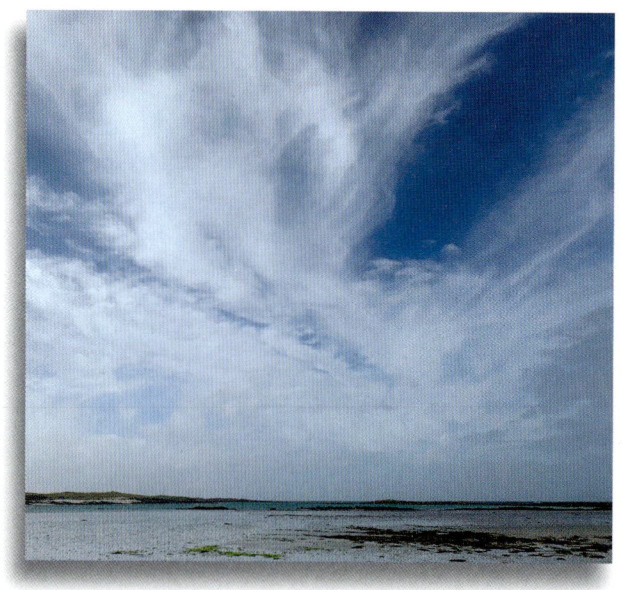

Windy Weather

Our cloud work so far has focused on using swirling and circular mark-making to create cumulus and stratus clouds. In this tutorial we will be looking at the effect of wind on the clouds and how to create delicate cirrus clouds – wispy and wild.

This will push you and develop your observational skills. More importantly, it will introduce you to the delicacy and subtlety possible with pastels. I've deliberately kept the palette quite restricted so that you can concentrate on the mark-making without the added complication of colour.

SELECT YOUR PALETTE

Here, subtle blue- and grey-based pale to mid tones are used for the sky, while a variety of complementary earthy colours – lilac, ochre, cream, white brown are needed for the beach. I used:

Sky colours BV9, BV10, BV11, BV12, BV3, LT1, LT12

Land LT5, BV8, BV1, BV16, G33, A52

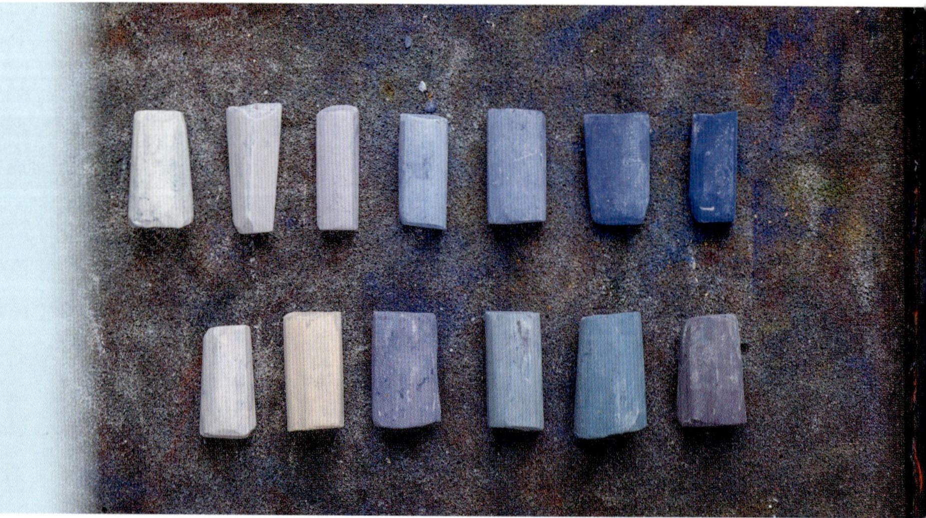

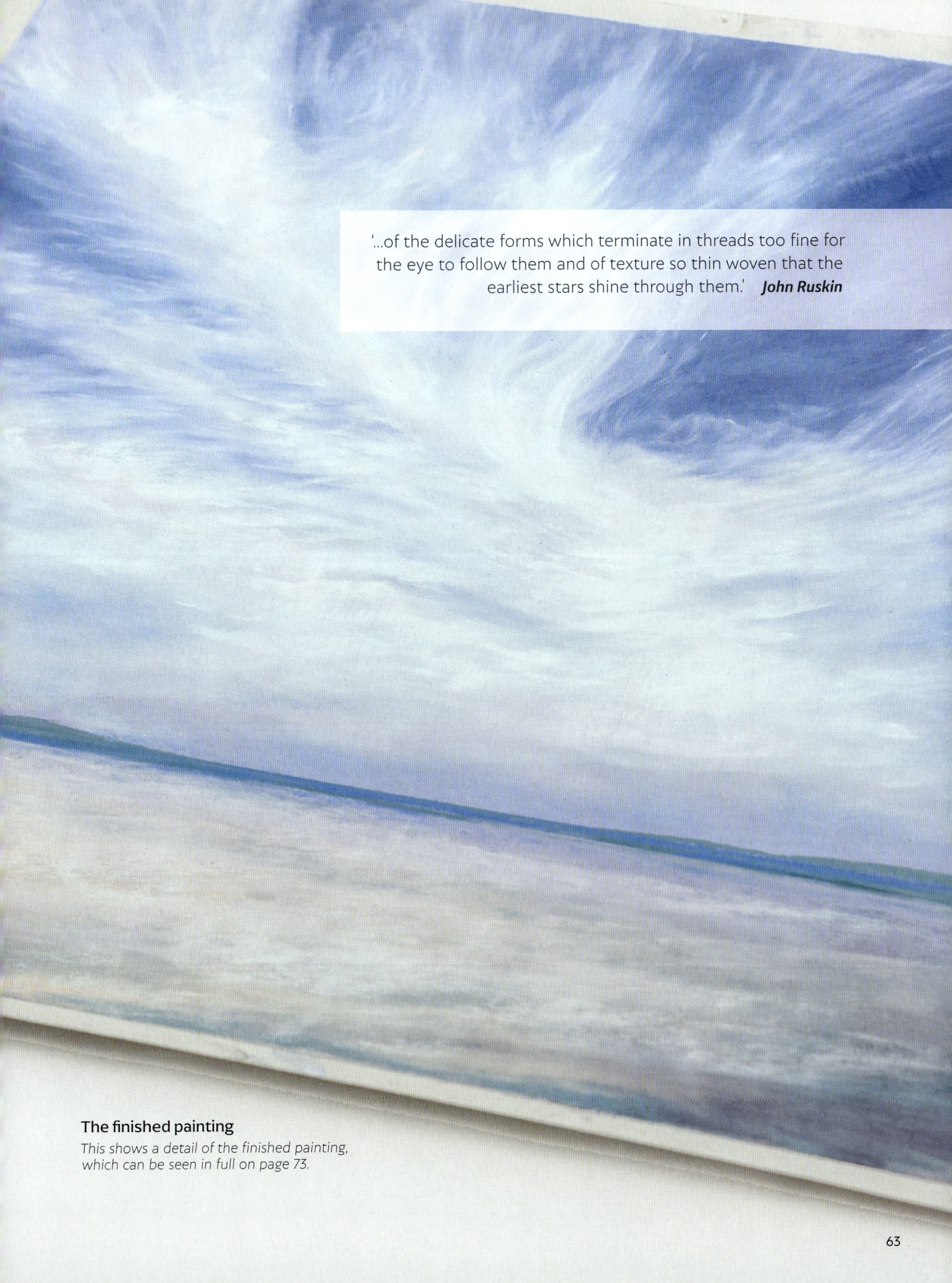

The finished painting
This shows a detail of the finished painting, which can be seen in full on page 73.

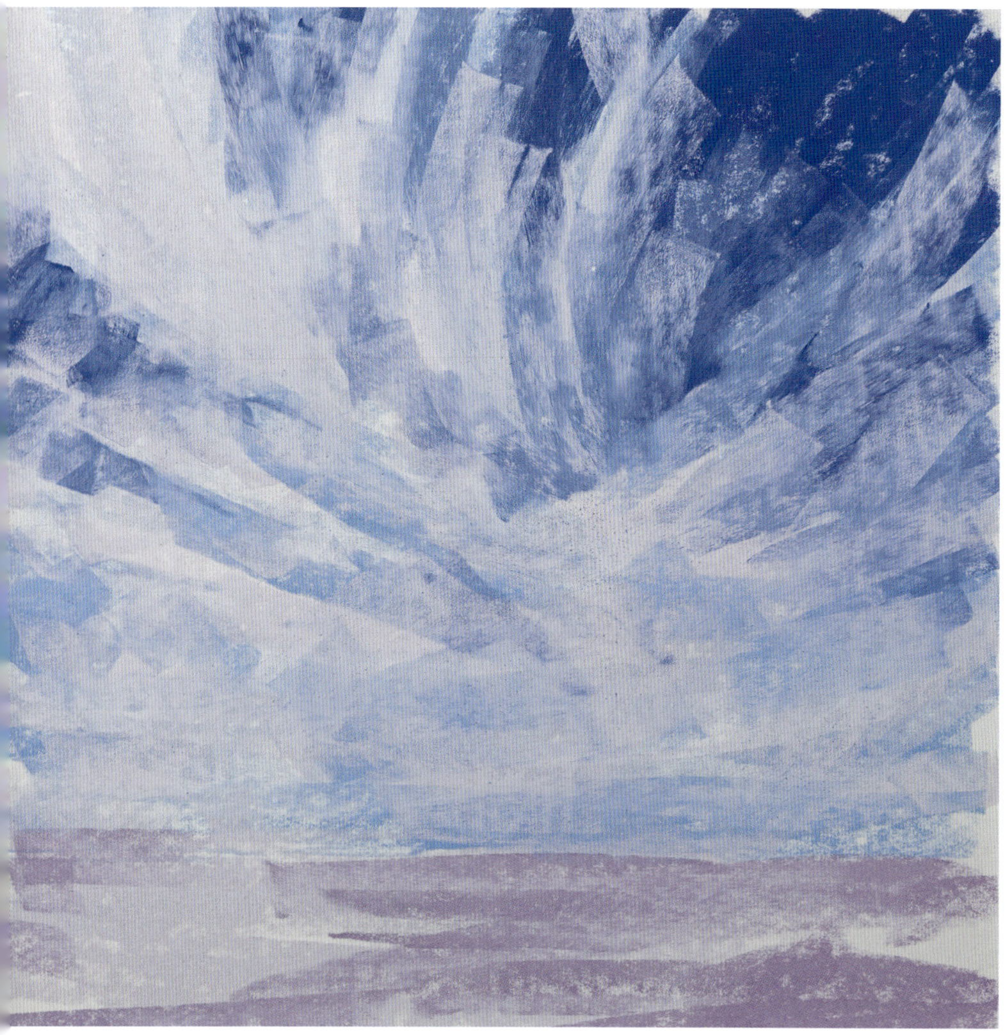

The painting at the end of stage 1 – initial marks.

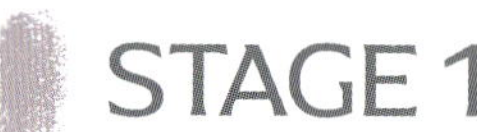# STAGE 1

Mark-making

- Start the picture by using the nib of the pastel to block in the basic shapes of the cloud formations and landscape.

- Use pale shades, chosen with the rule of three, in sweeping marks from the lower part of sky up towards the top. Use the photograph to inform the direction of the clouds.

- Add some darker grey towards the horizon. Use more controlled marks here, with less movement.

- Use two shades of blue to fill in the blue sky area. The sky is darker at the top and lighter towards the horizon.

- Build up the layers until you get to a smearable stage.

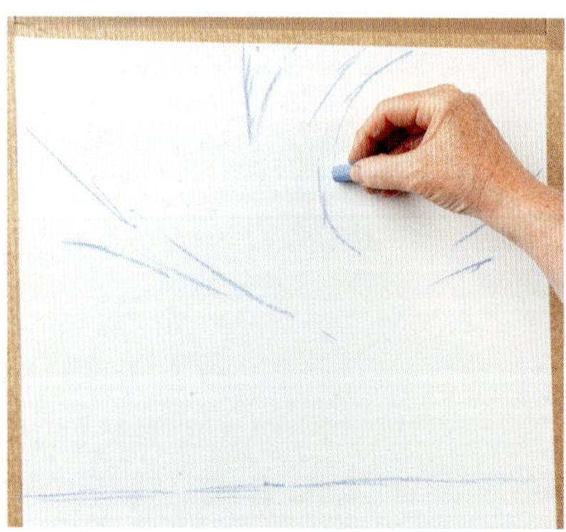

Initial layout

Use a pale sky colour to mark out the areas of blue sky and the horizon line. You don't need any more than that.

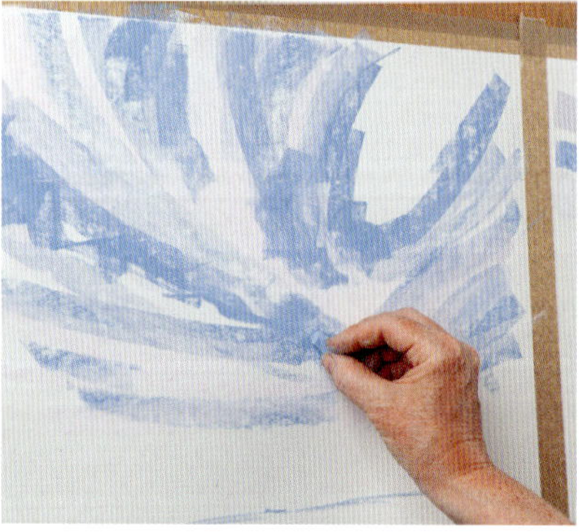

Work upwards

Angle your marks across then up. Normally with rounder clouds, you're working in small blocky marks. Here, you're using the side of the pastel to make big sweeping gestural marks.

Blending

- Start your blending with the deep, intense blue of the sky before moving on to the clouds.

- Rather than using circular movements, blend the clouds using pushing and sweeping marks up towards the top of the picture.

- Use tighter blending in the sky near the horizon.

- The land doesn't need any attention yet, so leave it unblended.

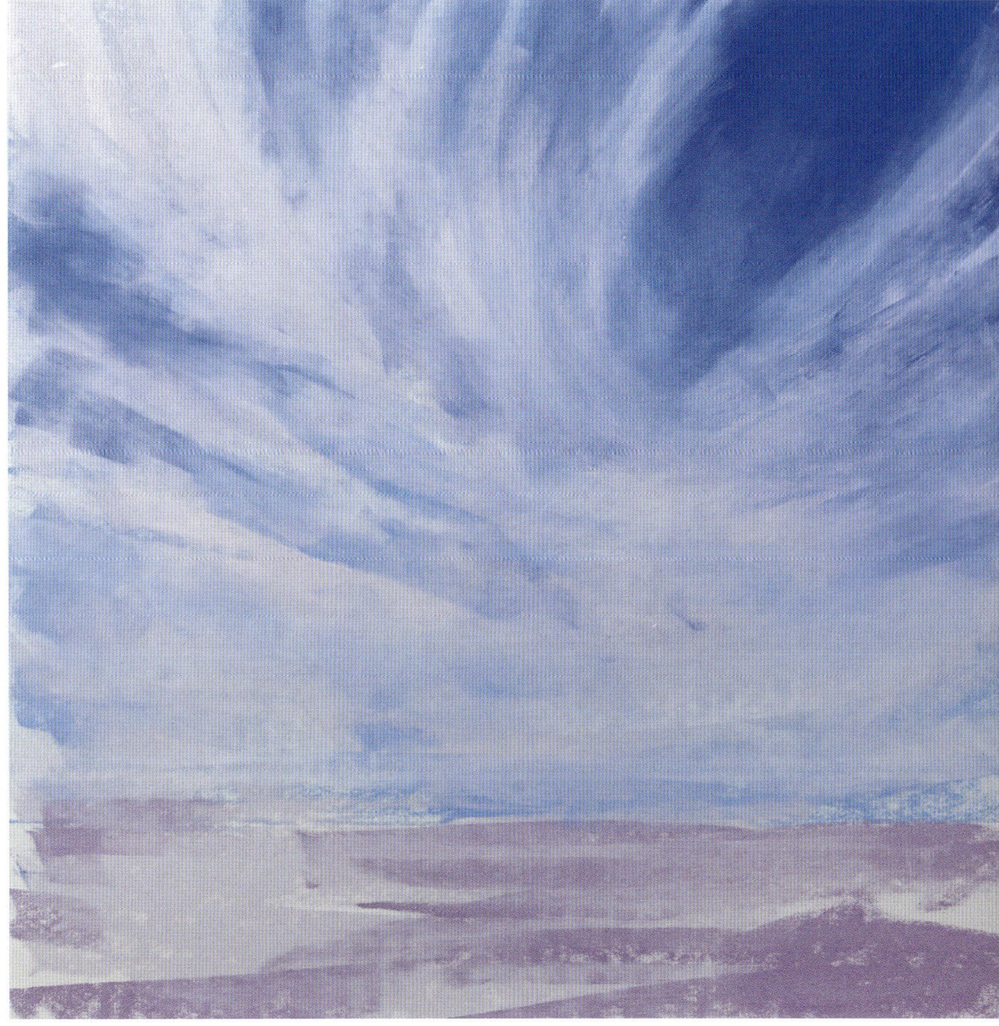

The painting at the end of stage 1 – blended.

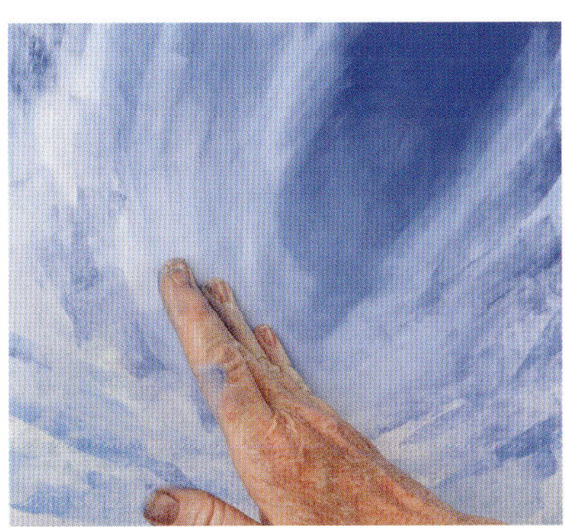

Keep out of the blue

We start with the blue sky area because we want to keep this vibrant. Don't work into this area from the surroundings; only out from it. This is the best way to keep the sky bright, clean and bold.

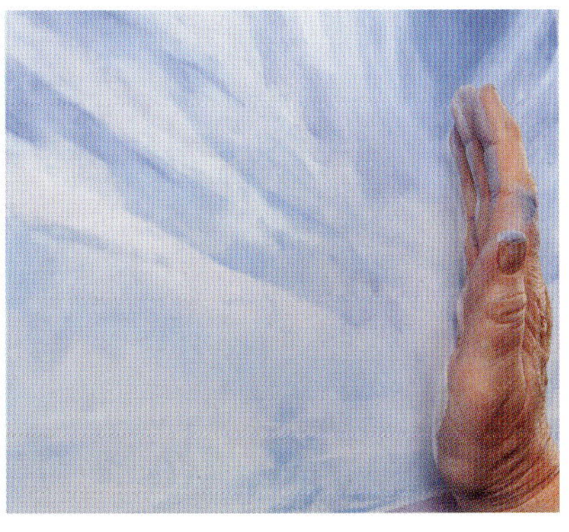

Big, bold movements

The heel of your hand is perfect for big expressive blending. The resulting marks suggest space and openness.

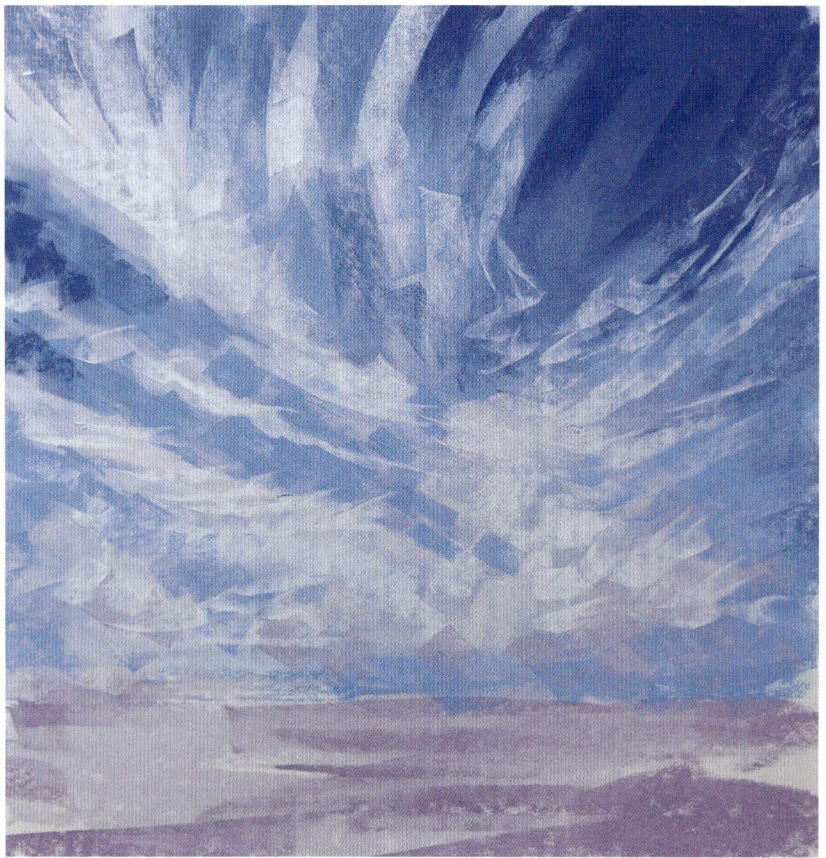

The painting at the end of stage 2 – blocking and structure.

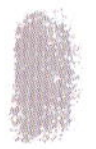

STAGE 2

Mark-making

- Start adding block marks to the lower part of the sky with pale pastels chosen with the rule of three. Allow the blocks to become longer shapes higher up to create movement.

- Work up into the middle areas of sky using angled gestures with very pale light tones.

- Cut lightly through the blue areas below the main part of the middle cloud, but use more solid mark-making for the cloud areas in the centre and on the left-hand side.

- Blend with sweeping marks, angling diagonally. Work with energy, but keep the pressure light for subtlety.

- Now add some more blue over the edges of the clouds – don't forget to vary it from dark to lighter as you come down the sky.

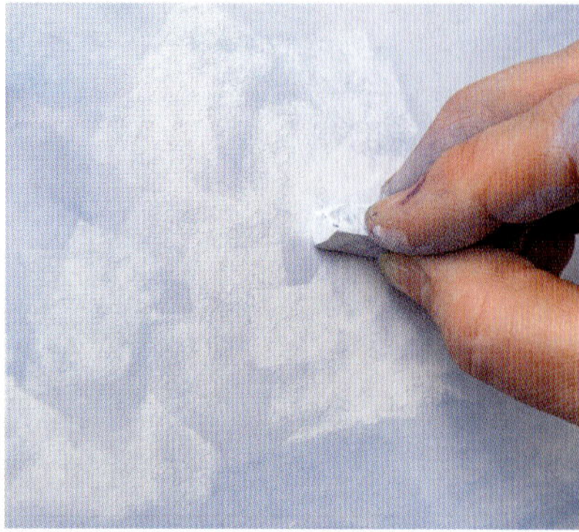

Block marks
Pay attention to subtle shapes and structures formed within areas of similar colours and tones.

Patterns and energy
These clouds often form quite distinct, rhythmic, repeated patterns in the lower part of the sky. Replicating these repeated marks is a good way to respond to what you're seeing.

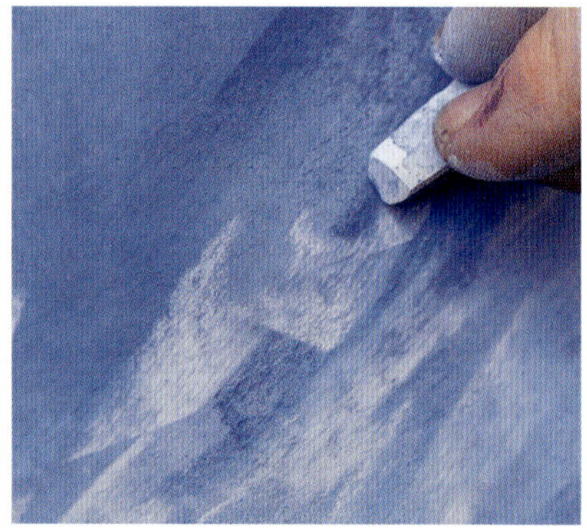

Flicking
To achieve the ethereal, wispy effect, you need to lift away the pastel as you work, and use energetic movements of the pastel to apply repeated light layers.

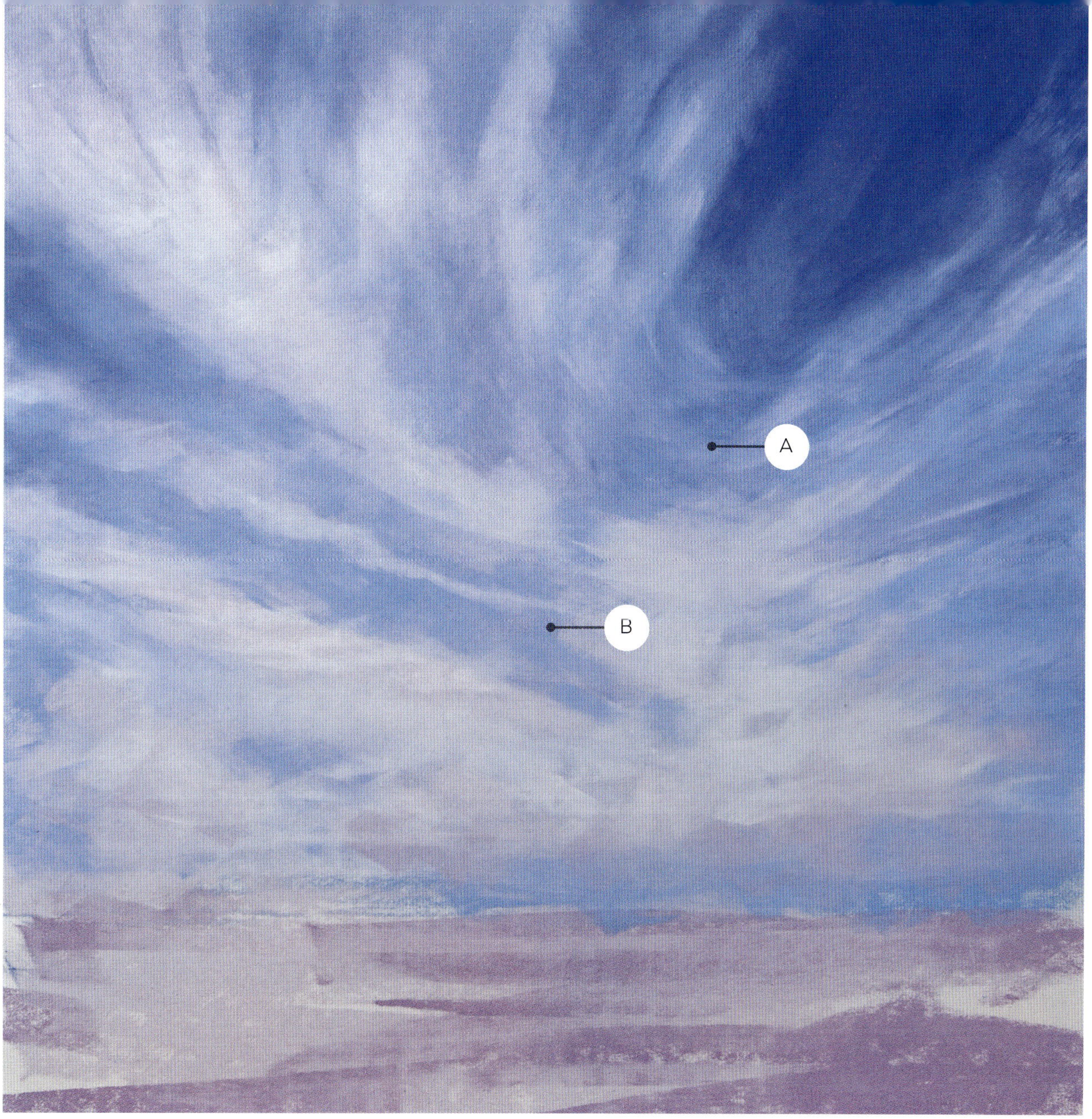

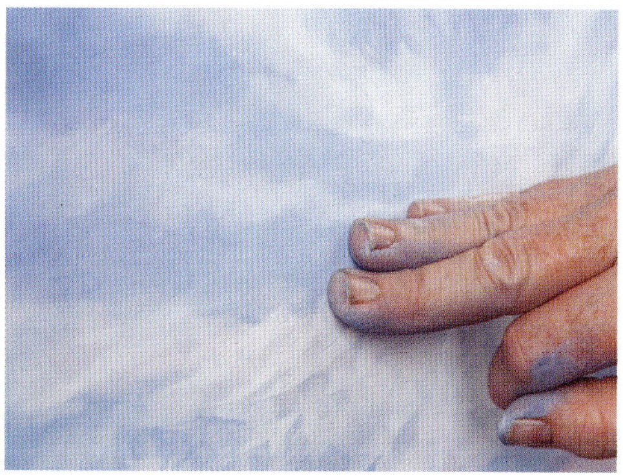

The painting at the end of stage 2 – blended.

Blending

- In the focal areas (A and B), blend lightly with just your little finger – try and keep the mark-making somewhat visible.

- Further out, work more decisively: switch to two or three fingers for blending larger areas.

- As well as following the directions made with your mark-making, work across them as well.

Considered blending
Small motions can work the pigment into the surface without sacrificing the interesting shapes you've made.

STAGE 3

Work more slowly at this stage to develop the form of the clouds more. The criss-cross layers and gentle arcs of cirrus clouds are delicate; so reflect that in your developing work.

- Repeat the earlier build-up of mark-making using layers of pale pastel to build the surface movement of the clouds.

- Use slicing marks to create the sharp lines at the edges of the light cloud, and through the central areas of the main cloud.

- Blend with the shaper, using pulling gestures to add movement and soften. Repeat as needed to build up.

- Use blue to work back into the edges of the cloud where necessary: redefine the sky where the pale cloud has spread too far. Use the shaper to blend on top of these areas to diffuse the results again.

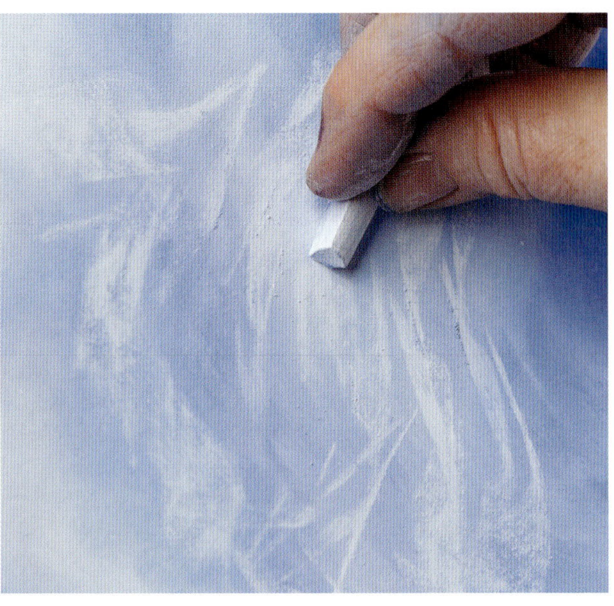

Small marks
Use the tip and edge of the pastel to focus in on particular areas. These fine, light marks build up to create the wispy, wind-driven texture of the clouds.

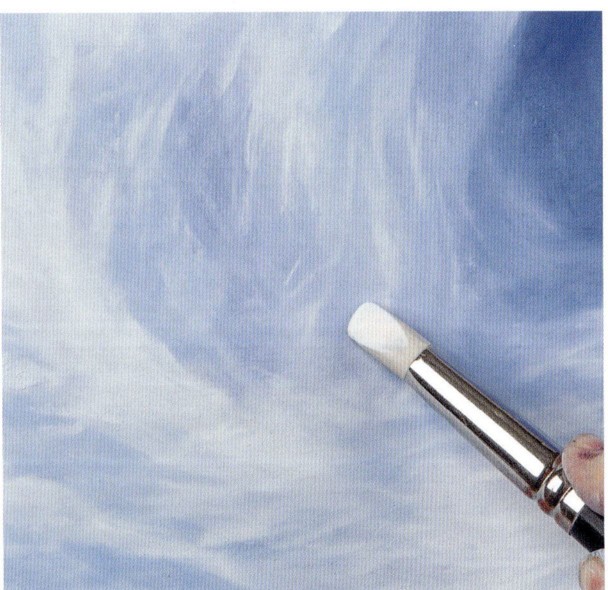

Colour shaper
This is invaluable at this stage, allowing you to keep the fine marks and wispy lines while integrating and softening them with the underlying colour.

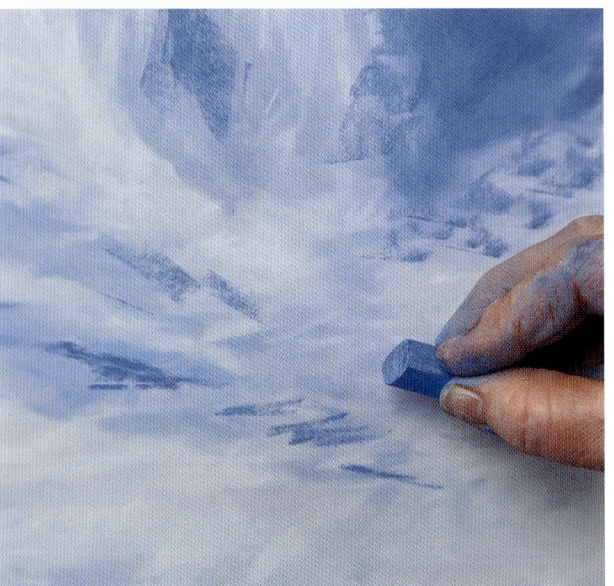

Bold blues
Don't be afraid to strengthen and reinforce the blue: it's important to have bold contrasts to set off the subtle veil of cirrus cloud.

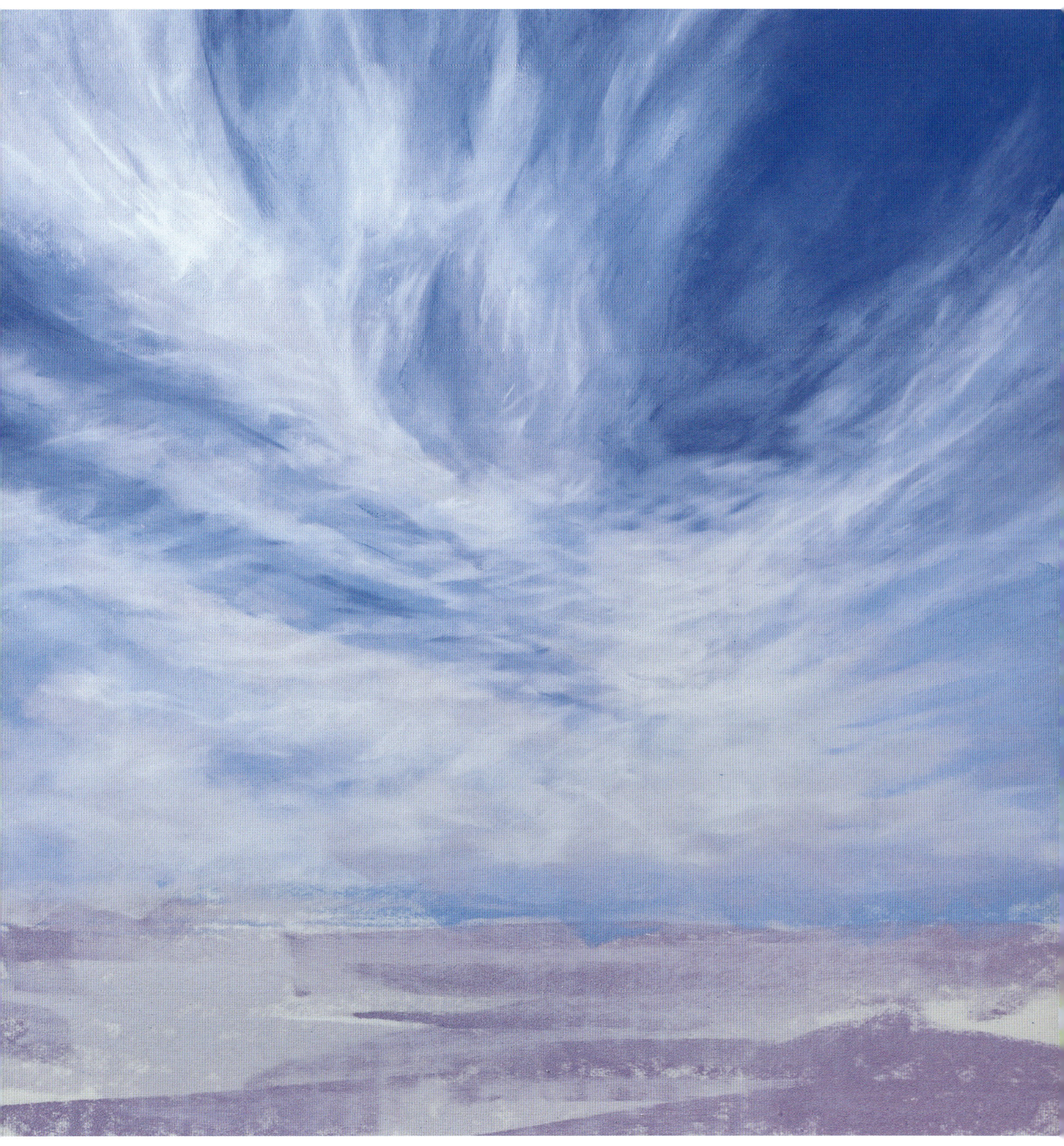

The painting at the end of stage 3.

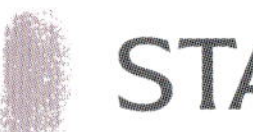

STAGE 4

- Use white pastel and the tip of the pale pastels to draw some wispy cloud areas out from the edges of the main cloud on the left and right. Combine this with some slicing marks for variety.

- Use the shaper to draw these marks out, simultaneously elongating and smoothing them.

- Tip the shaper up onto its edge and slice through the areas to add more movement – this will cut through the pale colours. You can smooth over the area with a finger if they remain too defined.

- To create smaller, finer wisps, add white to the edges of the clouds and use the shaper to pull and flick this new pigment into blue areas.

- Add soft grey near the horizon and blend the marks in with your fingers. Marks further down the sky should be made more broadly and softly, with less definition.

- Embolden some of the thicker areas of cloud by adding some blocking, then softening them in.

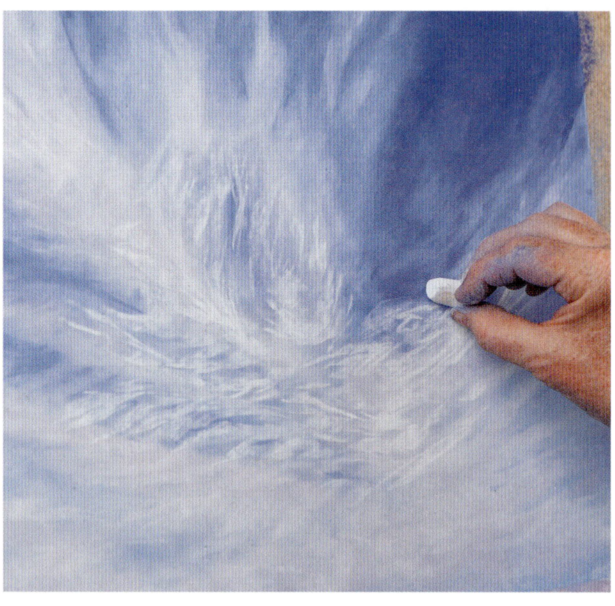

Focal point

Below the bold blue area of open sky is the first focal point. Use pure white pastel here, and tone down to just pale pastels further away, This will ensure the greatest contrast – between pure white highlight and deep blue – draws the viewer's eye.

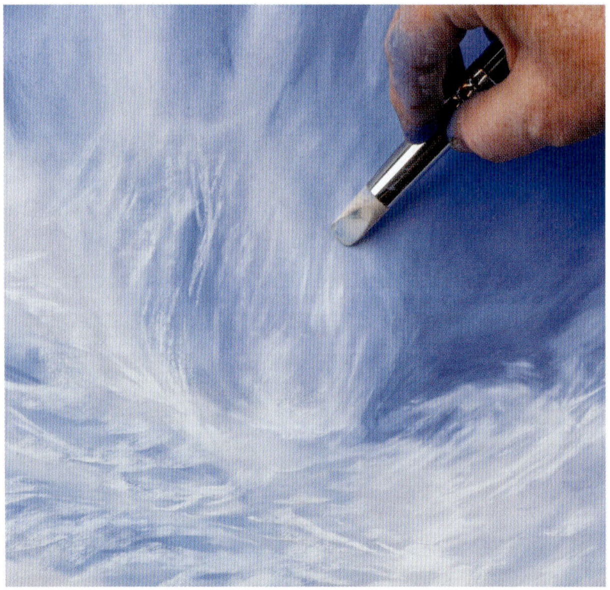

Be disciplined

It's important not to over-blend with the shaper, or you'll lose the rhythmic, wind-blown feel. Work over the small marks you've made fairly tightly, pulling them in the direction in which you made them.

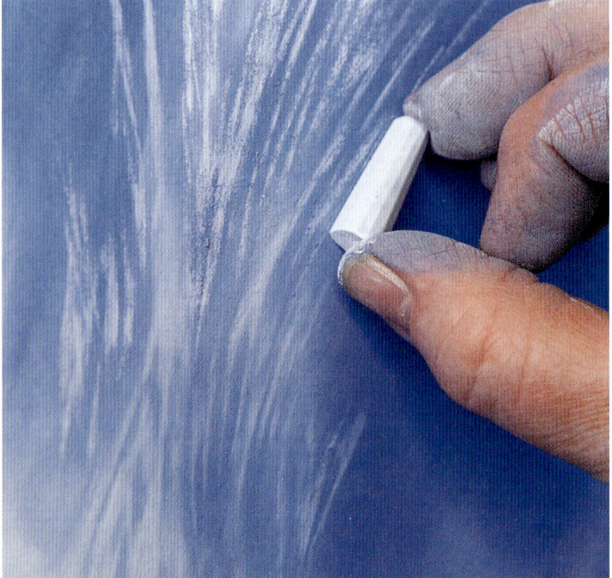

Stuttering slices

Because the cirrus clouds are wispy, the best way to tackle them is with erratic marks. Very lightly, and repeatedly, tap and lift the pastel away from the surface as you make your slice marks to create stuttering, broken lines.

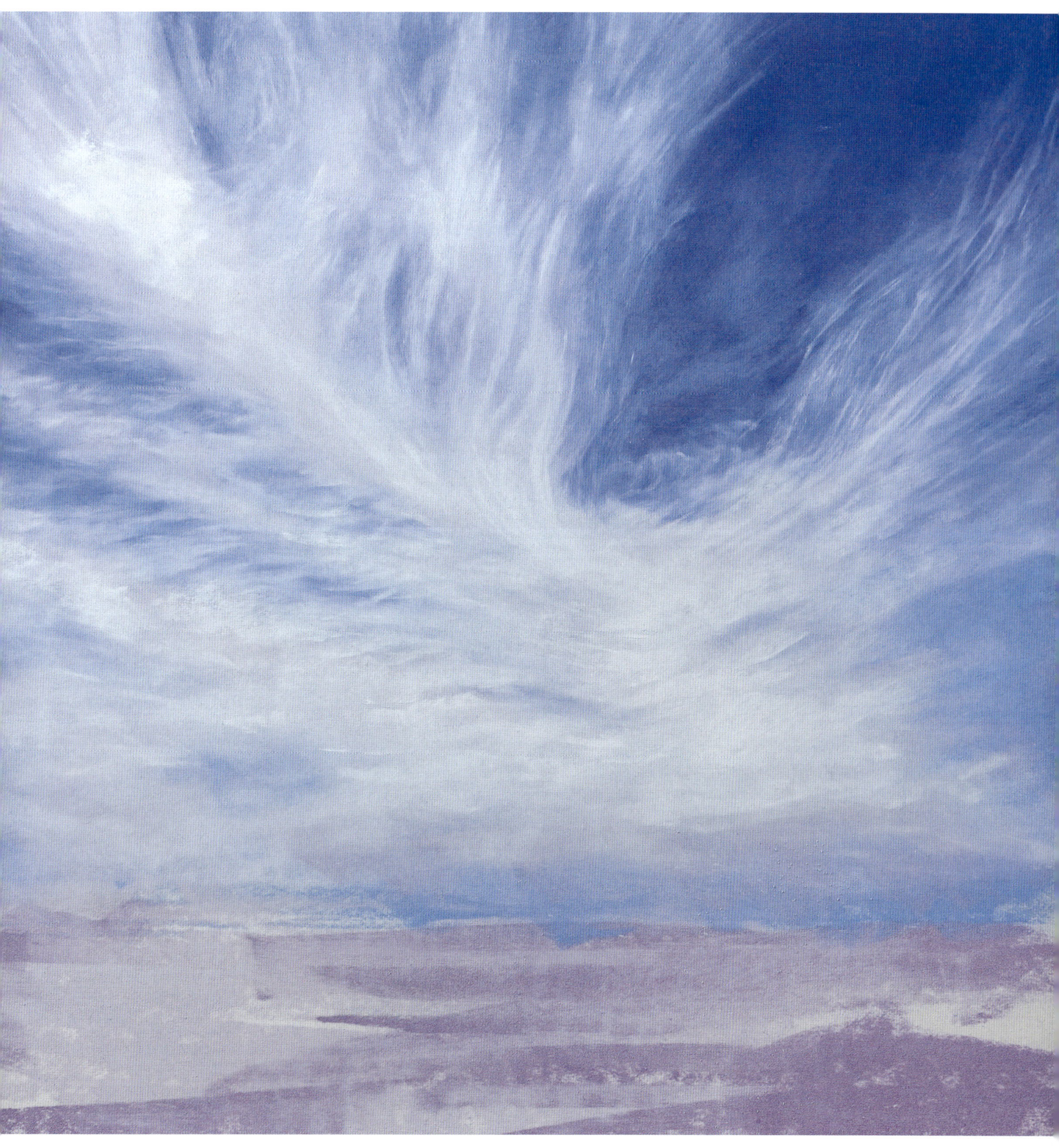

The painting at the end of stage 4.

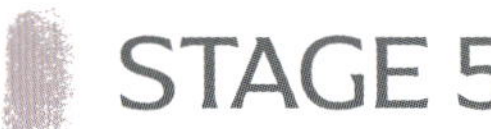

STAGE 5

- Add colours to the beach and blend them in lightly with horizontal movements. Use grey-greens to create the distant dunes. Define the horizon (see page 124 for tips on the horizon). Keep the top line fairly sharp and clear against the sky.

- Use the complementary colours of pale gold and purple-brown for the foreground seashore.

- Push and sharpen the foreground areas with the shaper tool.

- Add white and pale lilac pastel to the bottom of the sky on the mid-right near the horizon, and blend.

- Add more white, working diagonally from the horizon area up into the cloud, to lead the eye into the sky. Use the tip and tilt technique along with slicing movements.

- Add defining blues to the edges of clouds as needed. Keep these marks subtle.

- To finish, check over the piece as a whole to ensure the composition is balanced. Make sure the wispy effects are softer away from the focal areas. Ask yourself whether the wisps pull together towards the focal point, and whether the cloud structure flows well. If not, use your finger and shaper tool to work on this as needed.

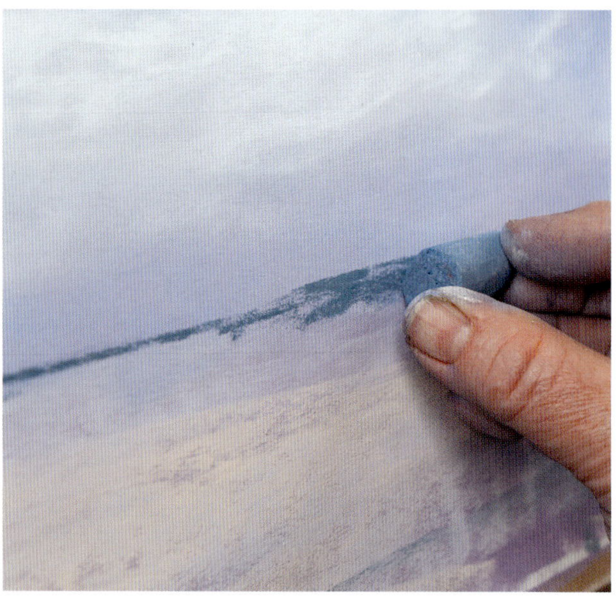

Horizon

Nibble downwards from the horizon line to define and add interest to the distant beach – blend in places but leave most of the texture.

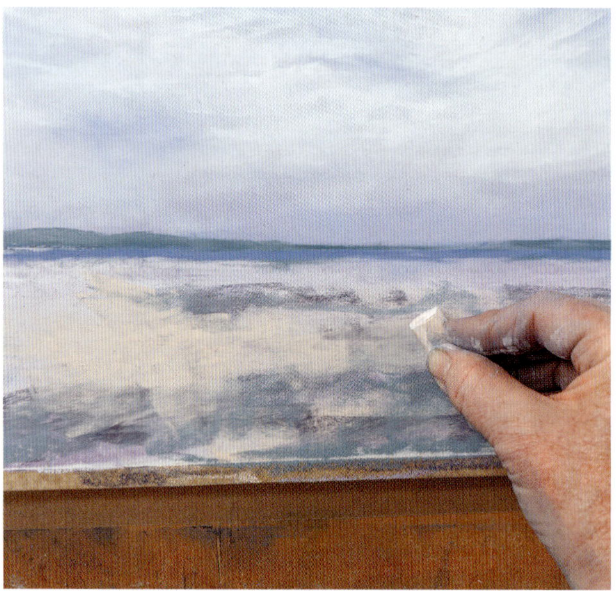

Foreground beach

After applying the colours with blocking, soften them in a little, then layer a pale lilac – the same used at the bottom of the sky – to harmonize the overall painting.

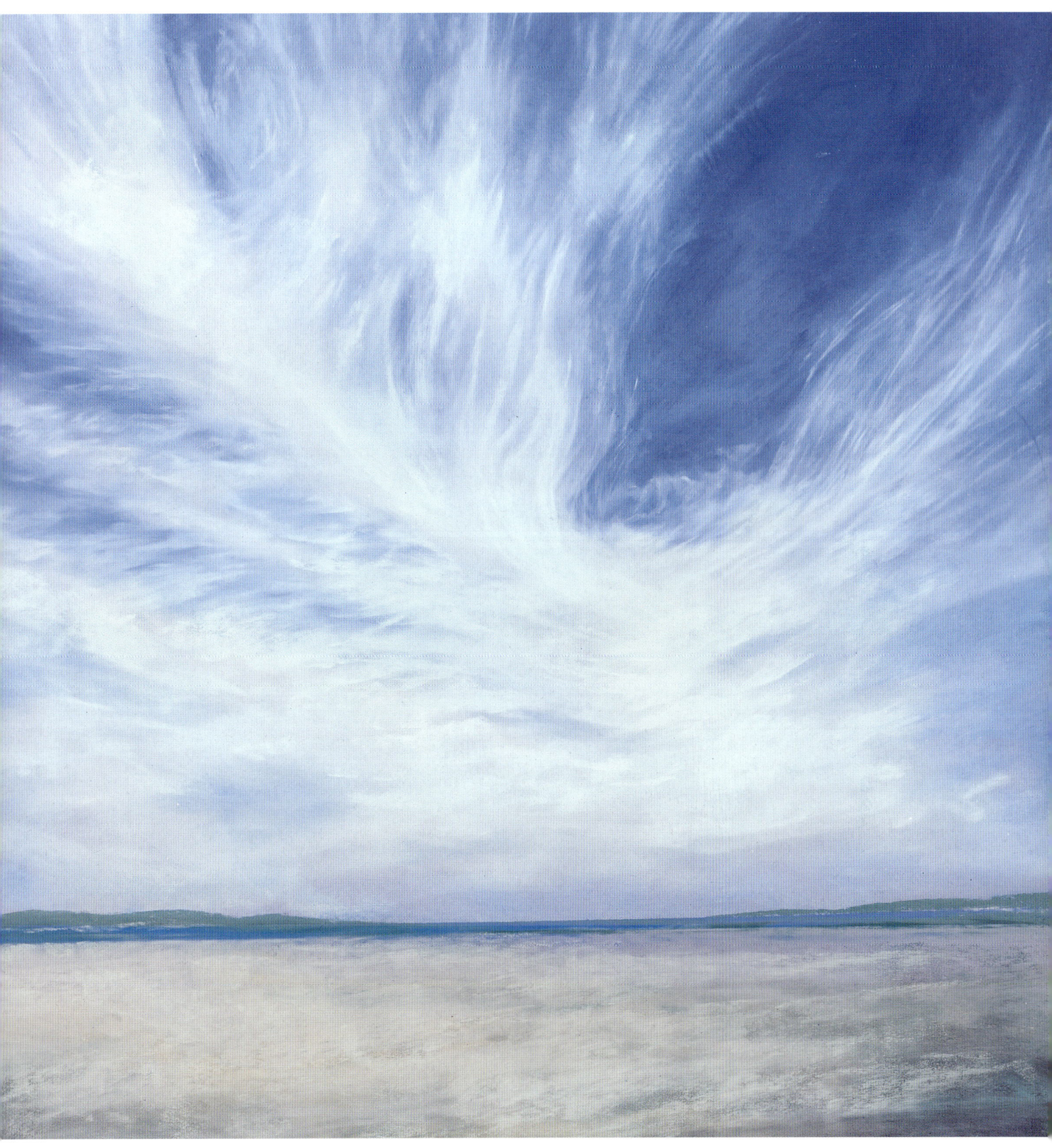

The painting at the end of stage 5.

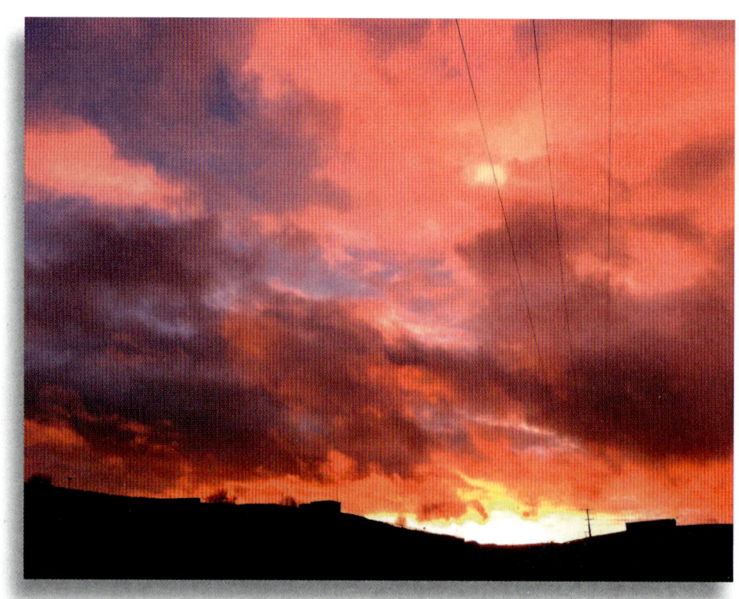

Vivid Sunset

Up to this point, we have been using a relatively muted and limited palette. You have explored different ways of building layers, applying marks and using the shaper. It is now time to really have fun with colour. This tutorial will show you how to control and use powerful colours to produce a beautiful sunset sky. We will also need to use bridging colours to control the blending process.

When using a range of very vivid, distinct colours, it's more important to keep your hands clean. Within stages, don't wet your hands: it's enough to brush them on your apron or a dry cloth. Between stages, wash your hands and dry them thoroughly – while basic, this advice is the best way to help control this colour challenge.

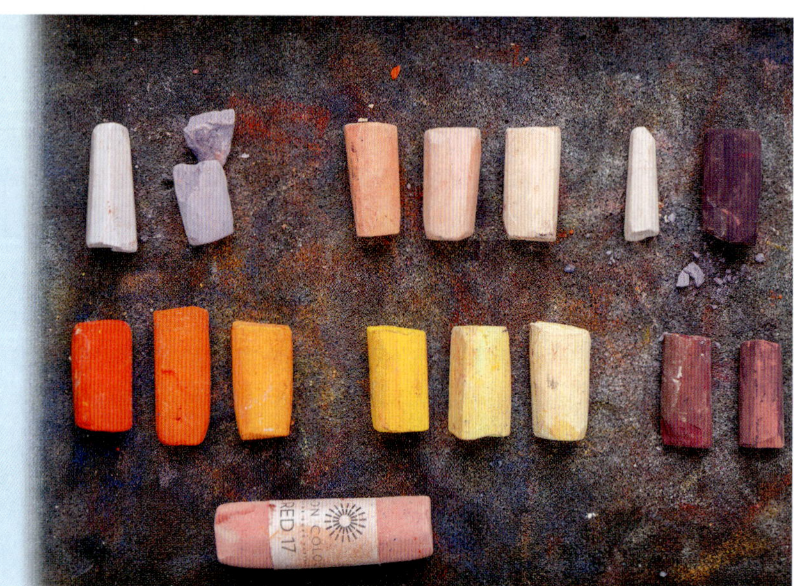

SELECT YOUR PALETTE

We need a rich range of warm reds, purples, oranges, and yellows, along with cooler blues, purples and pale lilacs – quite the range!

Note that the colours used for additional details aren't in the Sandra Orme Sky Set.

Warm sunset R15, A15, A14, O2, A12, A10, Y12

Darker clouds A36, R15, R16

Bridging colours R6, R18, LT12, LT5

Additional details BV1, R17

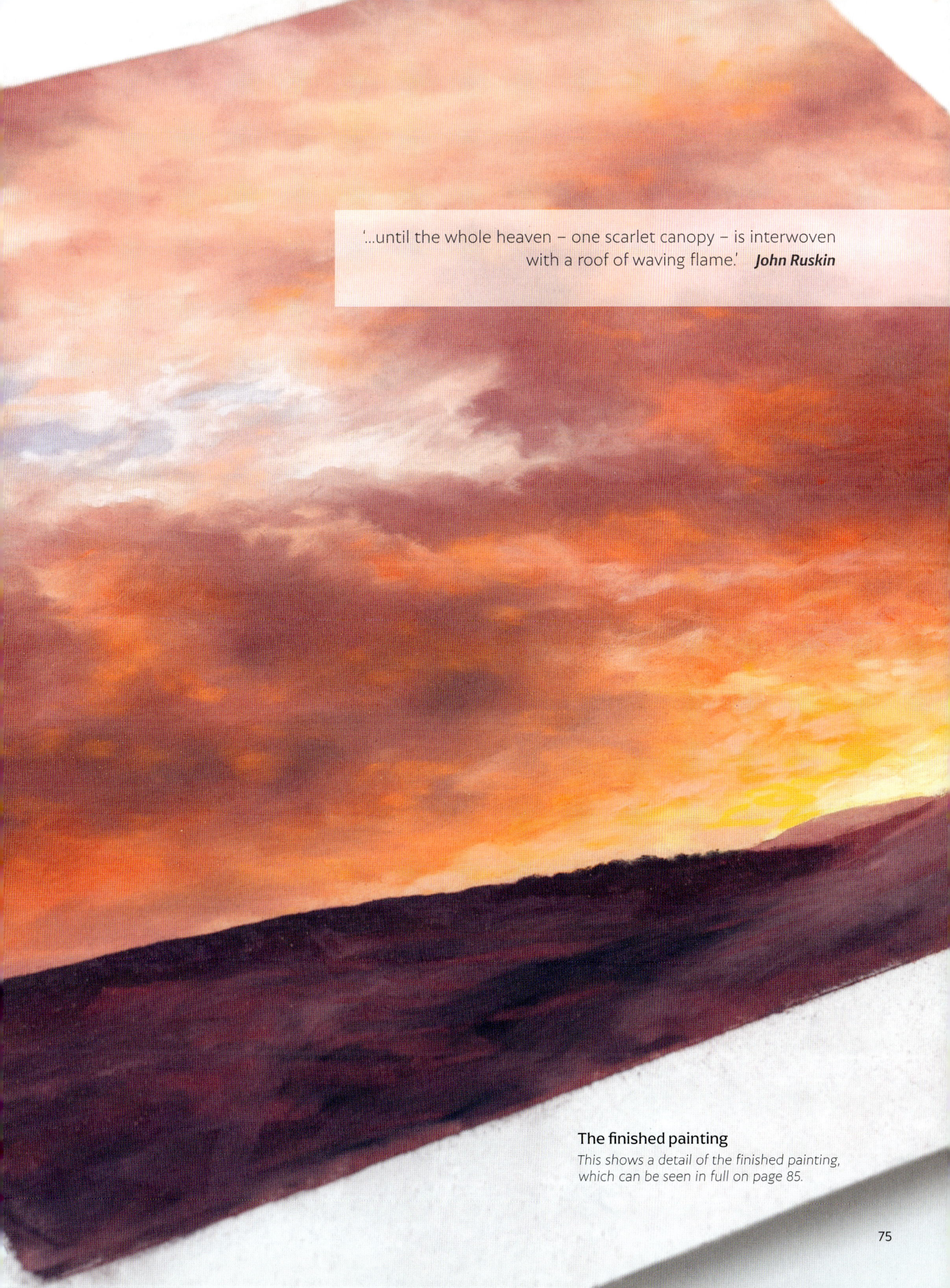

The finished painting
*This shows a detail of the finished painting,
which can be seen in full on page 85.*

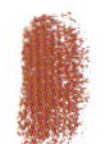

STAGE 1

Mark-making

We are going to add a base layer of vivid colours ranging from yellow at the horizon up to blue at the top the sky. There are a number of colour transitions to deal with so we need to be careful about colour placement and use bridging colours (purple and pink). Most importantly, we want plenty of layers of rich colours overlaying each other. That's what will give us a sense of depth.

- Sketch a line for the horizon using a pale pastel and the slicing technique.

- Add bright yellow near the horizon, then orange, then bright pink. Build up the shapes with a variety of flat marks using the side of the pastel.

- Use sweeping gestures and criss-cross your marks where the clouds are.

- Add purple over the edges of the pink along with other reds and pinks. Keep reds to the middle of the clouds, neither near the edges nor the purple areas.

- Add shades of blue, being careful to keep it in the right areas.

- Overlap bridging purple, lilac or pink around the edges of the blue in places.

- Add deep red to the land.

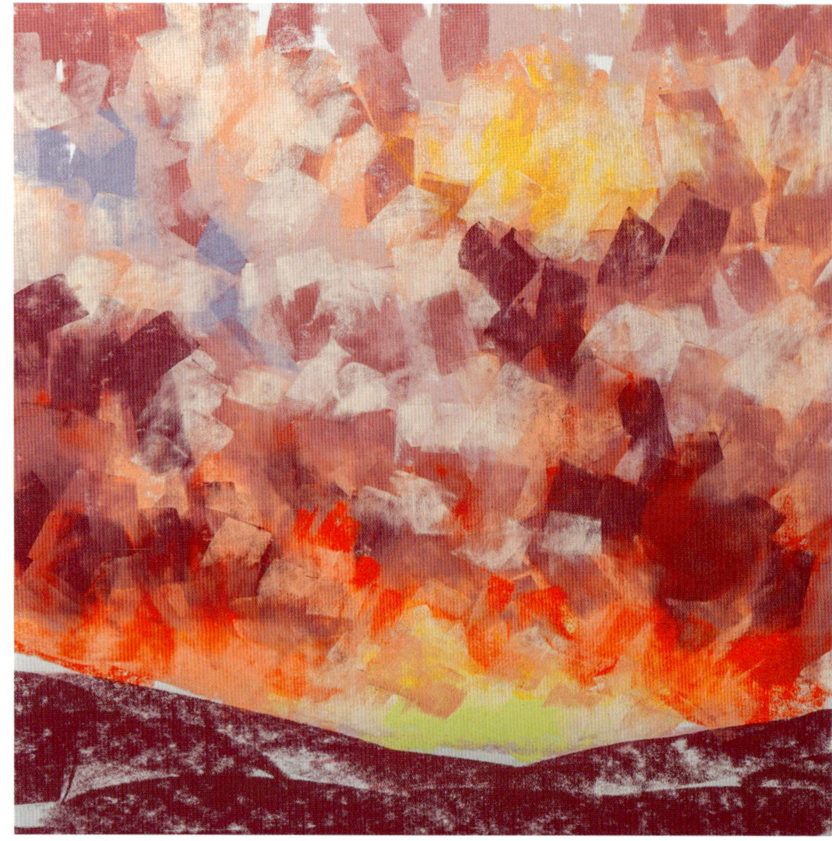

The painting at the end of stage 1 – initial marks.

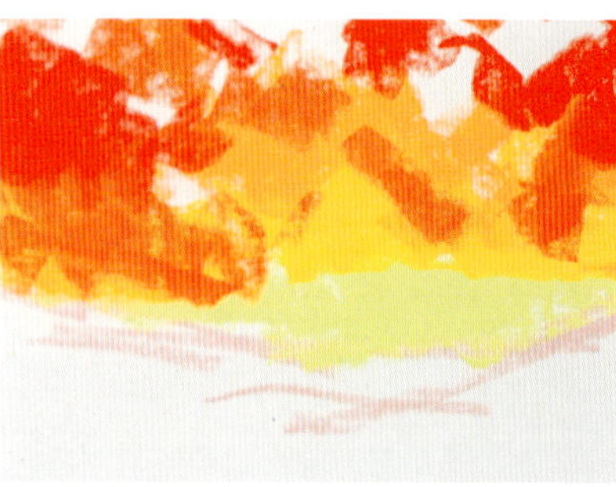

Horizon

The source photograph shows buildings, but we can turn these into the hill-line behind the buildings – the joys of artistic licence. The vivid colours above the horizon will give depth and richness to the colour on top.

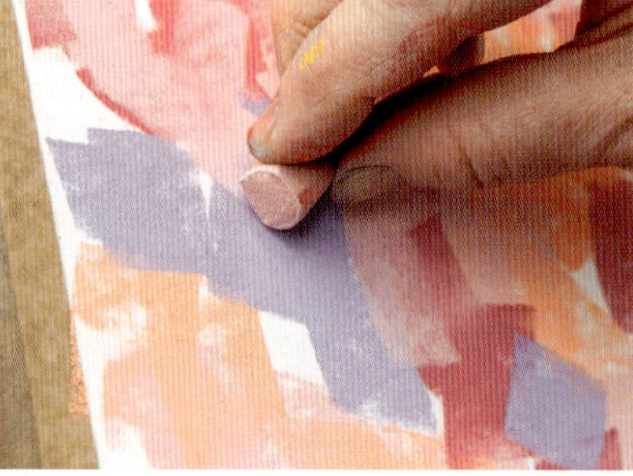

Bridging colours

Generally, it's best to establish the areas with extremes of colour – the reds and blues in this example – and then add the bridging colours (see page 34) into the gaps you leave in between these areas.

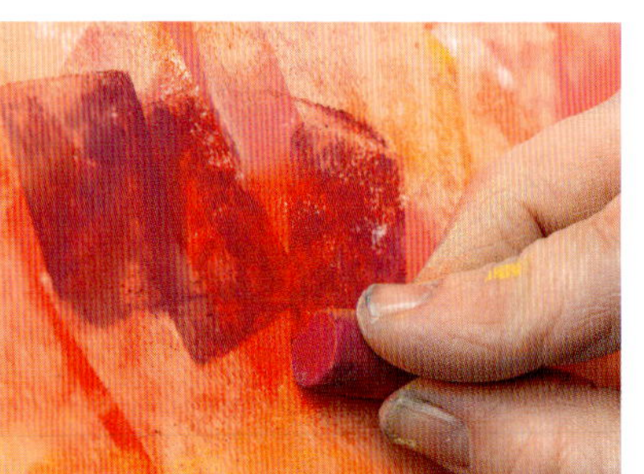

Three layers

To ensure depth and richness in the colours, try to build up at least three layers of marks in any area, with the dominant colour at the top.

Blending

- Blend carefully, using sweeping gestures along with limited circular movements.

- Keep the cloud areas where you want them by blending small areas at a time, and wiping your hands in between each.

- Be aware of how much pressure you're using when blending. The more pressure you use, the more the underlying colours will mix and rise to the surface.

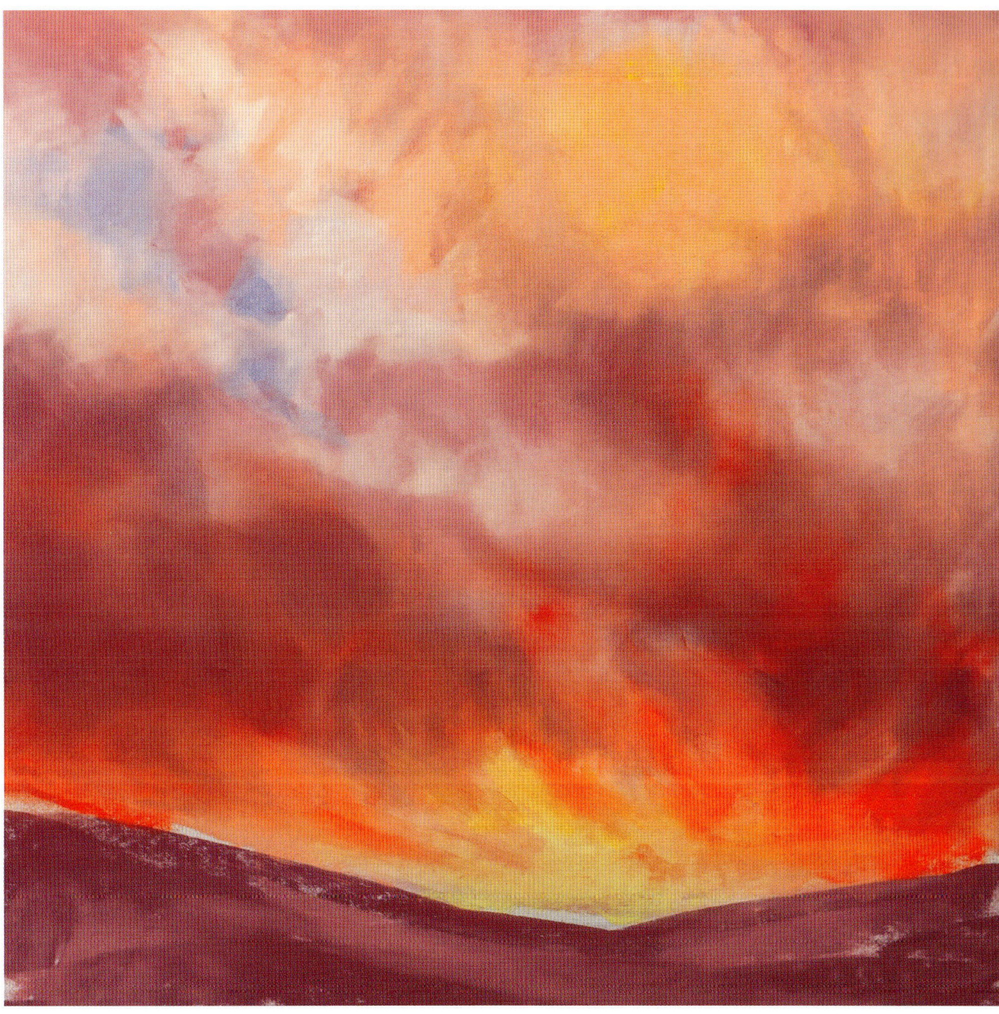

The painting at the end of stage 1 – blended.

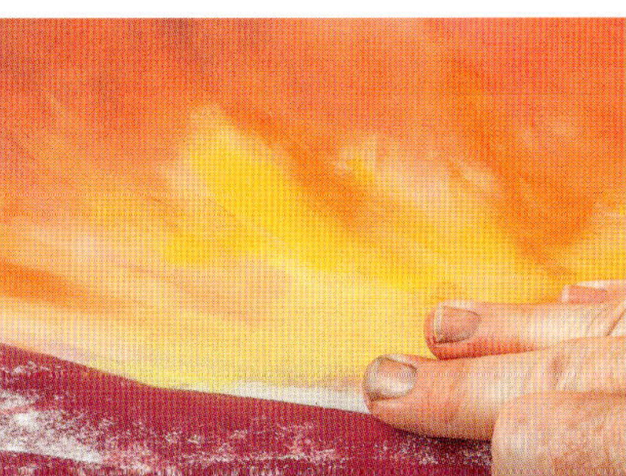

Vivid results

Avoid blending into the yellow sunset, or you risk losing the impact. Work carefully here, and only ever outwards from the yellow.

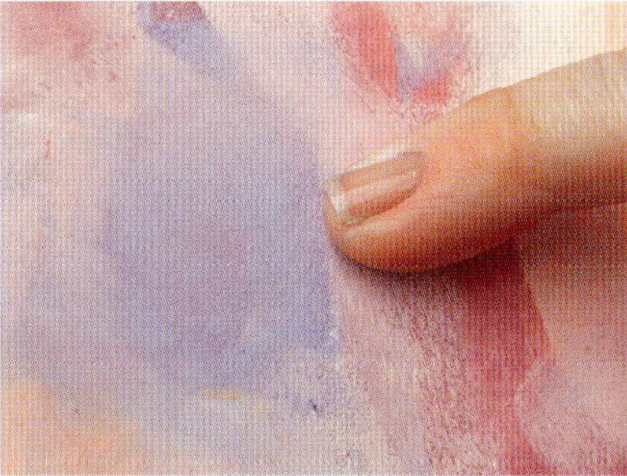

Blues

Only blend the blue into the bridging colours – not beyond, or you'll muddy the results.

STAGE 2

Colour combinations make it harder to assess the complete painting, so rather than applying marks and blending as a whole, for this project we focus on smaller areas in turn earlier than usual.

Note, however, that we are still using blocky marks in the main – there's very little variety of marks at this stage. That sort of refinement will come later, once we've established the richness of the overall picture.

- Select 'rule of three' deep pinks and purples. Use darker shades towards the top of the sky.

- Look for the dominant colour in each area, and reinforce it. Consider the angle and directions of the clouds as you add further blocking marks.

- Blend gently as you work – don't lose the mark-making. This is an energetic piece, but we want to keep the different areas distinct. Furthermore, blending too vigorously will bring up too much of the underlying colours.

- Add darker areas (such as 'A' and 'B') with deeper purple to break up the solid masses of cloud.

- Repeat as needed to build up the depth of colour and mark-making needed to create that interesting surface. Don't be afraid to add new dark and light areas to refine the overall shape.

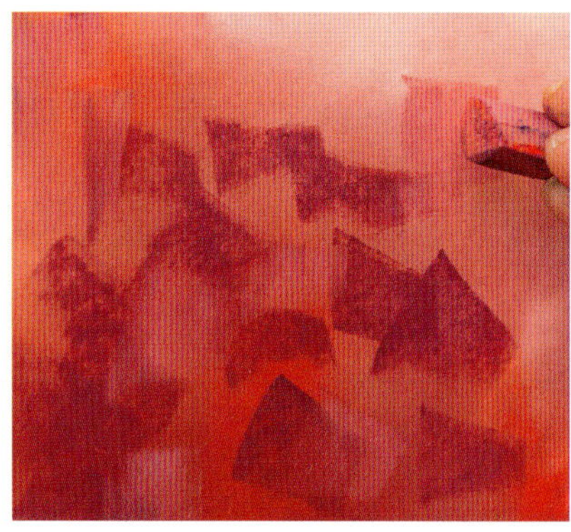

Deep purples

Blocking the deep purples and pinks over dark cloud areas helps you to build the movement of the clouds.

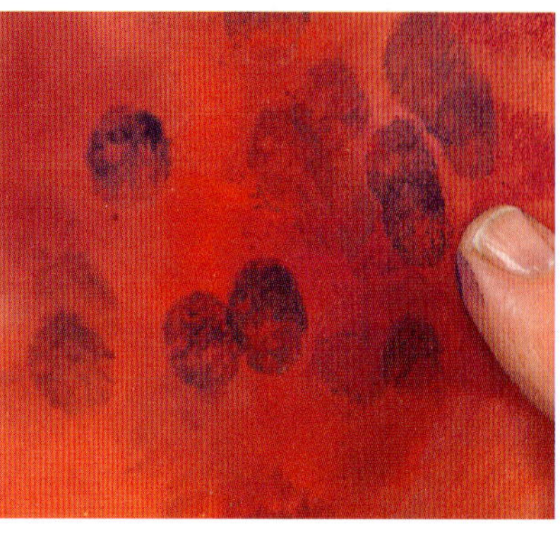

Fingerprints

Colour your finger with the pastel and tap it lightly and repeatedly on the surface. Once blended, this will create interesting swellings and 'bubbles' in the cloud.

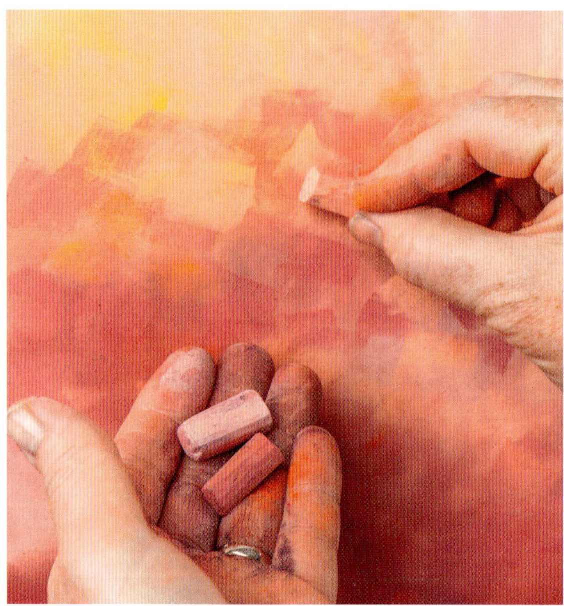

Rule of three

Select an area to focus on, pick three harmonious colours, and use them to refine the area.

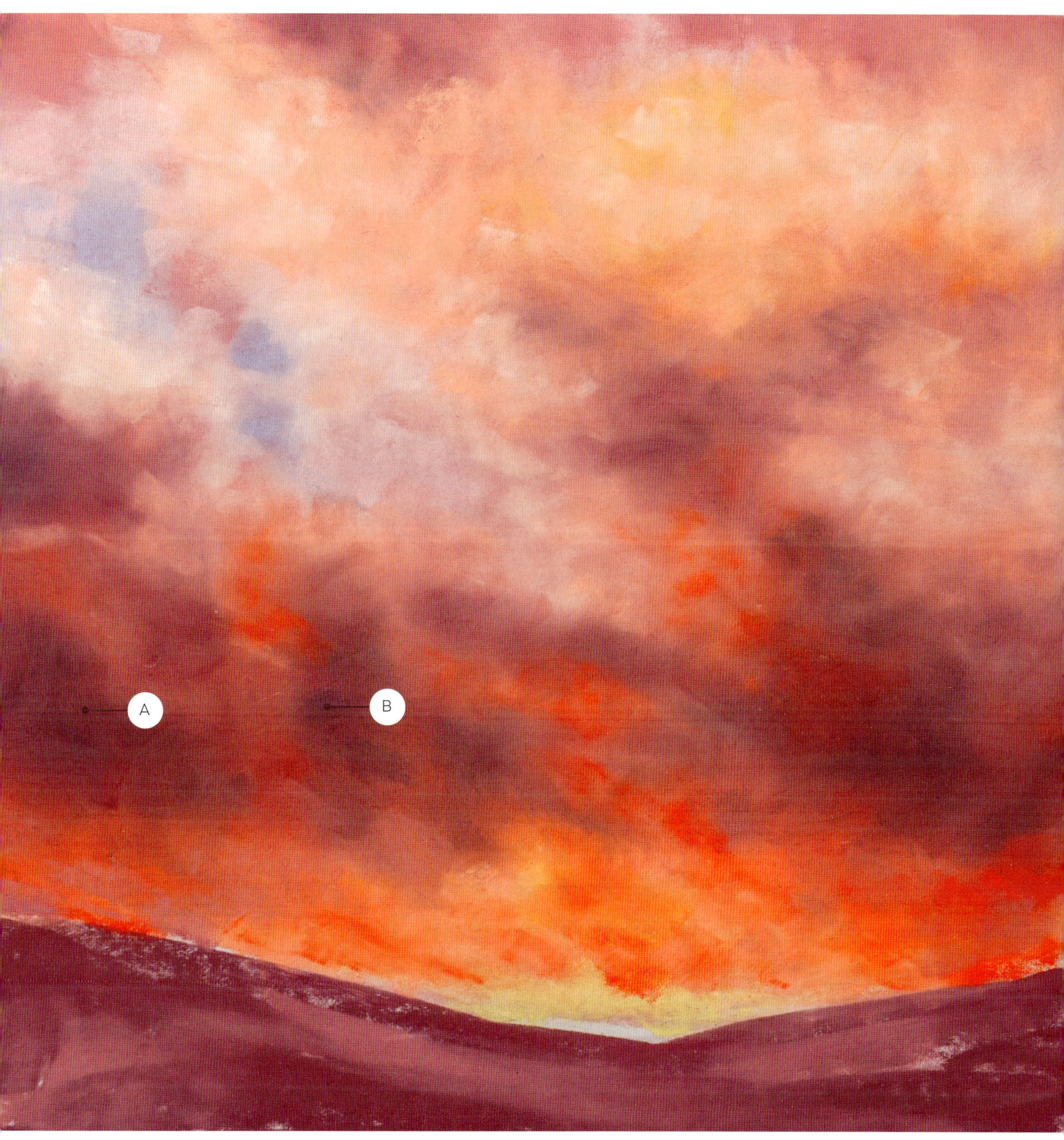

The painting at the end of stage 2.

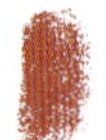# STAGE 3

As we move to refine the marks on the painting, it's worth pointing out that we're not necessarily trying to match the source photograph's colour, but rather to enjoy and develop rich colour ourselves. Refer to the photograph, but concentrate on your painting, not the inspiration.

The key at this stage is to build on the foundations and create the dynamism that we can develop later on.

- Use the rule of three to select yellows and oranges around the sun peeking over the horizon: use the tip and tilt technique to add this colour to the lowest part of the sky.

- Twist, rock and roll the pastels across the base of the clouds to create the vivid undersides.

- Use less pressure and work up into the darker areas, avoiding too much contact with the darker pinks or purples. Add some darker colours in between areas as necessary.

- Work gradually up the sky, refining as you go. Add more detail to suggest where the light breaks through the clouds with various marks.

- Blend using just one finger; even more lightly than in the earlier stages.

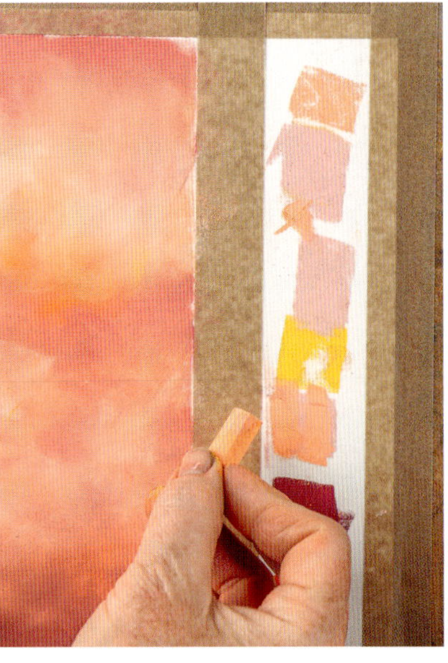

Colour swatches

Because of the range of colour combinations used, it's particularly handy to have your colour swatches at the side of the painting. Compare your pastels with the swatches to check you're applying the right colour.

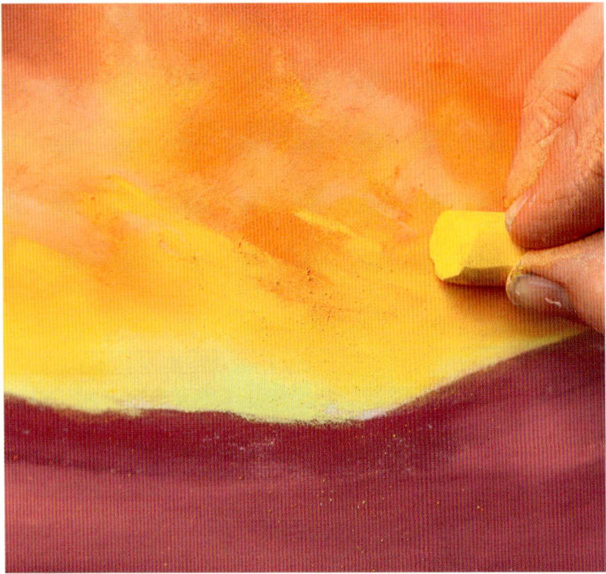

Lower part of the sky

Press firmly with the pastels – this applies more pigment to the surface and ensures a nice vivid result – and blend softly using the shaper tool.

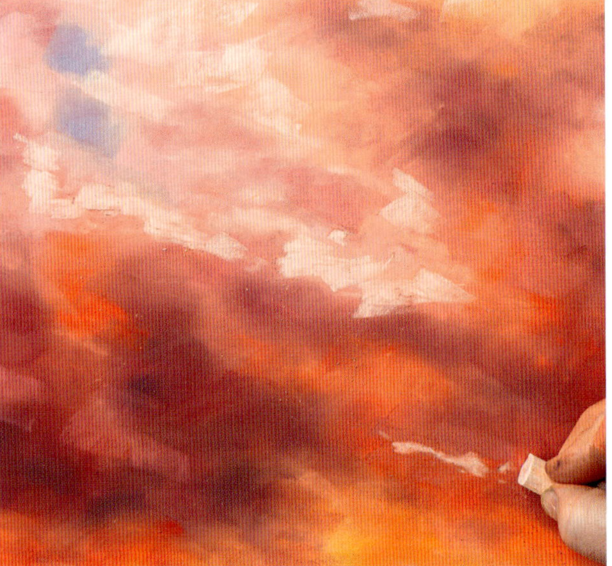

Edges of the clouds

Apply your three palest tones for the highlights, using a combination of techniques: slicing, rolling and using the tip of the pastel. Don't be tempted to use white – as you can see here, even pale pink looks white against the vivid colours.

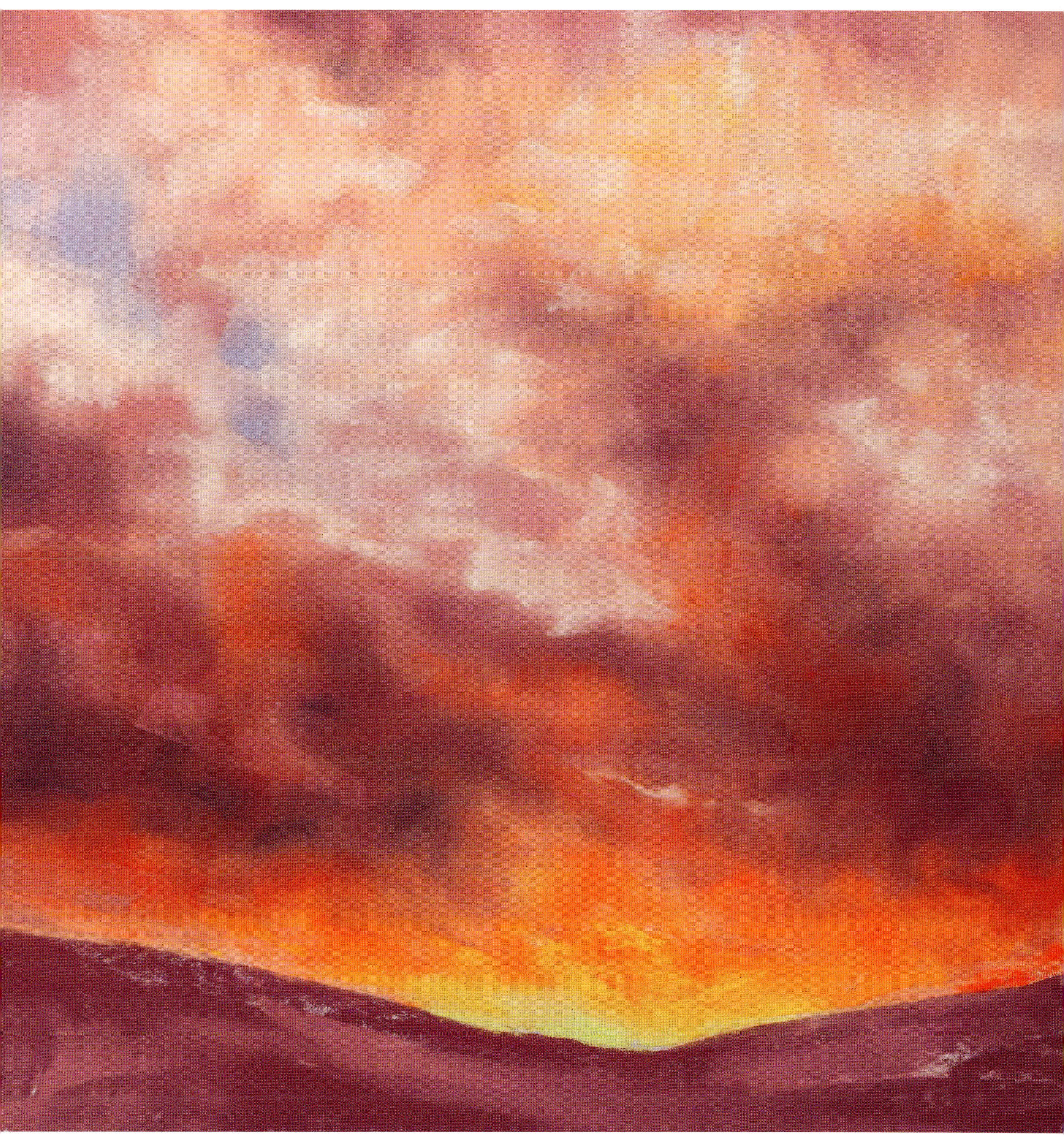

The painting at the end of stage 3.

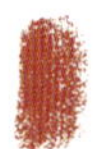
STAGE 4

Refinement begins at this stage, establishing smaller, clearer areas and carefully blending things in. With colour, this stage is particularly important.

- Use pale lilac to carefully draw in the bluer areas of sky. You might expect to use blue, but that would look far too vivid and unconvincing in the context of the warm sky.

- Use the rule of three, applying darker tones towards the top of the painting then lighter towards the base.

- Work edges in carefully using the tips of the bridging colour pastels, then use the shaper to push the colours along the edges to create cloud shapes.

- Repeat over the whole sky as needed. Take breaks, step back and assess to make sure the colours and marks are remaining in balance across the painting as a whole.

- Make areas further from the focal points (A and B) less defined and looser at the edges. In addition, deepen the tone towards the edges to keep the eye in the frame.

- Create cloud edges that lead the eye down from the blue sky in a zigzag to the sunset.

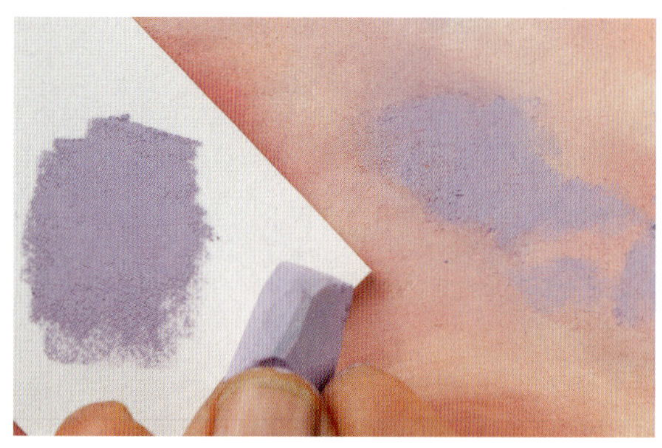

Colour relationships

Colours are informed by those nearby. This can sometimes lead to surprising optical illusions! Here, you can see a swatch of the same pastel (BV3) appears lilac on a neutral piece of clean paper, while against the warm-hued pink on the surface, it seems blue. Be alert for this.

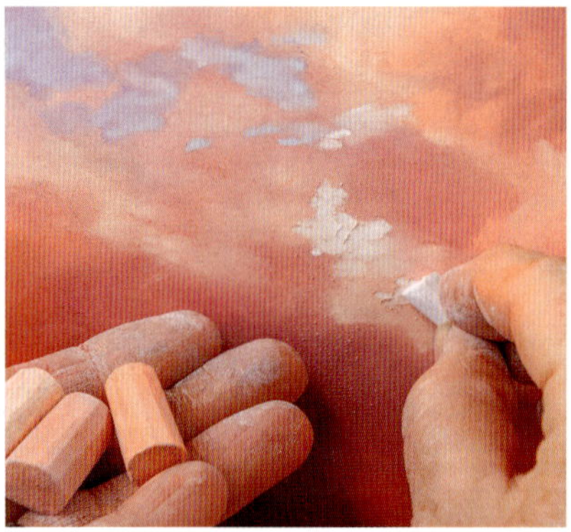

Sit the sky back

To prevent the lilac looking as through it's sitting on the surface, we need to knock it back using a range of paler bridging shades. Use the shaper to push pink or pale cloud in front of the gap in the cloud.

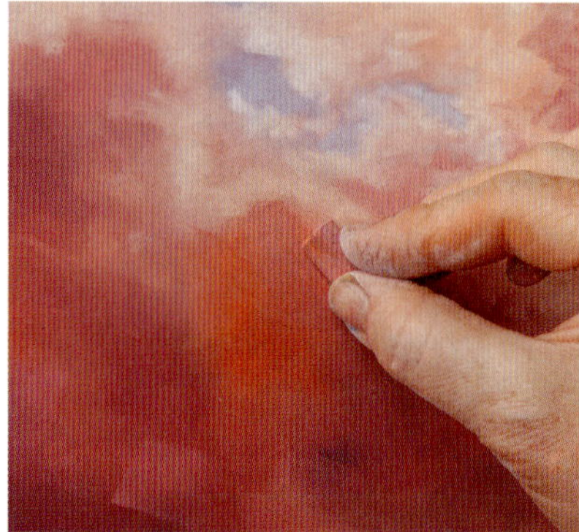

Limit the bridge

If you work too far out with the bridging colours, you risk them becoming dominant. Use them sparingly and in small areas so that the overall painting doesn't take on a muted feel.

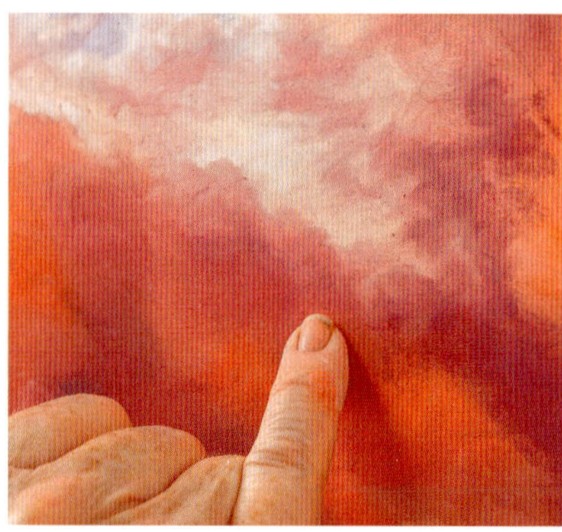

High contrast

After working in the paler tints, try adding areas of the darker tones. Blend the two away from each other with your finger, to leave areas of high contrast that draw the eye.

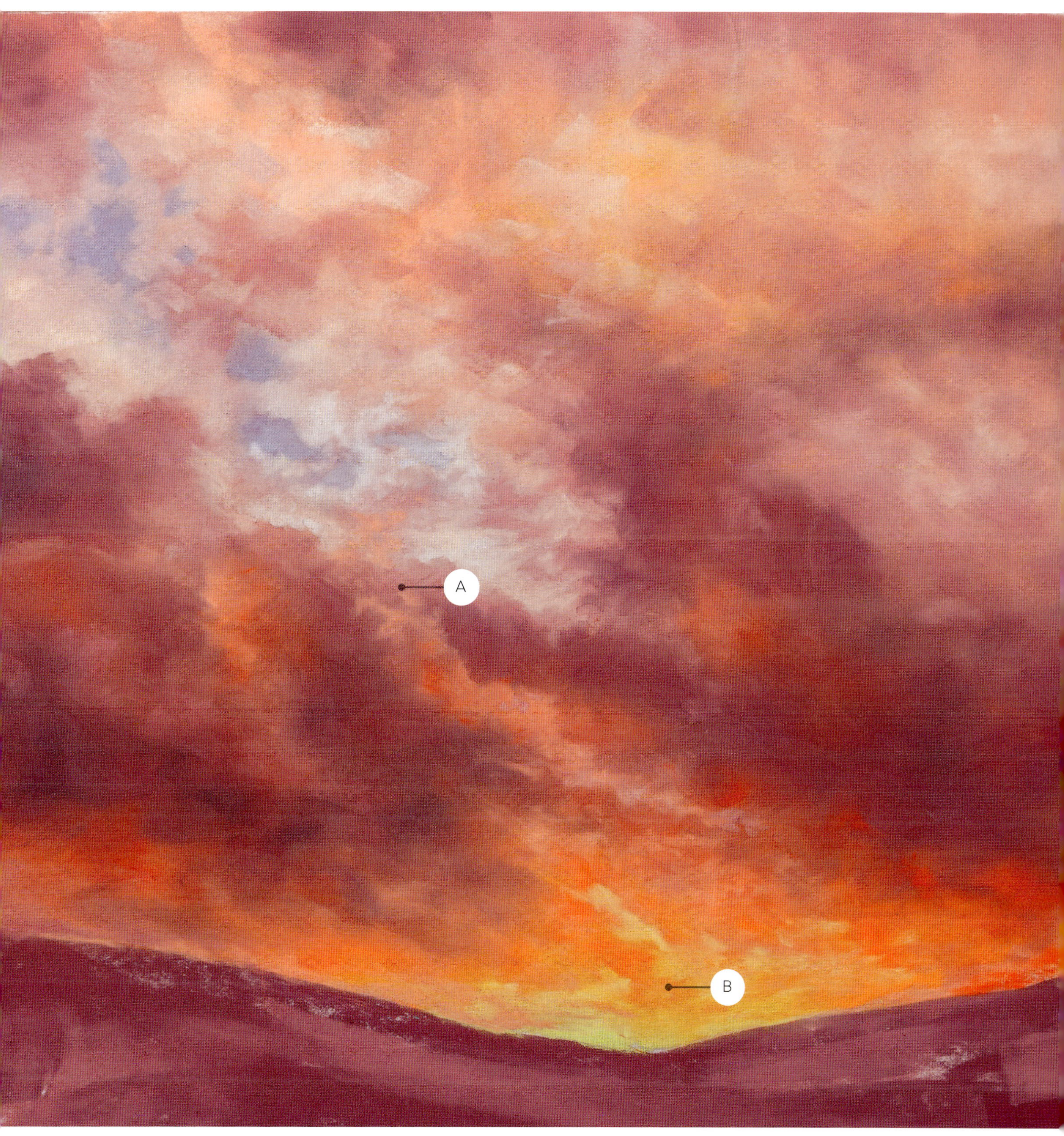

The painting at the end of stage 4.

STAGE 5

At this stage, we need to ensure the colours balance while drawing the eye through the picture. Step back and review every so often as you work. Before you decide you are finished, see page 111 for tips on ensuring you don't over-work the painting.

- Revisit the lowest part of the sky, where it meets the horizon. Add pale yellows here, slightly off-centre, to bring out the contrast and impact in the area.

- Add flickers of light and colour here and there using warm oranges. Use your artistic judgement and be sparing. Only subtle touches are needed.

- If you are happy with the lower area of sky, choose three mid and dark tones and draw heavily over the foreground to develop the hill shape against the sunset.

- Add further dark tones in the landscape to draw the eye towards the horizon. A stand of trees on the right-hand hill will help to counterbalance the light and blue sky on the upper left.

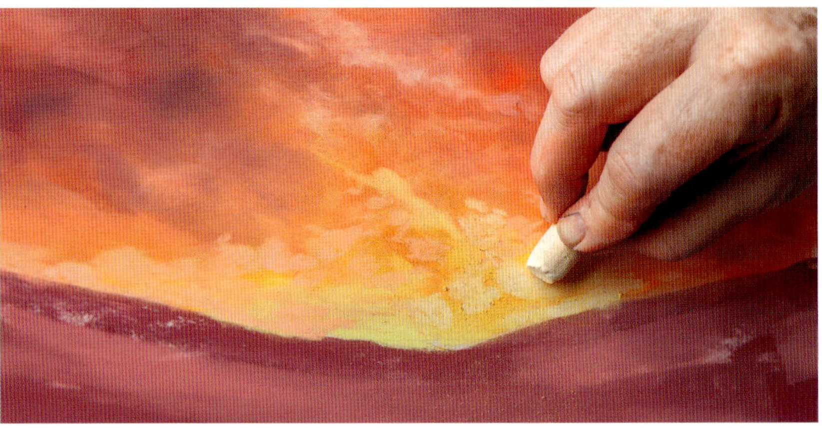

Sun

Use three or four yellows and oranges in this area; the key is to add hints and touches to prevent it looking separate from the surrounding clouds. The sky should look like a cohesive whole from bottom to top.

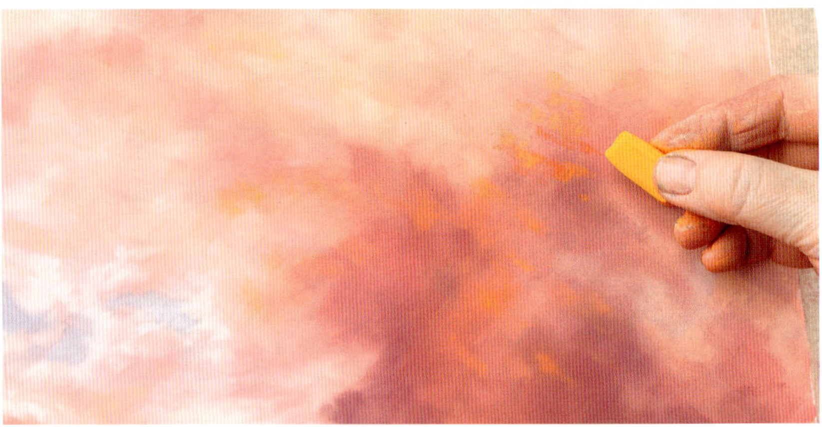

Warm the clouds

Keep touches of the orange minimal, and blend them in more thoroughly away from the sun.

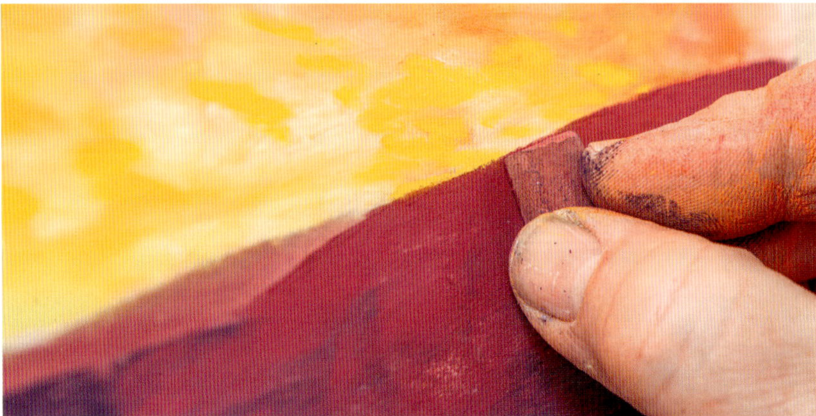

Foreground

Add layers of the mid and dark tones to the foreground using criss-cross motion with the flat side of the pastels. Tip and tilt the pastel to create a sharp edge on the horizon.

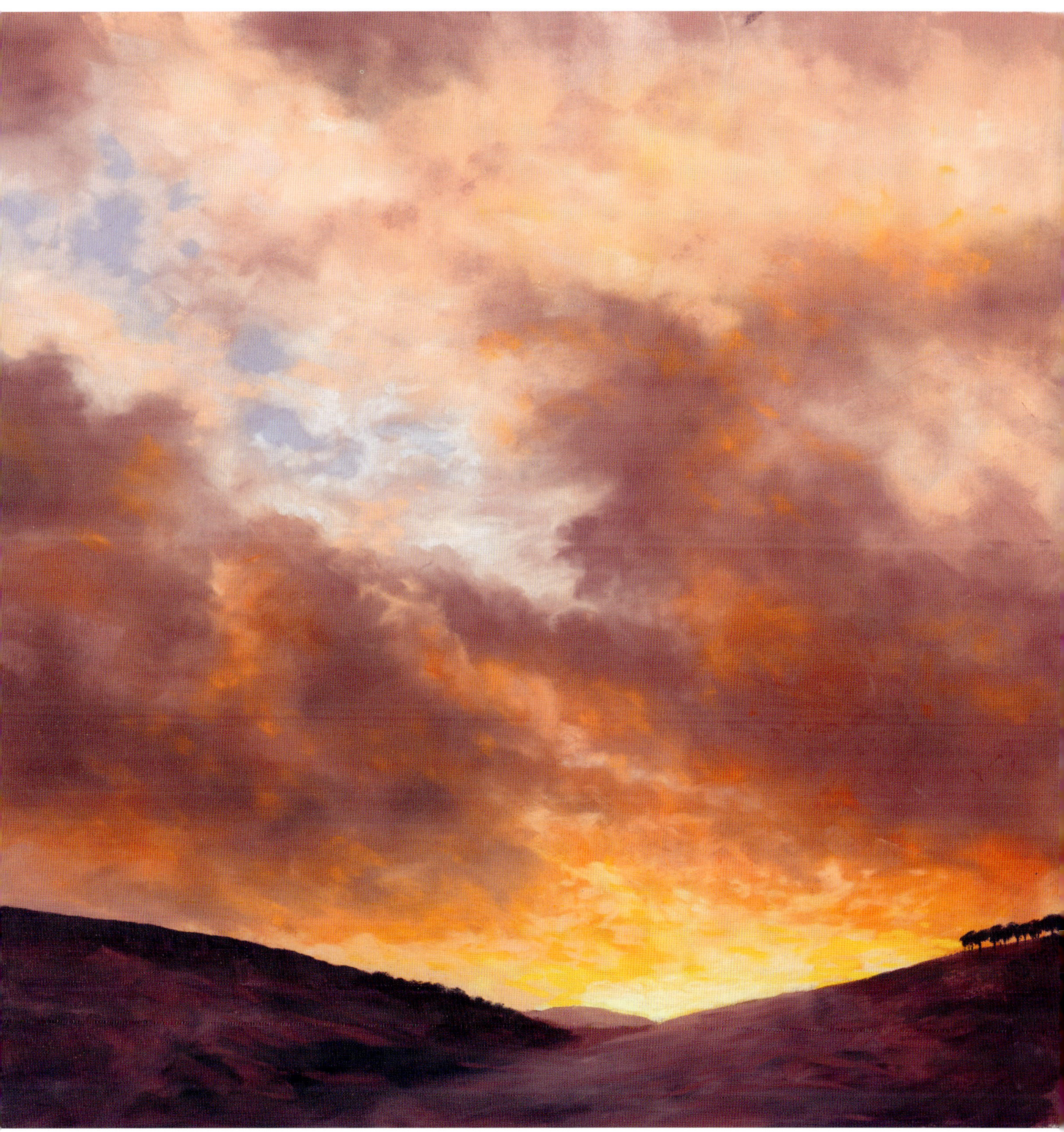

The painting at the end of stage 5.

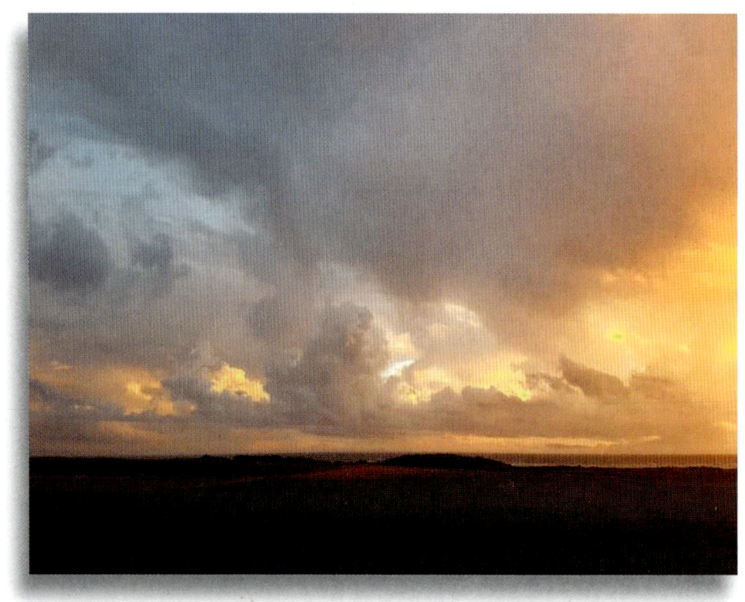

Stormy Sunset

This tutorial combines vivid colours with dramatic cloud shapes. The key here is learning how to deal with colour transitions in order to bring the best out of these striking clouds. We will take the lessons of the vivid sunset further and add more colours along with creating stronger cloud edges, movement and effects. You will explore moving from dark to light whilst transitioning through colours from orange to blue. The result will be a bold, exciting artwork that conveys the power of this stormy evening sky.

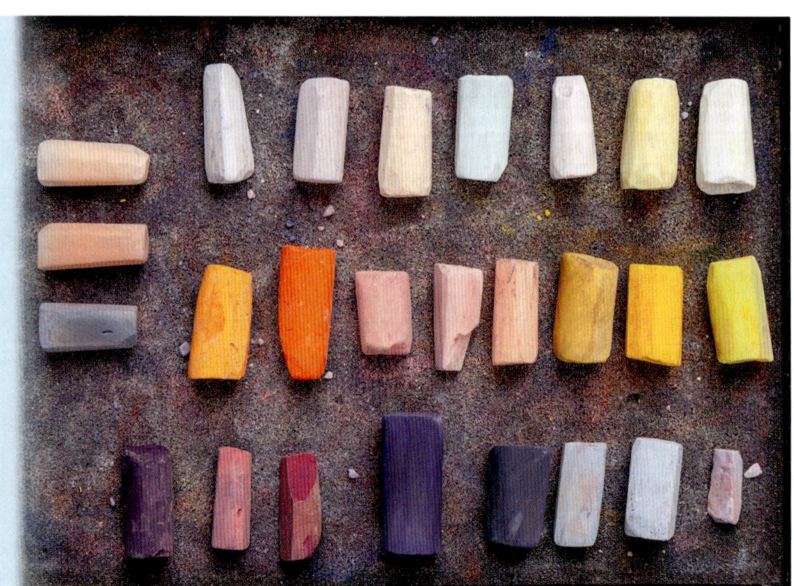

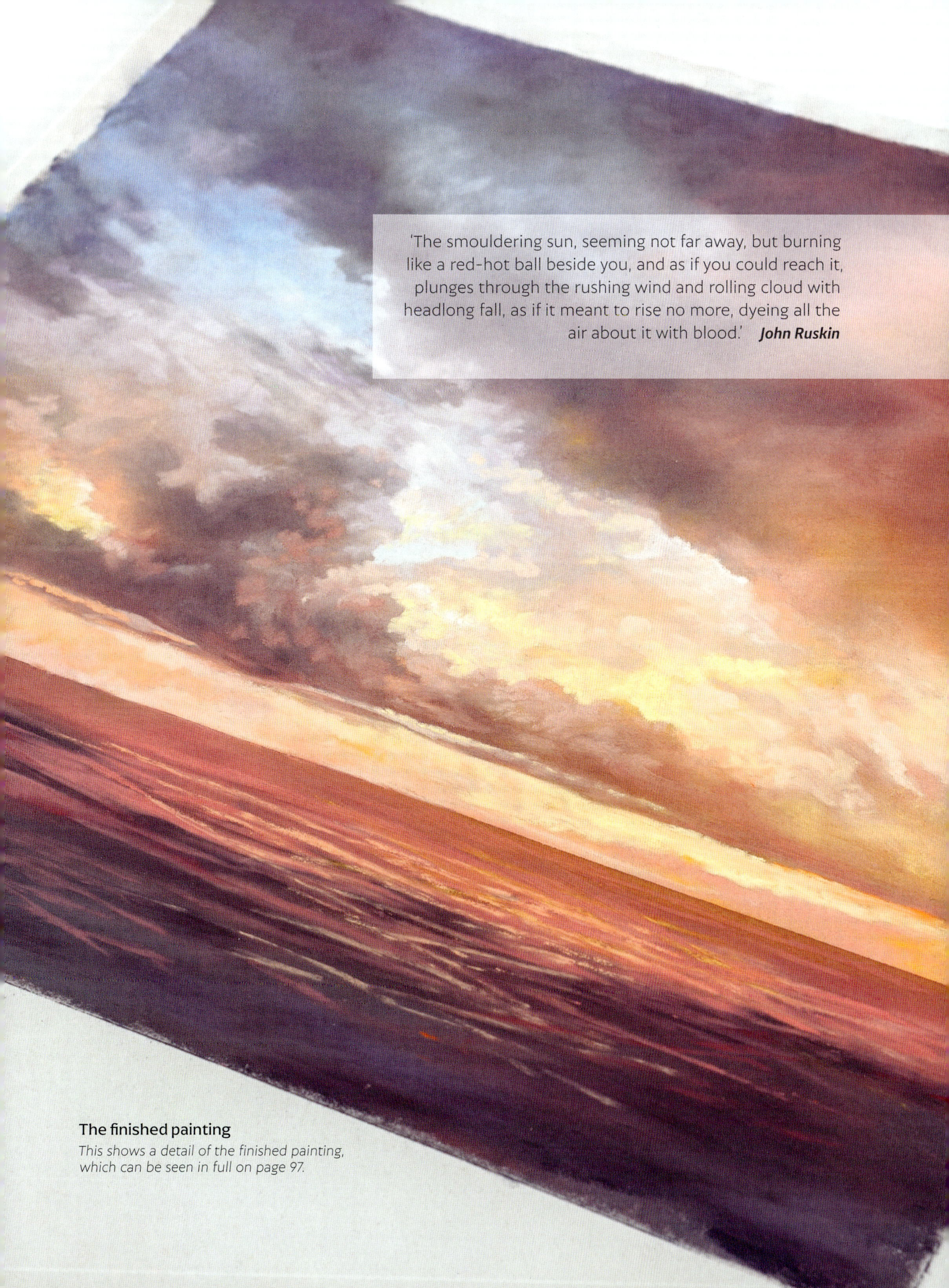

The finished painting
This shows a detail of the finished painting, which can be seen in full on page 97.

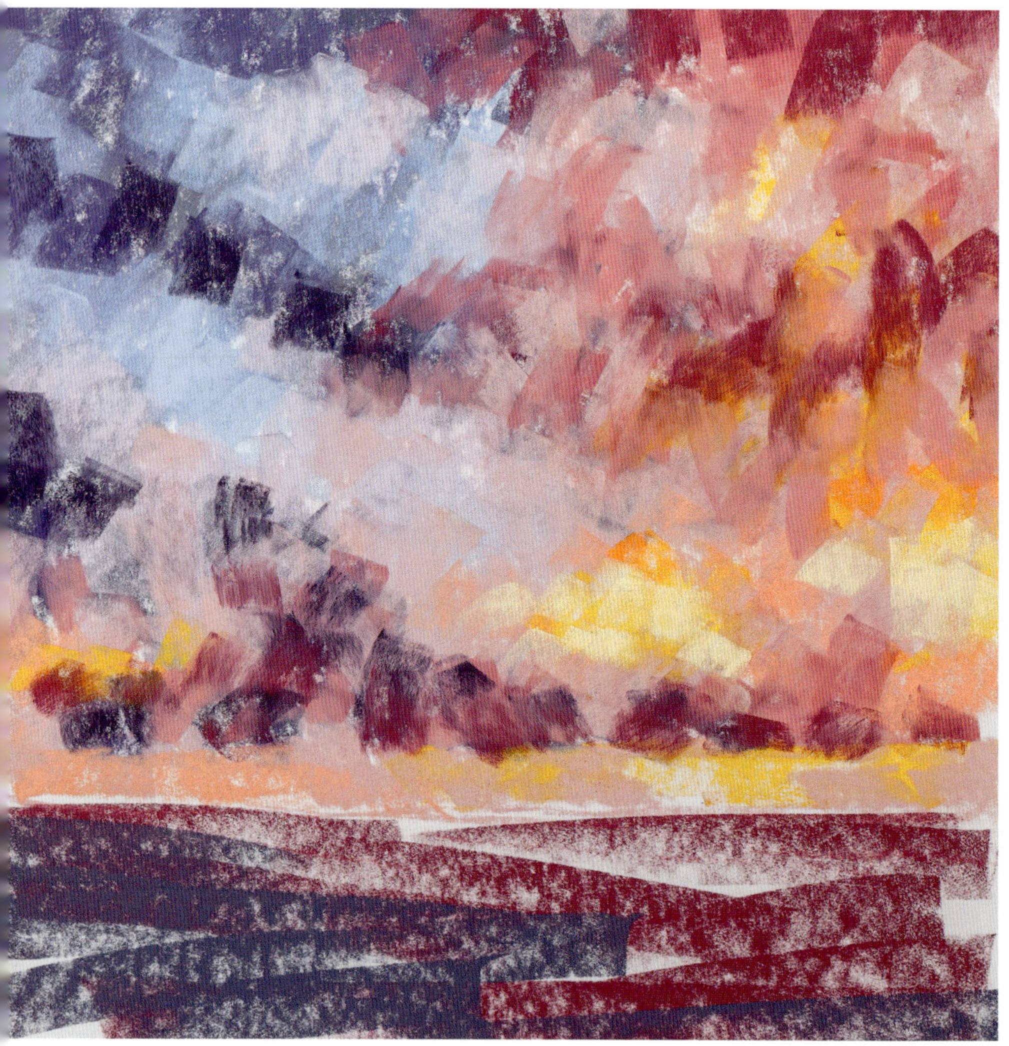

The painting at the end of stage 1 – initial marks.

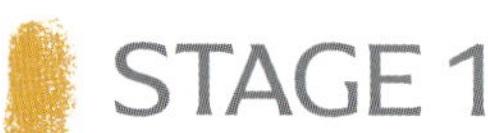

STAGE 1

Because we're working with complex colour transitions, these early stages of colour placement are particularly important. Take your time to establish solid, clear foundations for later refinement.

Mark-making

- Build up the colours across the whole surface slowly and gradually. You need to get to a stage where the colour is smearing (see page 24).

- Use sweeping marks with the side of the pastel and block over the blue and grey areas on the left.

- Add purple as a bridging colour towards the middle then add pink, orange and yellow in succession as you work across to the right.

- Add some pinks and lilac to the bottom of the sky. Add some lights to the paler areas.

- Apply horizontal sweeping marks with the side of the pastel for the sea.

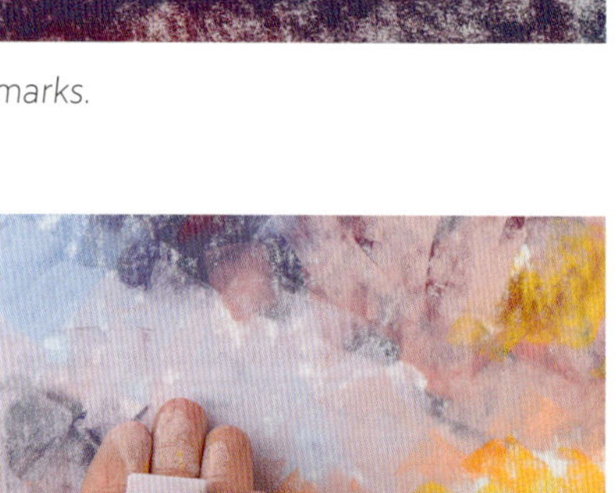

Sketch with bridging colours

Sketch in the main diagonal shapes using a mid-pink bridging colour – that way it'll fade in regardless of what you work on top.

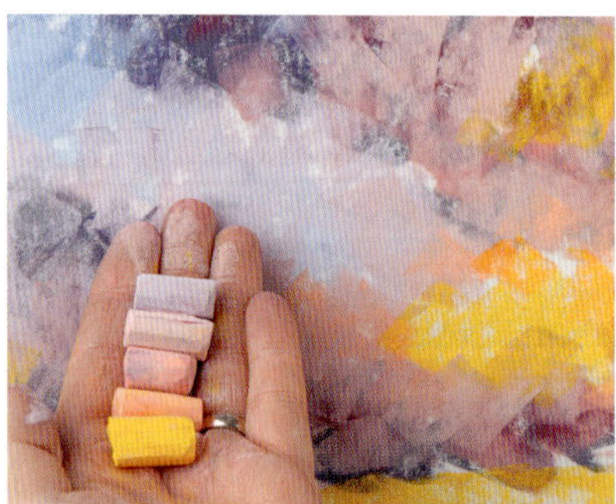

Use the rule of three

This stage means you need to concentrate on the broad colour transitions. The fewer other considerations you have, the better. Stay disciplined with the rule of three, particularly on the bridging colours, to avoid having to think of which colours to use on the fly.

Blending

- Blend using circular movements to build banks of different coloured clouds on the left- and right-hand sides.

- Add further layers of colours to build depth in the dark cloud areas.

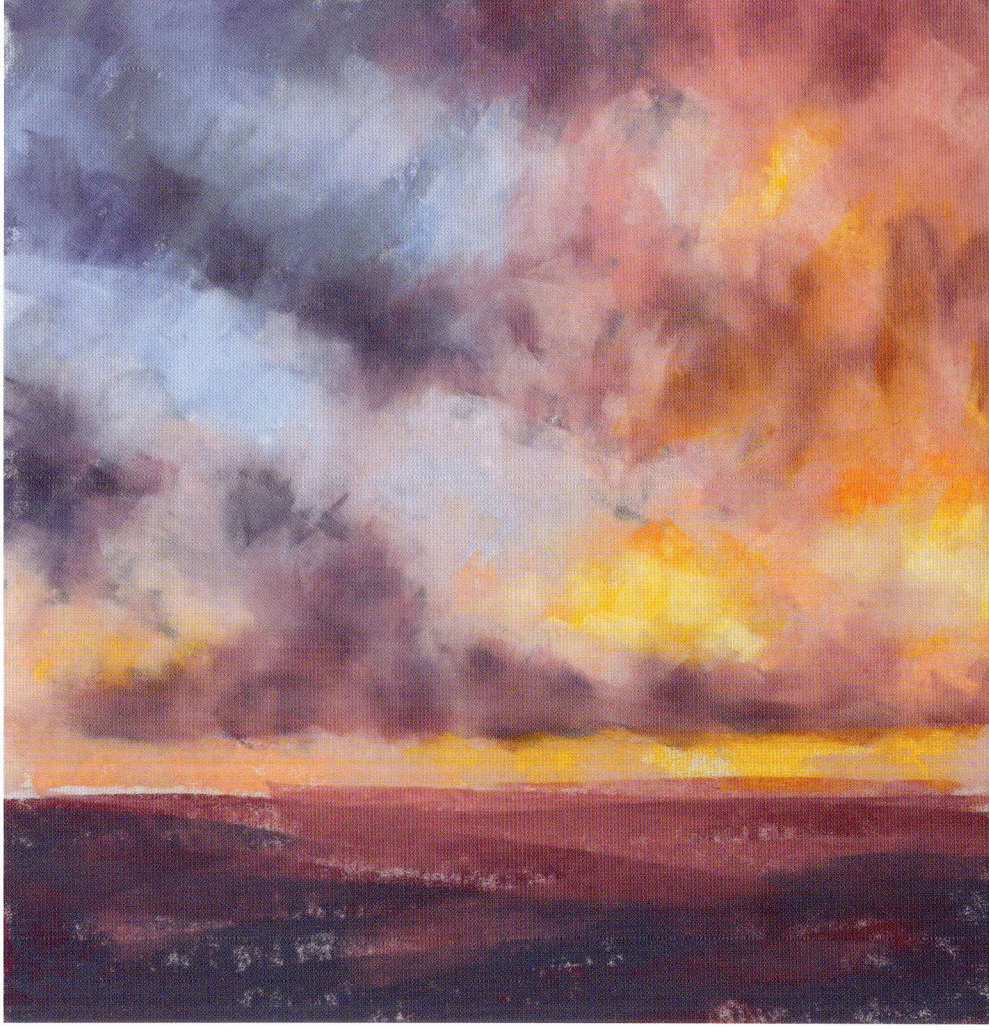

The painting at the end of stage 1 – blended.

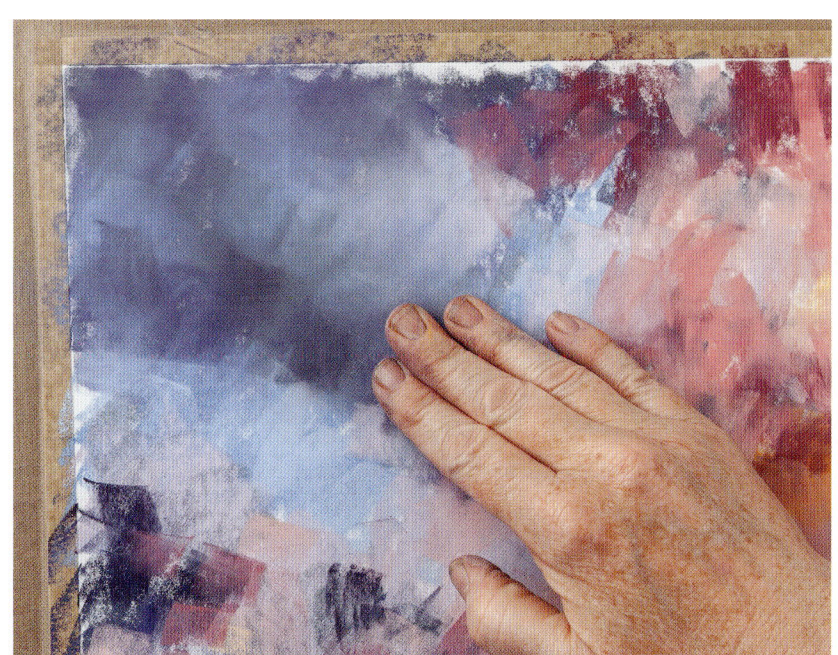

Keep colours separate

Keep dark, vivid or differently coloured areas distinct. Blend each area in isolation, then blend between. Keep cleaning your fingers!

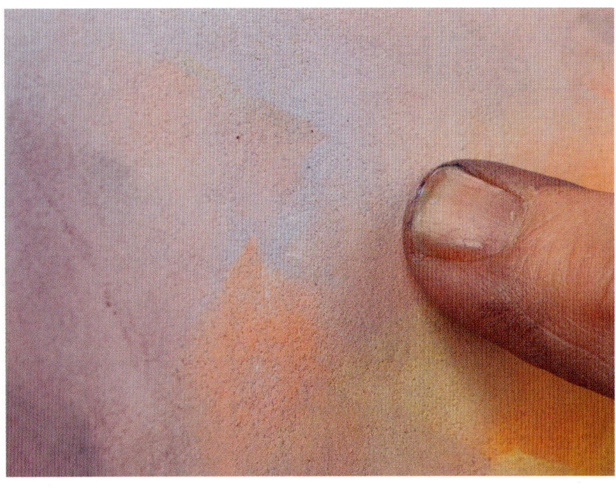

Tough blending

As there's not as much pastel on the surface as usual, when we start to blend, you might find that blending takes a bit more work, and feels more abrasive and resistant.

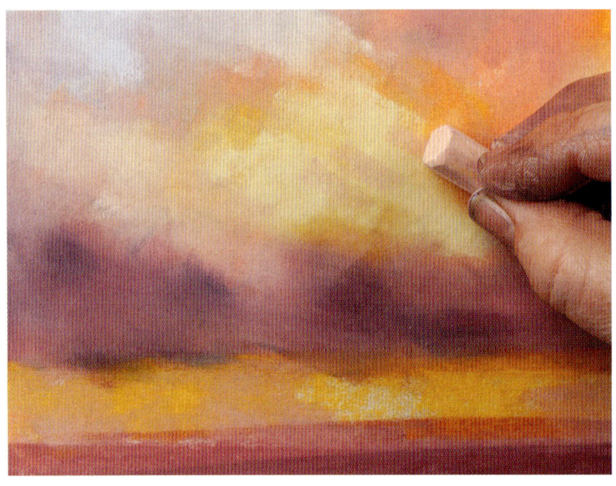

Low clouds

Don't get caught up in detail here at this stage, just concentrate on getting a good foundation of bright colour and interesting mark-making.

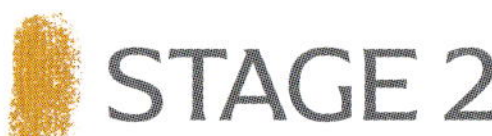

STAGE 2

Mark-making and blending are intertwined in this painting early on. This is because there are so many colours involved that you need to evolve more organically than in previous projects, and adapt as you go. Instead of applying marks all over the painting then blending in one go, you need to apply the pastels and blend area by area.

- Use blocky marks to build colour on the blue-grey clouds. Add tints of purple and pink, then blend gently, using swirling marks to retain a sense of movement.

- Work towards the right using bridging colours, then add more orange and gold tones.

- Blend gently to avoid over-mixing and to add some richer tones on the surface.

- Work down towards the horizon, applying smaller marks, using the rule of three to choose colours for the paler areas and the smaller clouds.

- Build up some low cloud banks and the patch of sunlight loosely.

- Work over each area a few times to loosely form the shapes and structure; and blend within each area.

- Look at the areas between shapes and add some transitional colours to start to join areas together.

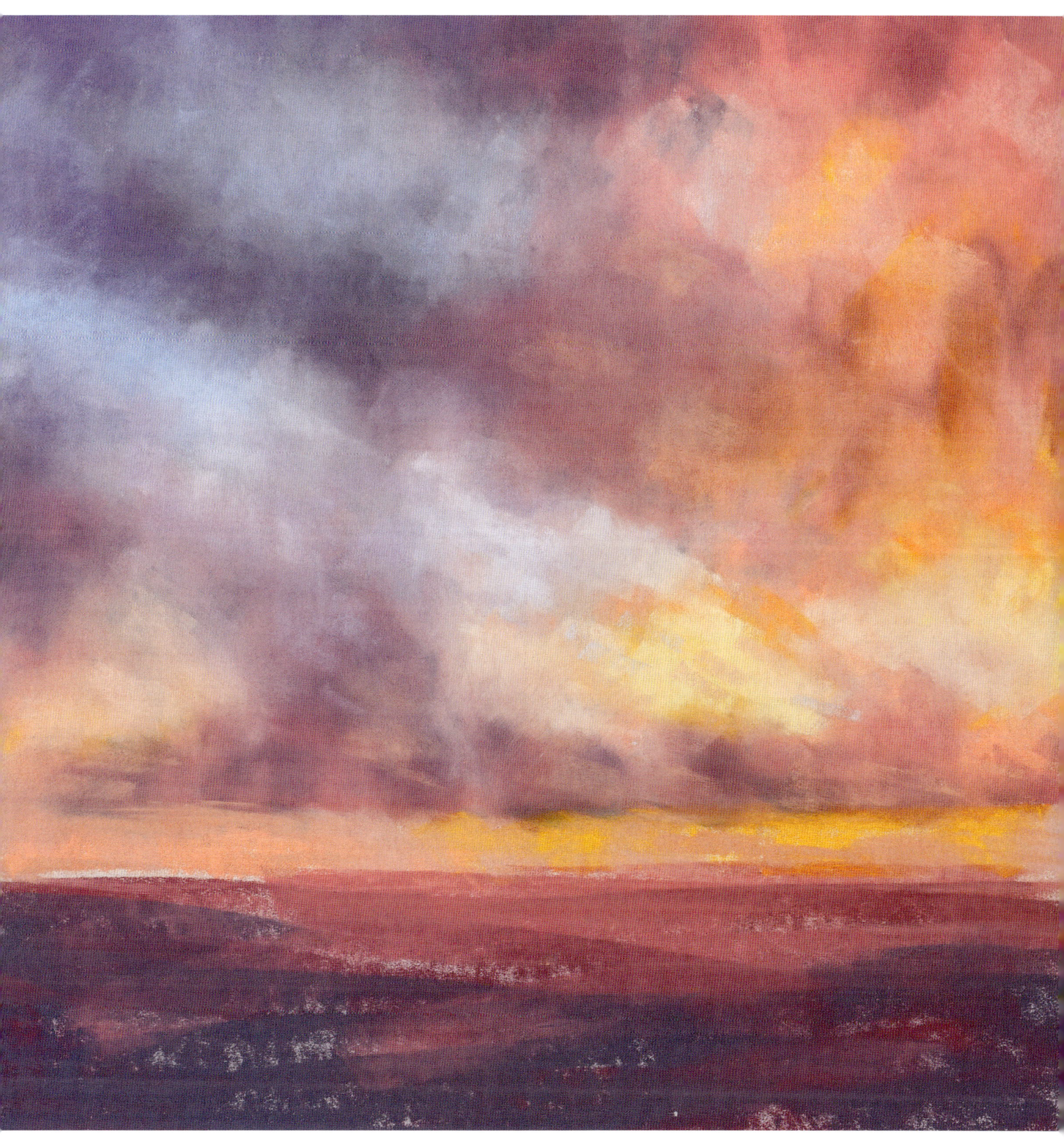

The painting at the end of stage 2.

STAGE 3

- Focus on the lower cloud area. Work across the cloud bank, using smaller block marks. Transition from lilac and greys to gold and copper colours.

- Build up the edges of the cloud bank using the bright colours from the sunlit area behind it; then carefully blend using the shaper tool.

- Add some stronger yellow and orange shades as you work your way up into the sky.

- Create the shape of the cloud bank using bright yellow and pale shades to develop light behind the cloud. Use the tip of the pastel to create the intense colours.

- Blend lightly to avoid muting the colours.

- Add darker shades as needed.

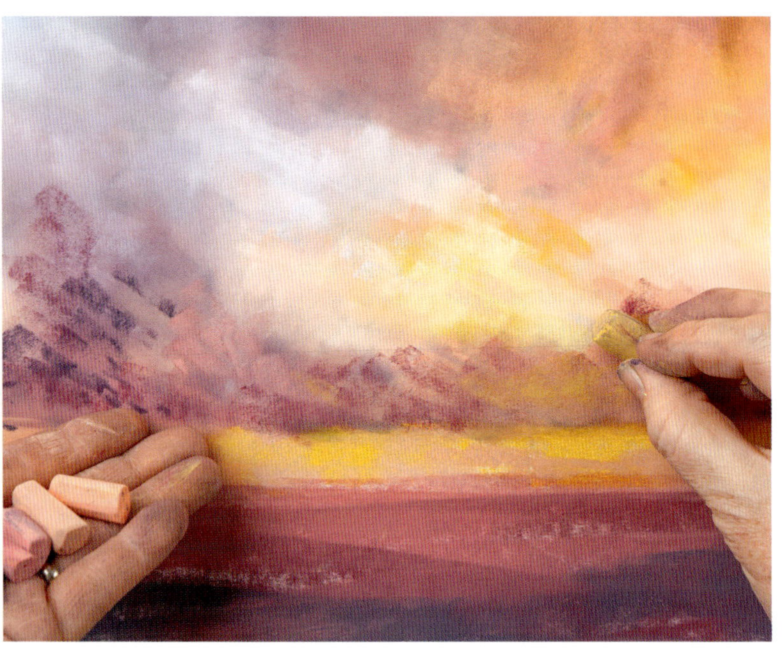

Lower cloud bank

Treat this large bank of clouds as a single area that transitions from deep purples to rich golds and coppers. Have all the pastel colours you'll need close to hand, and work steadily from one side to the other.

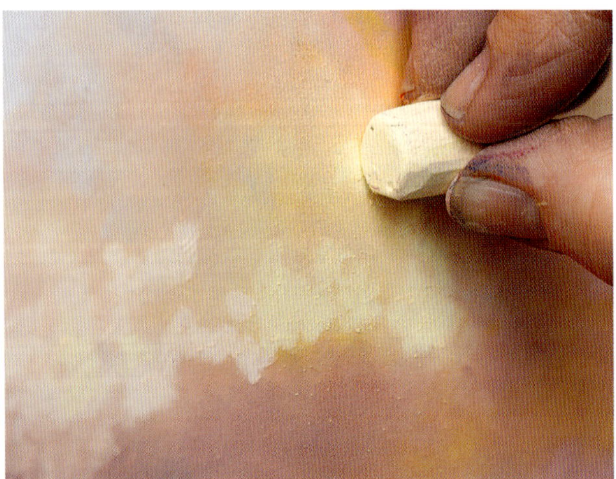

Cloud edges

When defining the edge, tip and tilt the pastel to create an interesting edge, rather than a solid line. Use these marks away from the edge, into the surrounding cloud.

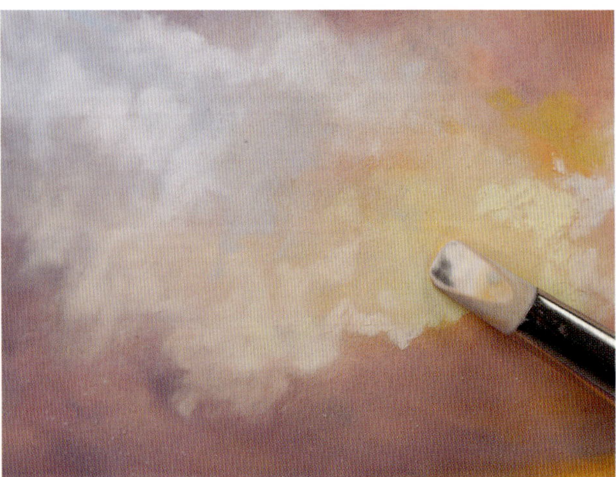

Blending with the shaper

Be careful to maintain the edge when blending. Work into the area of light, rather than back into the cloud. This will leave a crisper edge on the cloud bank. Push the dark cloud of the cloud bank into the light as necessary.

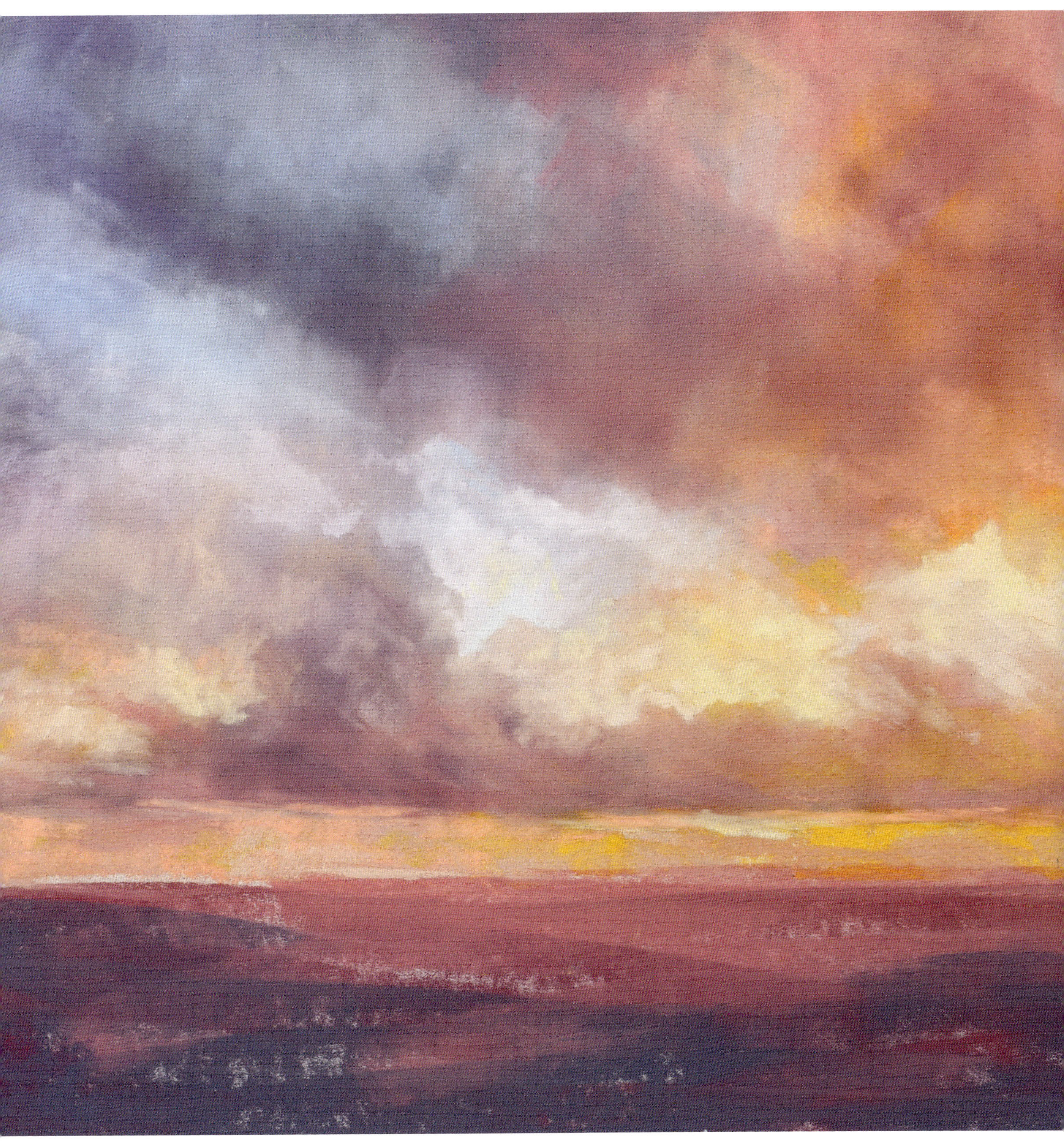

The painting at the end of stage 3.

STAGE 4

- Revisit the cloud bank edges with the same pastels and techniques as in stage 3. Focus on particular clouds to bring out further details.

- Apply the same techniques to the dark side of the cloud; create irregular and interesting dips and bumps.

- Add details along the underside of the cloud bank using the slice, tip and tilt techniques. Bring in some additional colours, similar to those used at the top of the cloud bank, with the nibble technique.

- Work up into the underside of larger clouds further up to create some edges within the cloud bank – but be wary of drawing too much attention to areas that are away from the centre.

- Add pale tones as needed to create distance – particularly on the left, then work your way along the horizon to add warm tones. As with the point above, don't over-define the detail here.

- When you are happy with the colours of the lower part of the sky, place a strip of tape along the horizon and use a strong warm magenta to apply the sea's colour. Blend down away from the sky, then remove the tape and add further textural details as needed. Allow your colours to become stronger and more detailed in this focal area.

- Add a hint of colour in sea – use the nibble technique to apply the pastel and blend it gently. The colours used here are the same as in the top part of the sky.

- Develop the foreground with blocking and slicing using the darker pastels. Blend vigorously.

- Add lilac and pale tones to create the gap in the clouds at the upper left of the sky.

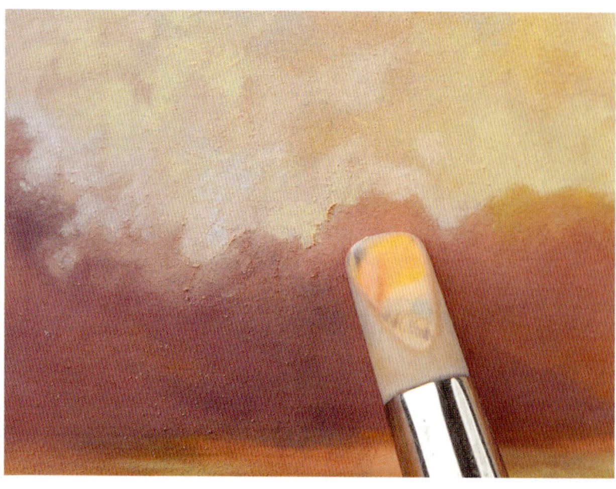

Dark side of the cloud
To create a natural look, avoid being too consistent and regular along the cloud edges.

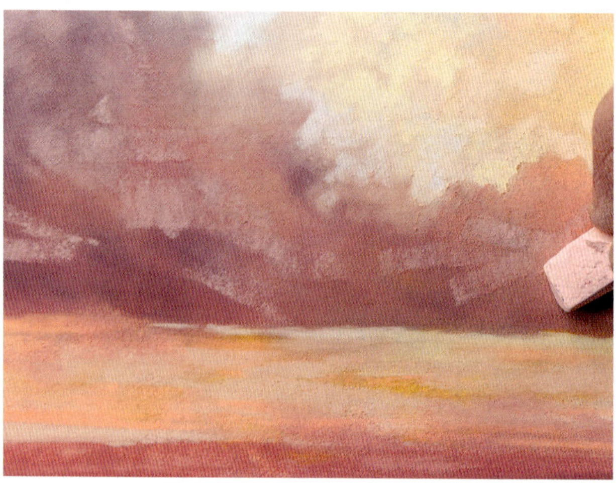

Dimensionality
After working the top and bottom edges, you may find your cloud looks a bit like a silhouette. Adding small details brings out the form and helps it feel more part of the overall painting.

Horizon
See the pastel clinic on page 124 for more on how tape helps with creating a flat horizon.

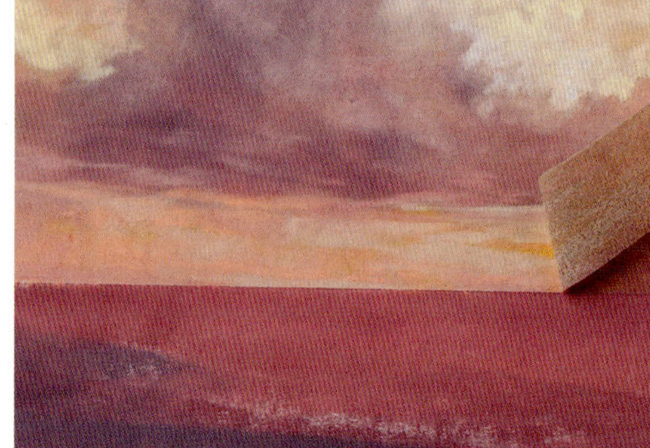

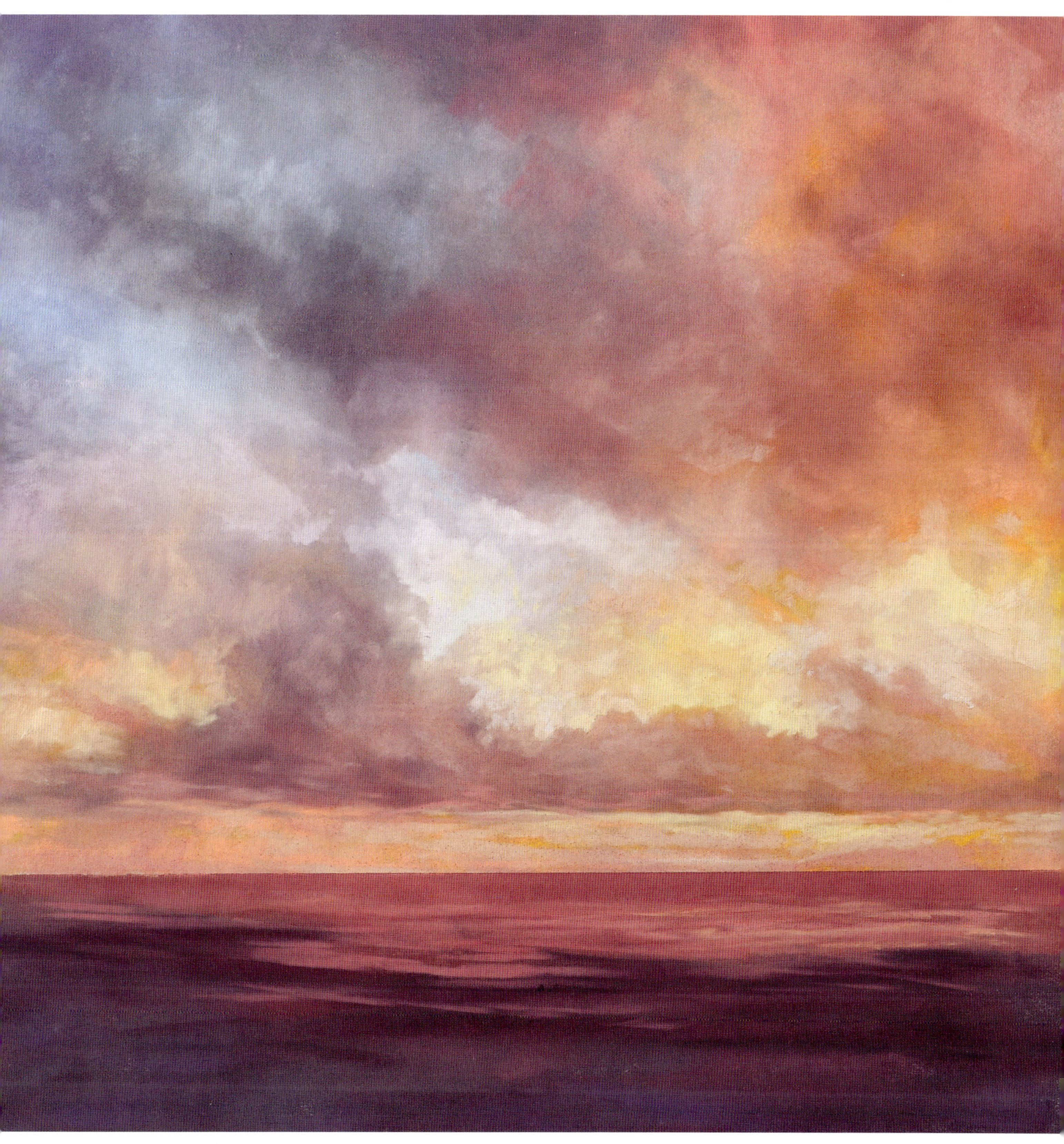

The painting at the end of stage 4.

STAGE 5

This closing stage is where we assess the image as a whole and apply balancing colour to unify it – adding more vivid, brighter or moodier areas as needed. You need to balance colour transitions with details. Use your judgement to decide where to add extra details to draw the eye, and where you should soften and blend to make areas recede.

- Using your pale pastels, add 'windows' of bright colours to show the sky behind the cloud on the left-hand side. Use the tip of pastel and press very firmly, before smoothing them carefully with the shaper.

- Use the other side of the shaper (i.e. the clean side) to push darker edges of cloud over these windows so that they recede. Repeat as needed.

- Work the windows of light diagonally down from mid-left to above the horizon on the right. Blend them carefully to soften them into the background.

- In the focal areas above the cloud bank on the right, use 'rule of three' pale colours, bridging colours and then cooler shades to add fine cloud details.

- Add a unifying colour, like warm pink, to the lower cloud bank and upper cloud areas to add warmth and pull the picture together.

- Add distant clouds near the horizon to create perspective and depth.

- Use the slice and nibble techniques to add light on the shoreline and water below the focal point.

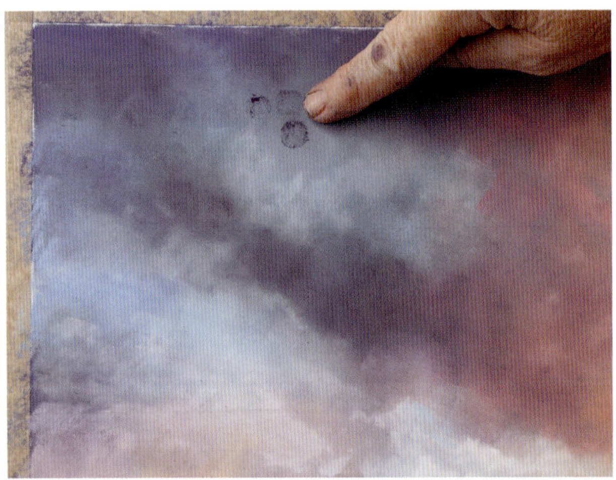

Balancing

On consideration, I felt the dark sea needed balancing, so I sparingly added some dark fingerprints to the sky before softening them in.

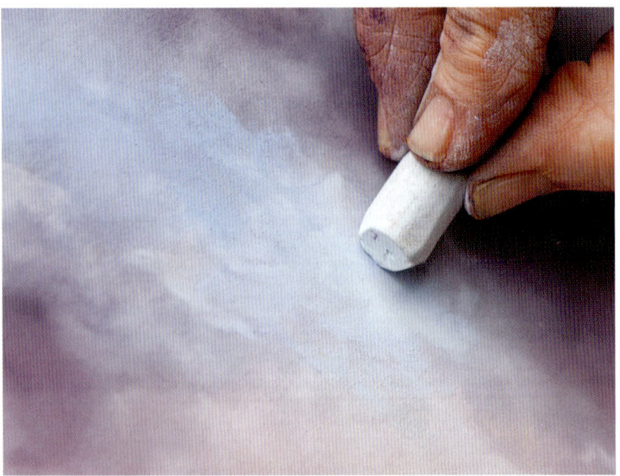

Cloud windows

The trick – and the challenge – with these small areas is getting the tonal balance and level of detail right so that you don't draw too much attention from the focal point.

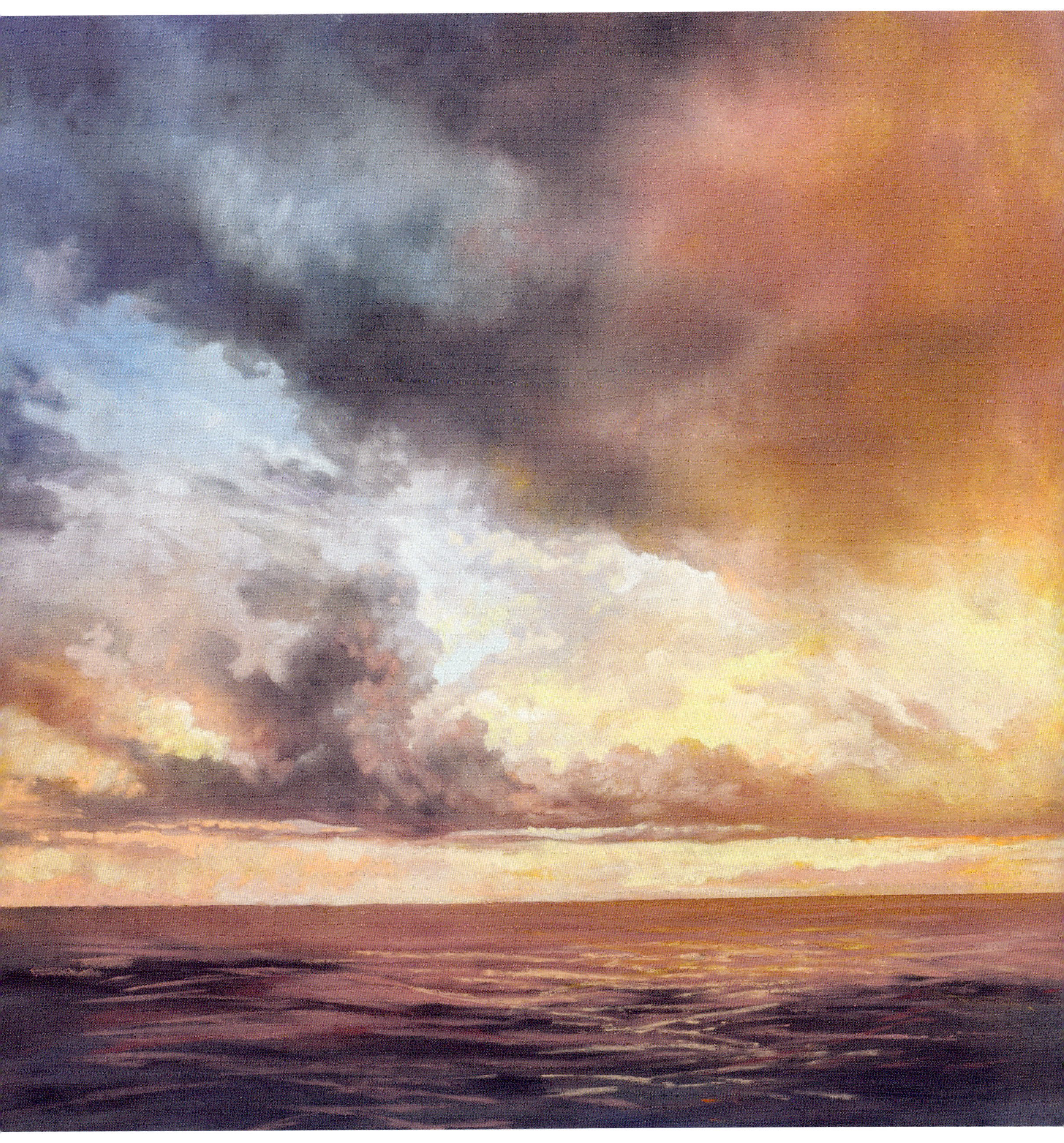

The painting at the end of stage 5.

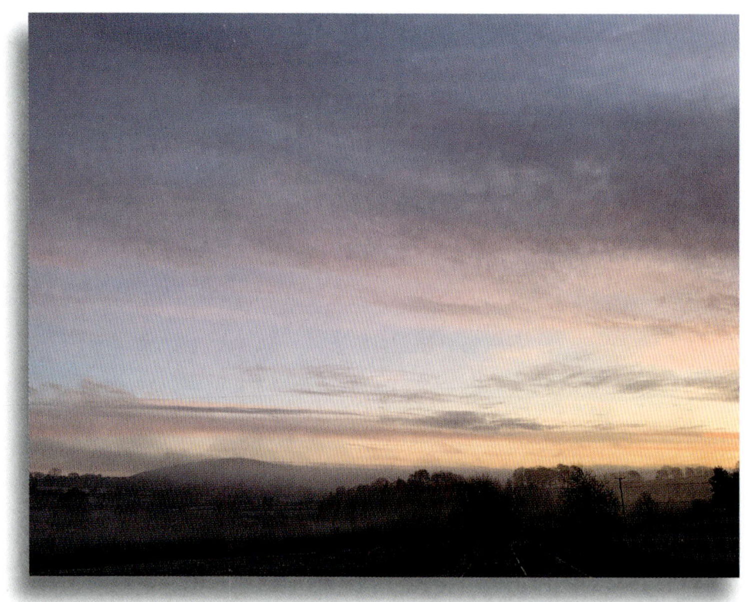

Delicate Sunrise

We have tackled both using a limited palette and using vivid and dramatic colours.
Now its time to explore applying these skills to a more delicate dawn sky. This is
a chance to use your colour mixing and shaper skills to create feathery edges and
gentle wisps of cloud.

   Sometimes being subtle can be the hardest thing and this is good practice for
learning to control the amount of pastel you apply, as well as the way you use the
shaper. This project is a great way to explore the importance of pressure, in terms of
pastel application and how you blend.

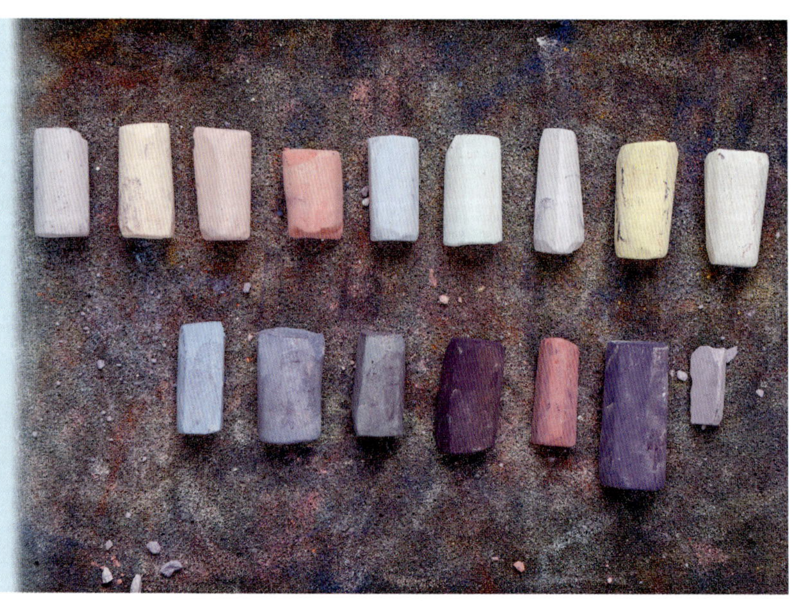

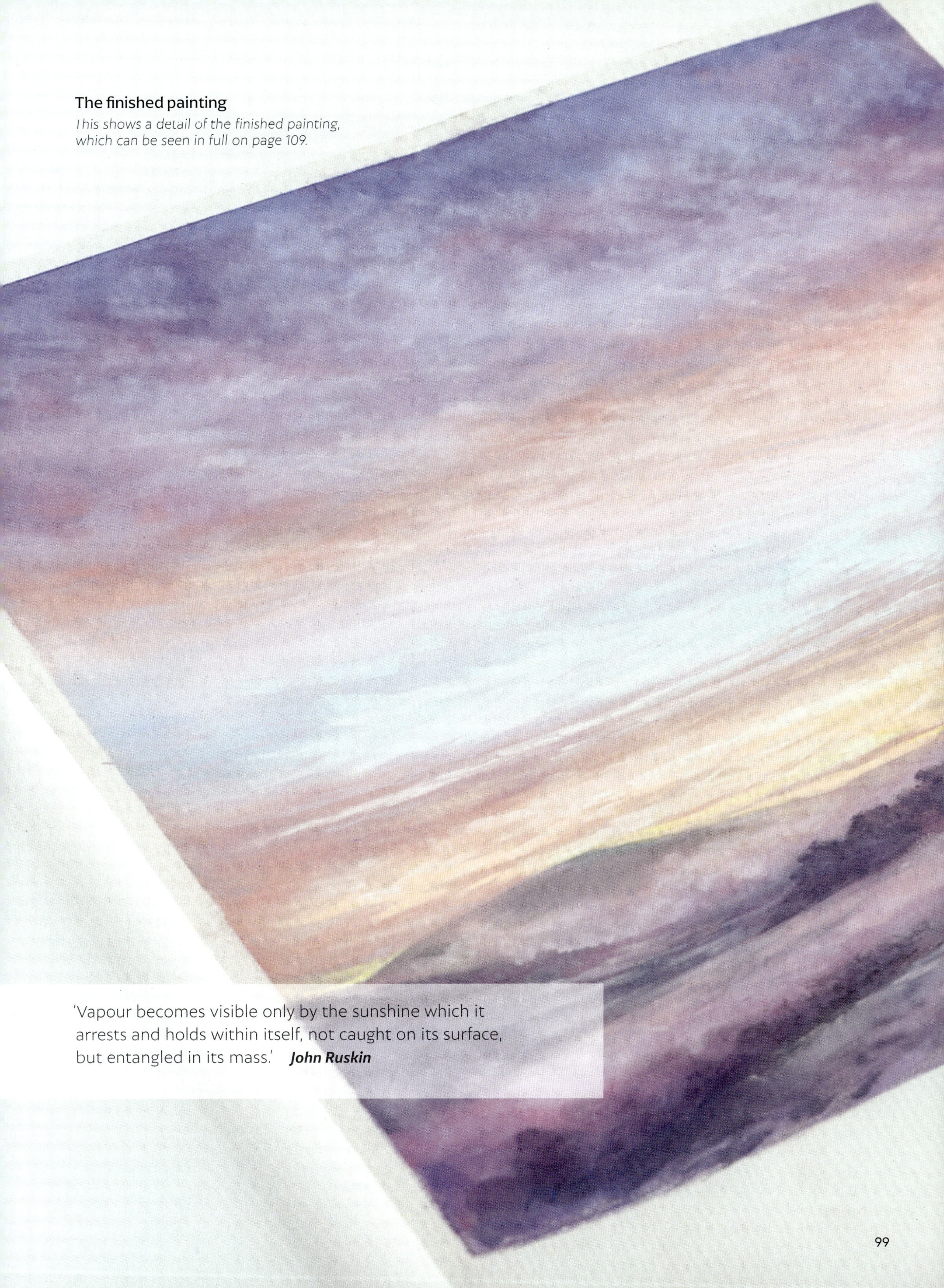

The finished painting

*This shows a detail of the finished painting,
which can be seen in full on page 109.*

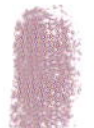

STAGE 1

We start by building up layers of the subtler hues to create a delicate effect. Avoid adding too much of the stronger, more dominant colours at this point, as they'll complicate the blending.

Mark-making

- Make a quick sketch, in a neutral pale colour, to show the edge of the hills along the horizon.

- After organizing your palette, apply broad strokes of the base colours, starting from dark lilac at the top, down to pink, blue and then more pink before adding orange and yellow.

- Establish a light few layers of the colours to get the placement right, then go back and add more of the colours to build up the surface and introduce the detail.

- Think in terms of subtleties – this project is all about a light touch. Use undulating strokes with the flat of the pastel.

- Avoid trying to add the 'dark' fingers of cloud at this stage. We will be using pink and lilac for that later.

- Add further layers using some paler and darker tones to add subtlety to the base colours.

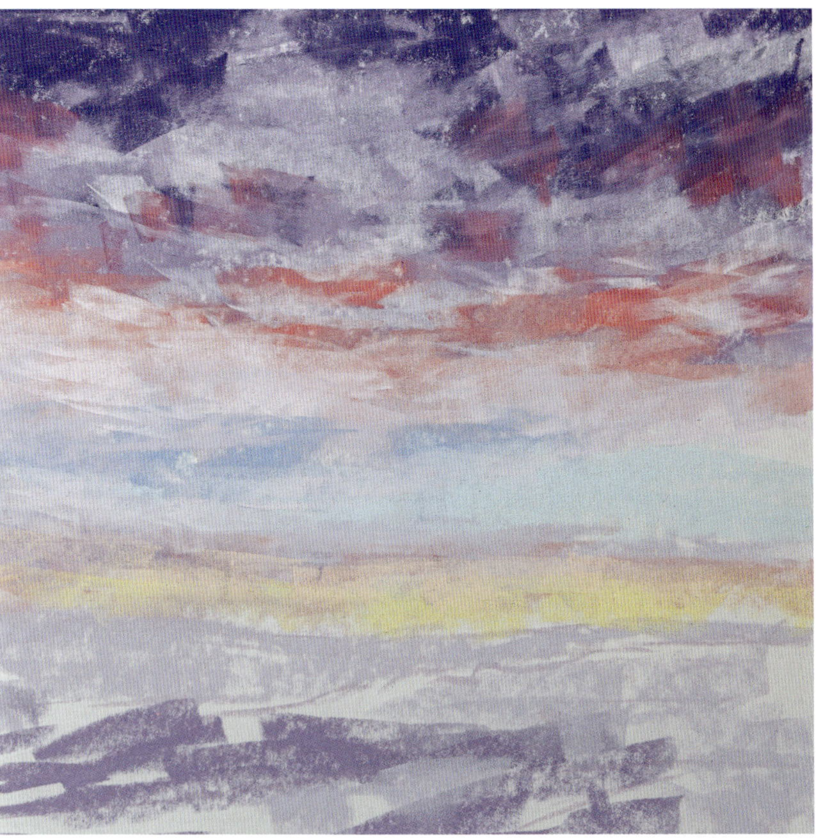

The painting at the end of stage 1 – initial marks.

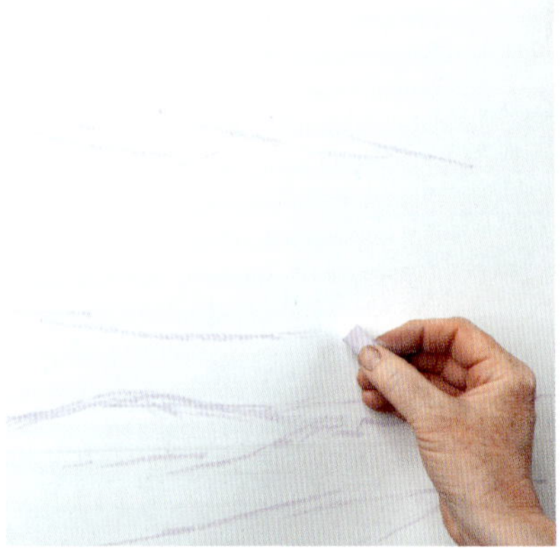

Sketch

We use a neutral bridging colour for the sketch so that it can be blended in and hidden among the subsequent layers without muddying the hues.

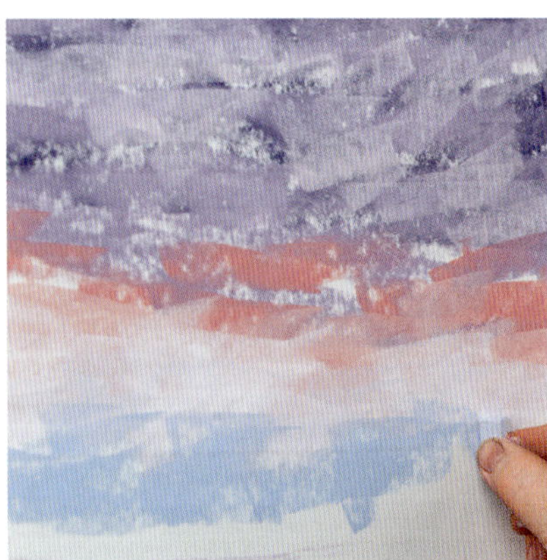

Gradient of the sky

Work down from the top, making broad overlapping strokes using the flat of the pastels. Don't work in solid bands; overlap the colours in turn as you work down, introducing each gradually, and using earlier ones less and less until you abandon them entirely. Don't forget your bridging colours.

Blending

- Start with a gentle circular blend in particular areas, then develop the movement into firmer horizontal strokes.

- Wipe your hand in between blending each of the major bands of lighter colour, and avoid working back and forth.

- As you move further down the picture, use softer movements, particular in the blue area.

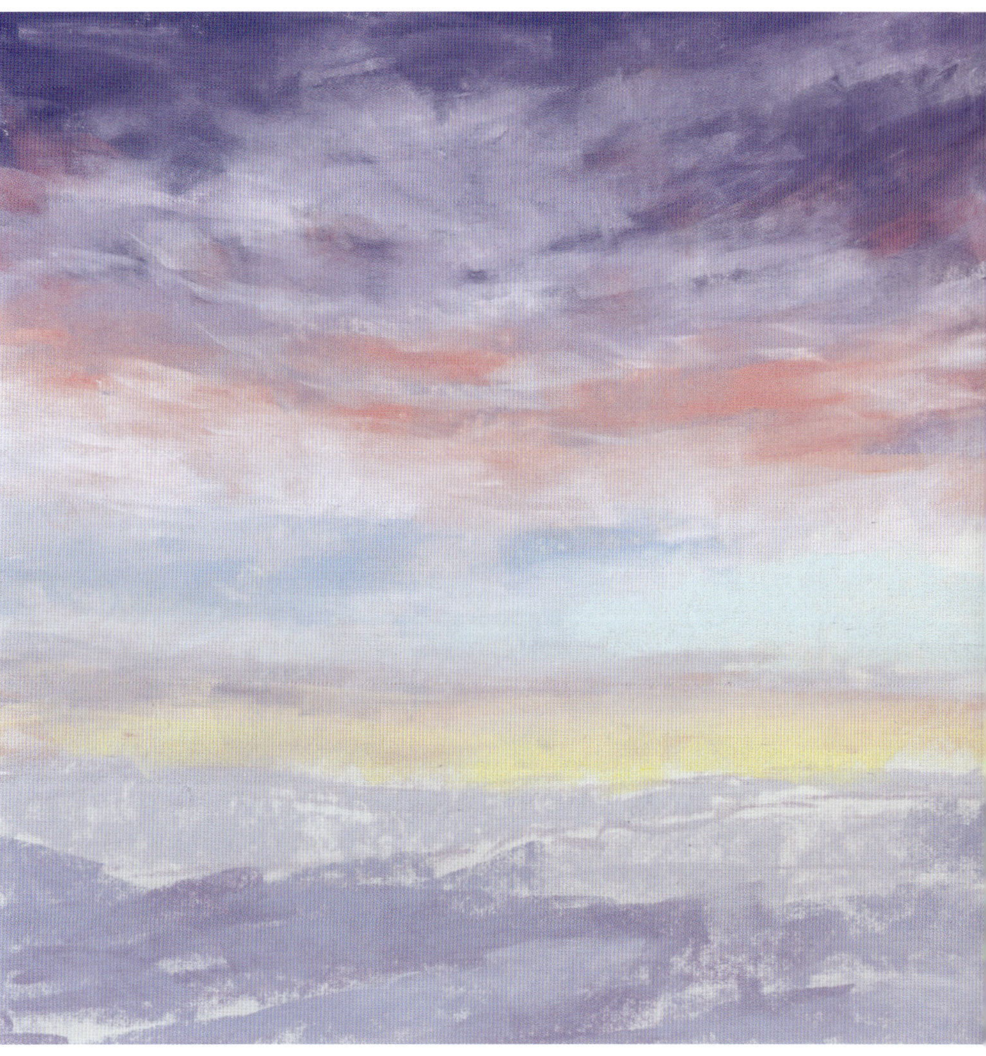

The painting at the end of stage 1 – blended.

Blending the sky

Work hard to keep the clarity and brightness of the light you've established: use the heel of your hand in large, single strokes across the lighter bands to avoid muddying them.

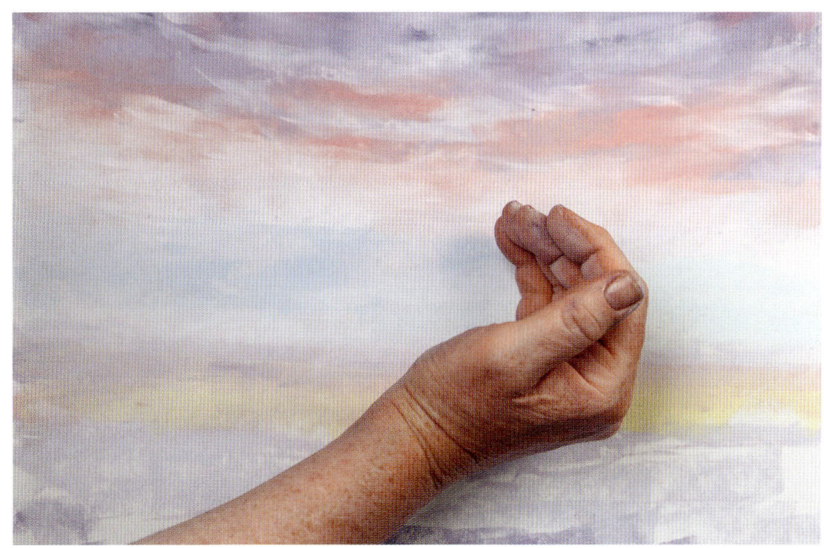

STAGE 2

Mark-making

- Using pastels chosen with the rule of three, work over the top part of the sky, using blocky marks to create the subtle variations of dark and lighter areas.

- Work downwards, blending carefully between the broad bands of colour. Keep building up the layers gradually with light blocky marks.

- As you move down into the bank of cloud above the horizon, go back to the lilac and pink and add those across using horizontal marks. Add pink and orange towards the right of this and a little darker lilac on the left-hand side.

- Using pale pink, pale orange and yellow, develop the brighter sky directly above the hills.

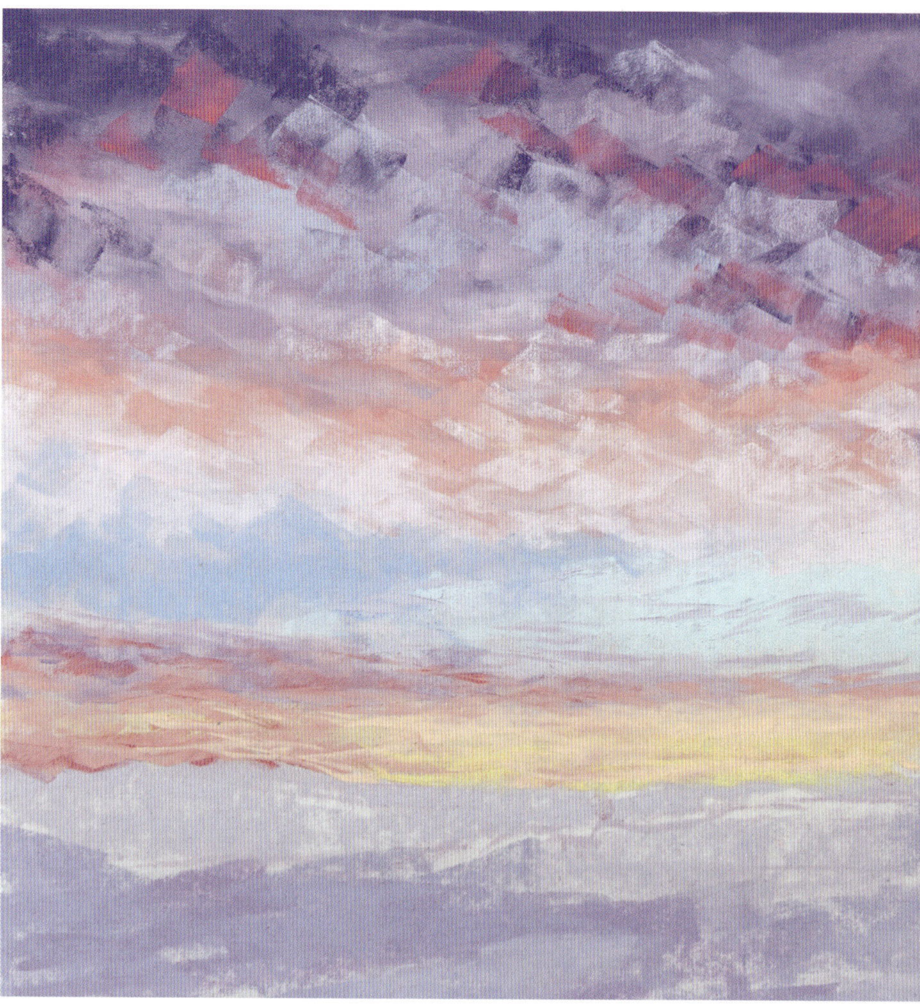

The painting at the end of stage 2 – developing the marks.

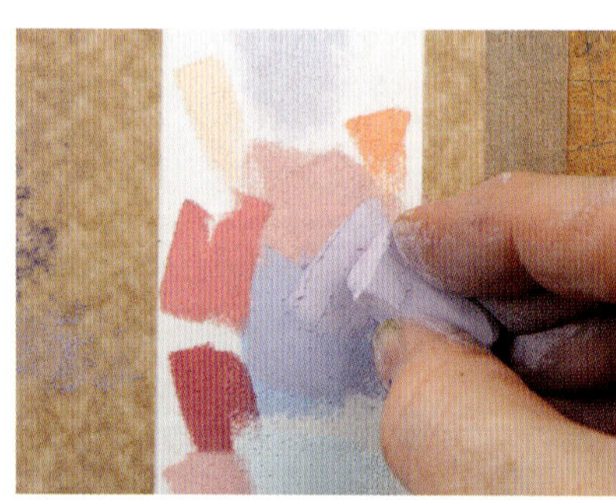

Bridging colours

When transitioning between the purple and pink, use pale lilac and pale pink as bridging colours. If you're unsure on which to use in a particular area, test the colour on the area to the side of your painting first to see whether it has more of a blue or more of a red tinge.

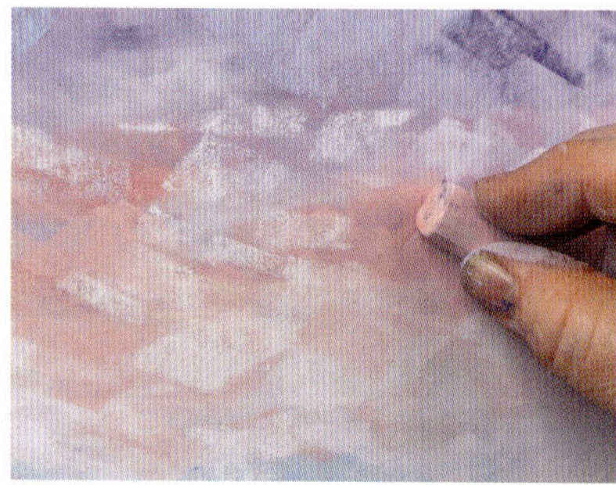

Dawn blush

R16 is a stronger pink that is great for suggesting the distinctive dawn light. Add some touches in the cloud banks, both at the top and bottom.

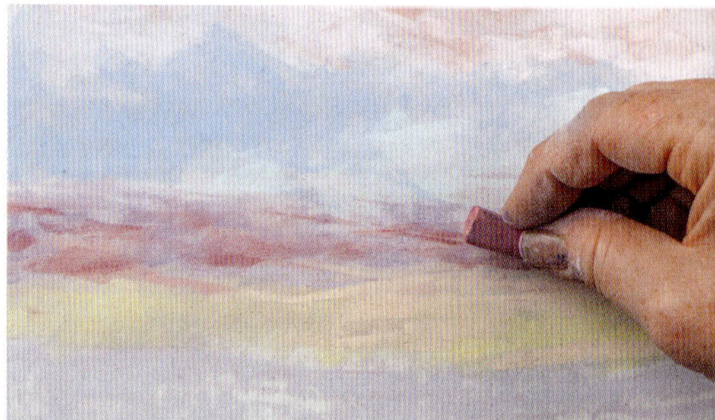

Blocks and slices

Make your marks light and choppy, with little pressure in the upper part of the sky. This will help to evoke the thin, subtle clouds.

Lower down in the sky, make your marks with horizontal slicing actions.

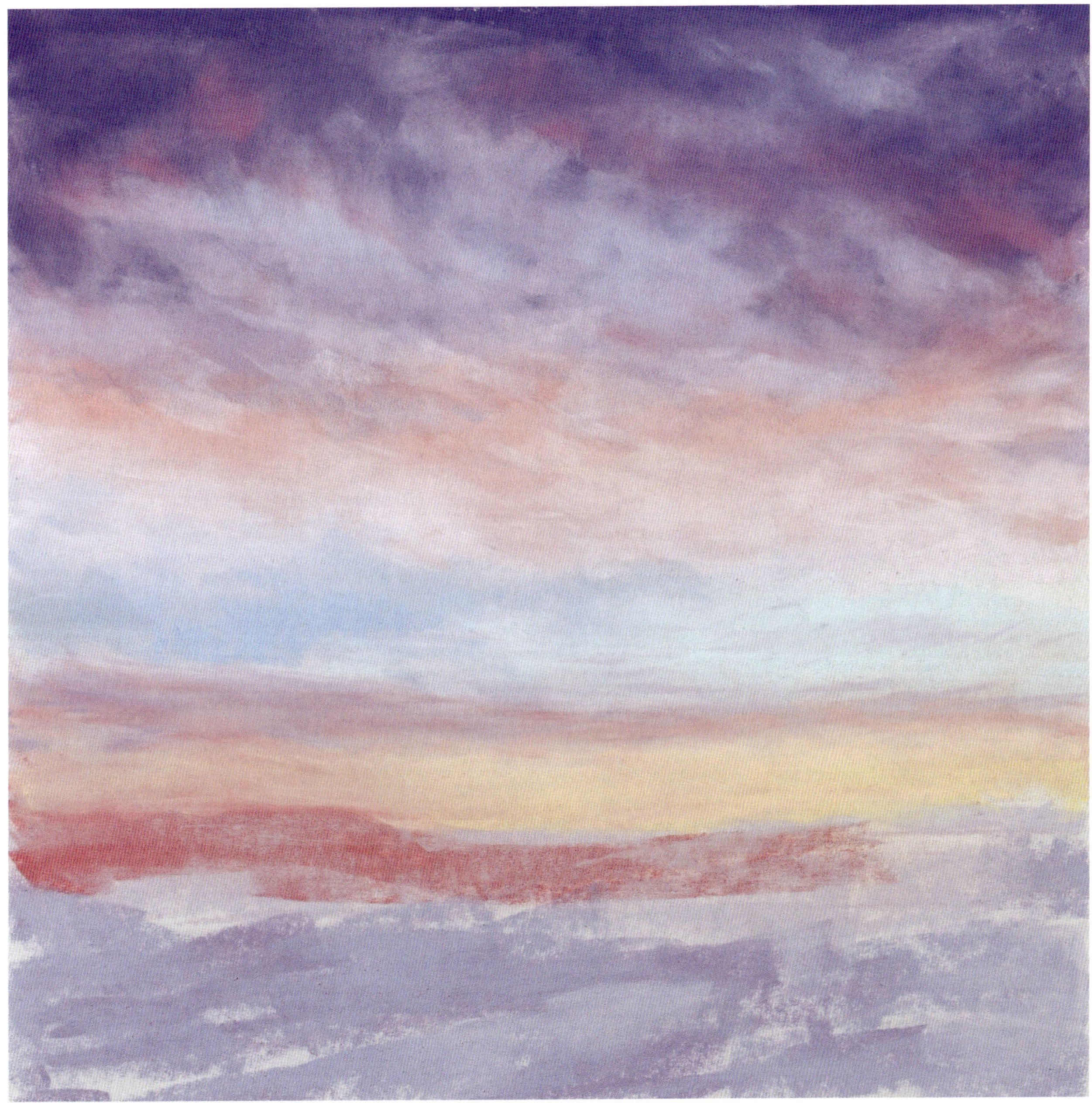

The painting at the end of stage 2 – blended.

Blending

- Blend with sweeping horizontal movements.

- Be vigorous, but controlled. Keep the colours within their broad bands.

- Blend the band of brighter colours below the cloud bank using circular movements to help evoke the mistiness and stillness.

STAGE 3

- Using the tip and tilt and and slice techniques, add pale pinks to make small mottled marks across the bottom of the thin cloud, then use the shaper to blend vigorously within the area. Repeat this process of mark-making and blending until you build up the right effect.

- Add a hint of blue into the top of the sky with very light blocky marks. I used BV4.

- Next add the lilac and pink to develop the dark wisps of cloud. Use the shaper to push these across diagonally – but don't spread them too far into the surrounding sky. Use a single finger for control if you want to soften the marks further while blending.

- Use pale sky colours to slice back through the wisps to break them up. Don't use the same colour all the way across – make sure you use at least three different tones of pastels.

- Alternate between adding dark and light marks and blending until you are happy with the effect.

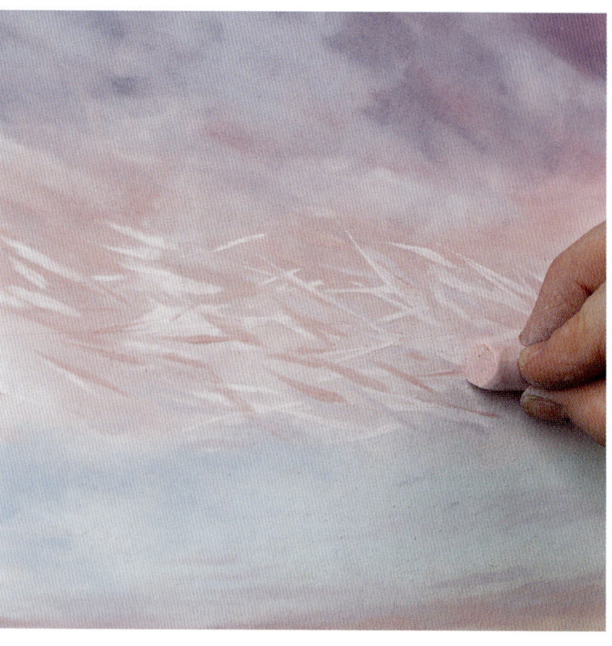

Bottom of the cloud bank

Use a combination of diagonal and criss-cross movement over this area to develop the distinctive mottled marks.

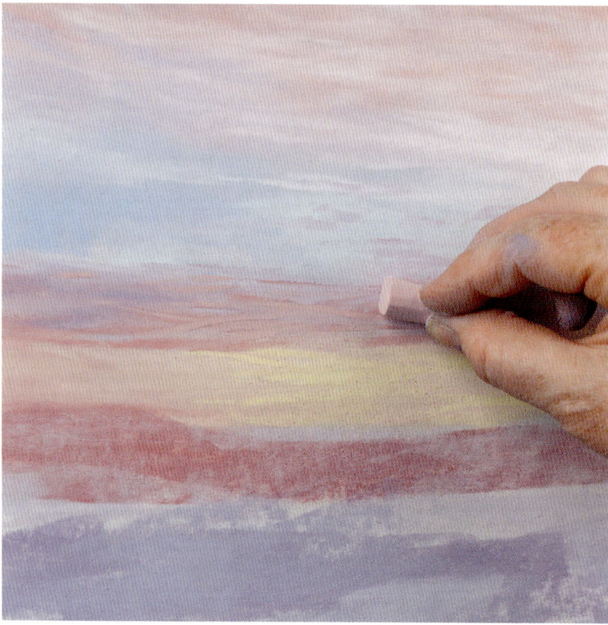

Wisps of cloud

Remember that if you have a colour against a light area, choose a lighter tone as it will appear dark against the light area. Don't worry if the wisps stray a little too much into the areas above or below, as we can cut back over them later.

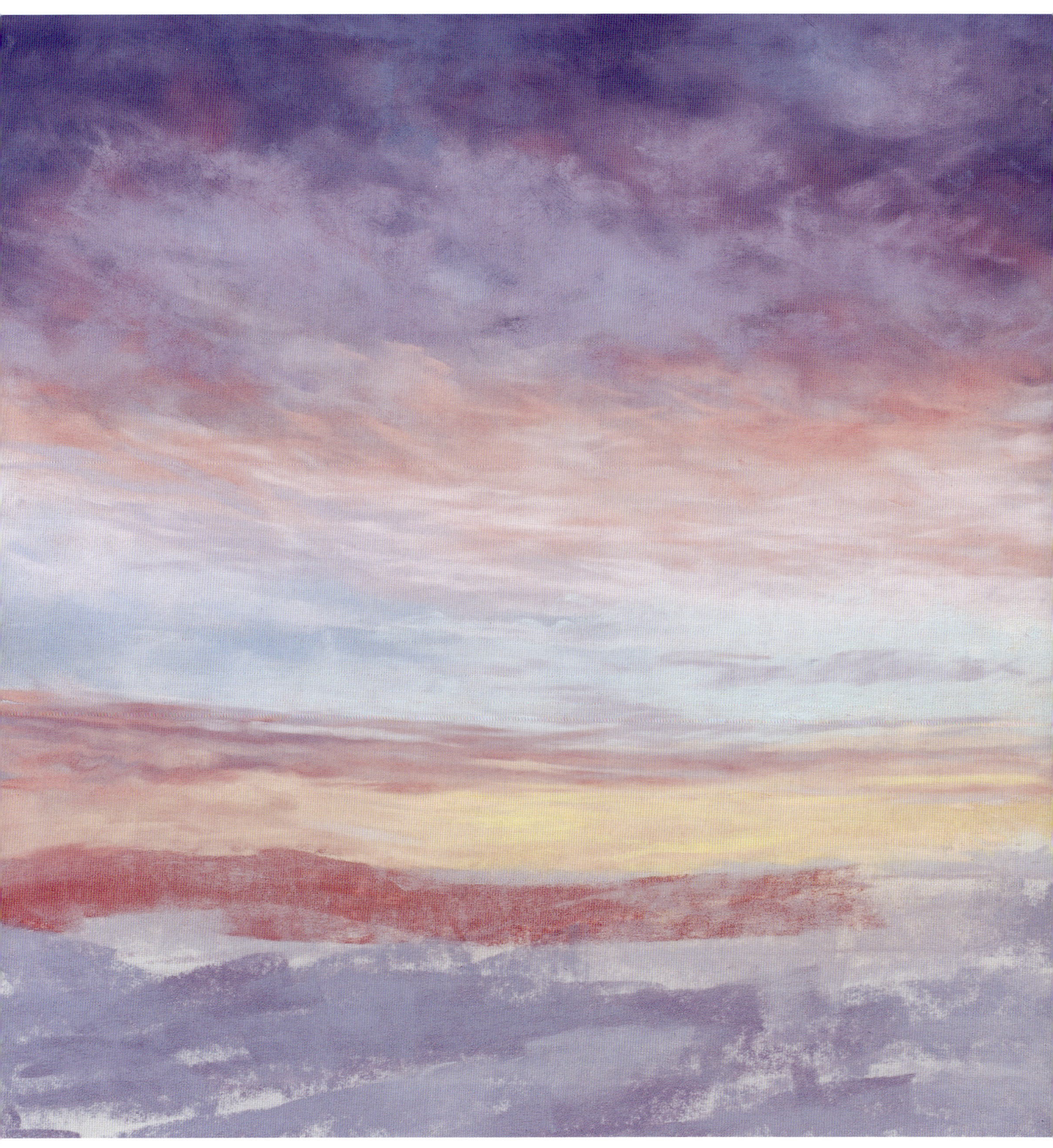

The painting at the end of stage 3.

STAGE 4

- Apply pinks and lilacs over the lower area of cloud to start suggesting the fingers of cloud and add more detail. Work across the cloud using elongated, flattened criss-cross marks with the slicing technique. Work these in with the shaper, and repeat.

- Go back under the cloud with some bright gold and add areas of light to suggest the fingers of cloud. Blend these gently with your little finger to soften the underside of the cloud.

- Use small amounts of pastel on your finger to create wisps of darker cloud under the main cloud.

- Build layers of dark colour and lilacs on the landscape, then blend them in.

- Use the side of a dark pastel to put in the distant hill shape. Blur and soften to suggest the mist.

- Add layers of pale pastel to create misty cloud and block in tree areas using circular movements.

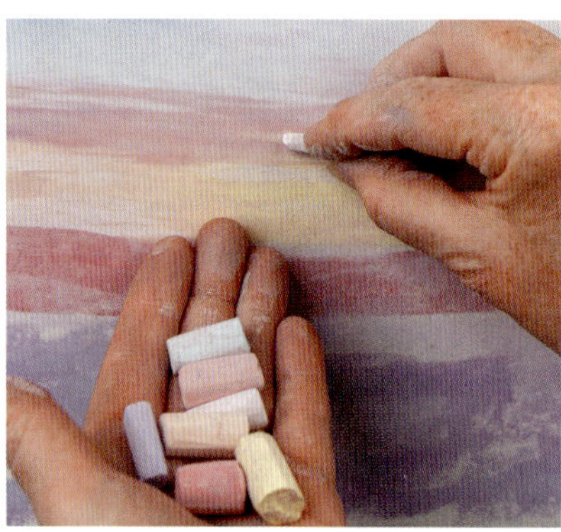

Lower clouds
Use a combination of pale and mid tones to build up depth and interest. Variety of hue and tone is key.

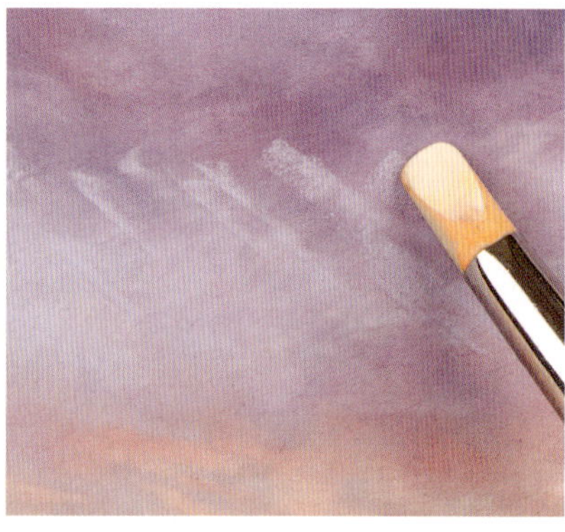

Wind effects
Use the shaper to criss-cross and pull pastel throughout sky to create the wispy clouds caused by the wind. Make a series of short slice marks in one diagonal direction, then use the shaper to work across them to create the effect.

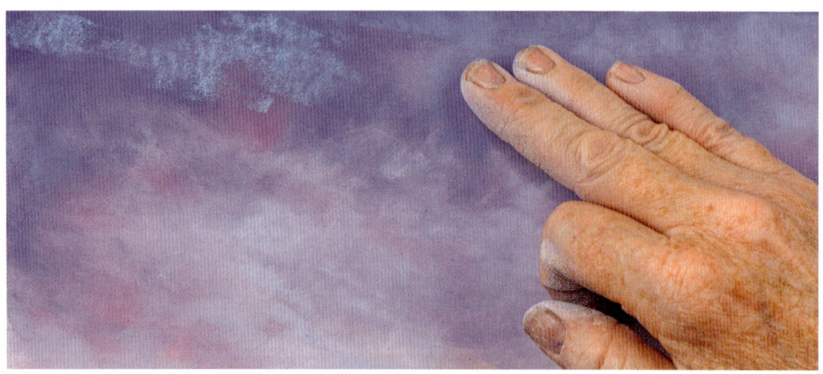

Softening
Soften any shaper mark-making you feel is too strong. This is particularly useful for the less defined upper parts of the clouds.

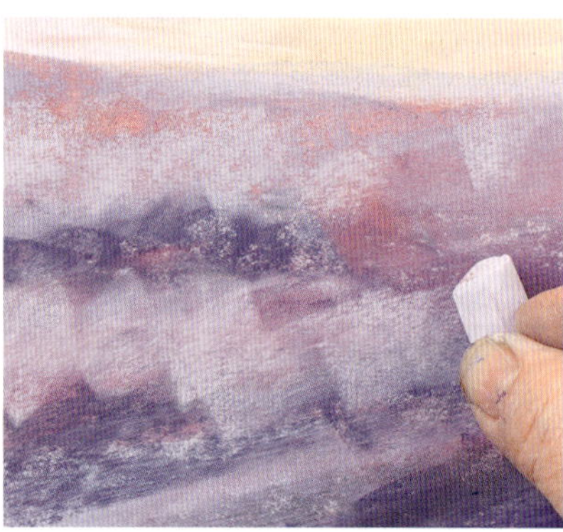

Mark-making in the landscape
Use a variety of chunky marks here, but include some light pastels for mist.

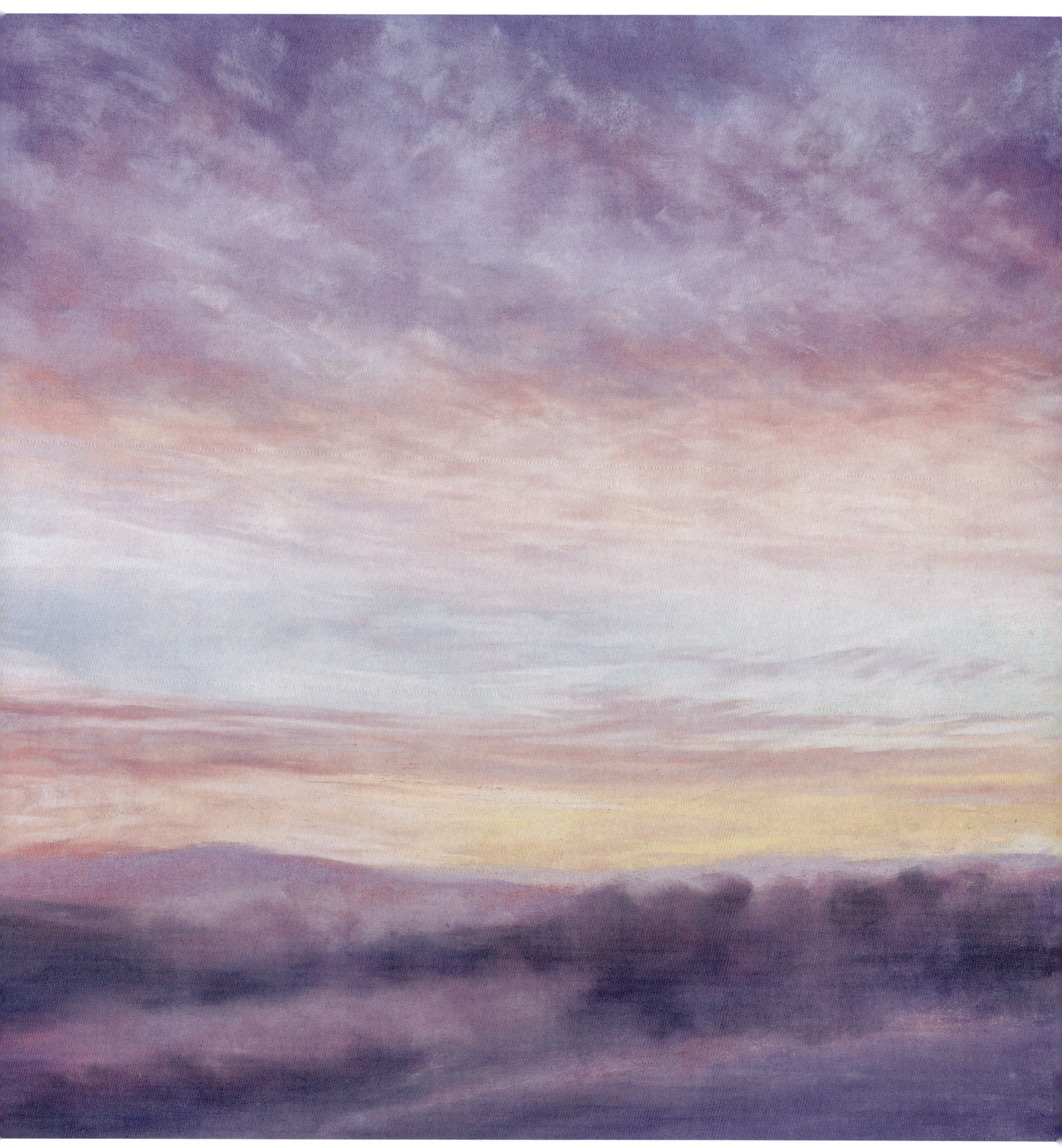

The painting at the end of stage 4.

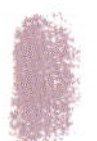

STAGE 5

Mood and atmosphere are more important than photographic accuracy, so try not to fixate on individual points in the clouds. Instead, aim to evoke the calm and peace of early morning by creating an overall impression Use soft blending touches to keep things misty.

- Add some pink on the horizon line and soften it into the top of the landscape – the mist means that much of the horizon should be hazy and undefined.

- Using the tips of the pastels, add any brighter final light areas; particularly at the focal point on the left of the horizon line above the hill. Barely blend this in.

- Add some pale lilacs to create more mist as needed. Use the shaper to redefine the tops of trees and bushes emerging from the mist, by pushing the darker colours up from below.

- Use the carbon pencils to add tree details and texture in the foreground. Add these sparingly, and only in the very foreground. Soften them into the mist with the colour shaper.

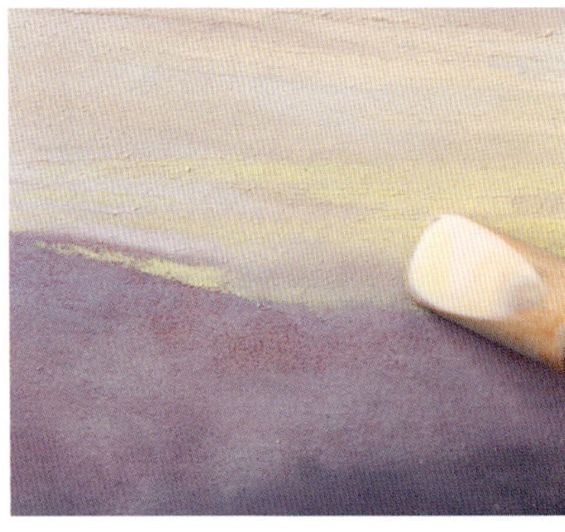

Horizon line

Haziness is important in this painting, and best achieved by softening and blending selectively. Consider where you need to keep distinctions between areas, and where you want the eye to glide over.

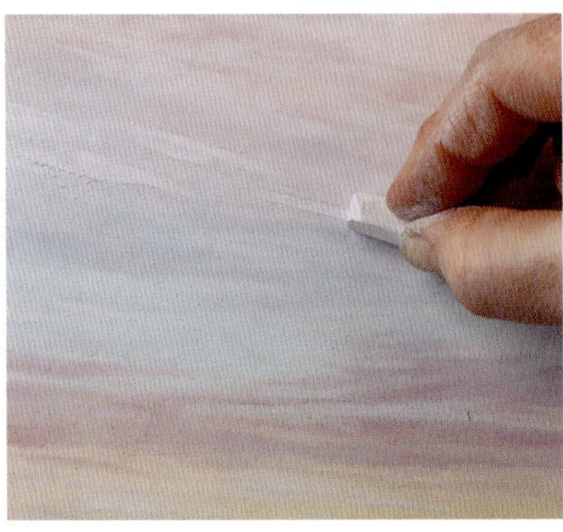

Directional lines

Even blended in, the marks you make will subtly guide the direction and speed of the viewer's eye, so consider the direction in which you place them.

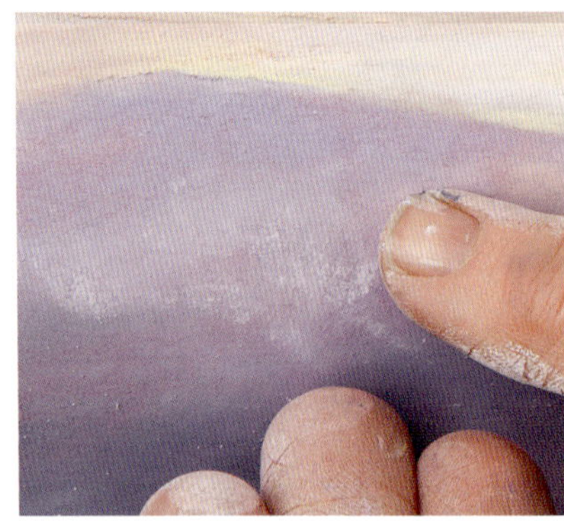

Foreground mist

Use your finger in very small circles to apply the mist, and use a combination of different pastels. Three is the sweet spot. Fewer, and the area will appear flat and dull, too many more and the colours will become muddy when blended.

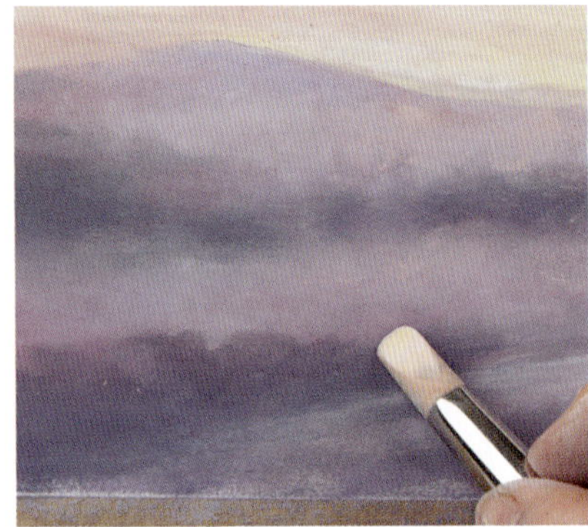

Fields

Use the tip of the pastel to suggest fields. To suggest recession, make the more distant marks finer, smaller and closer together. Soften these in with the shaper, using gentle horizontal strokes. Add lighter colours and leave the marks more textured in the closest field.

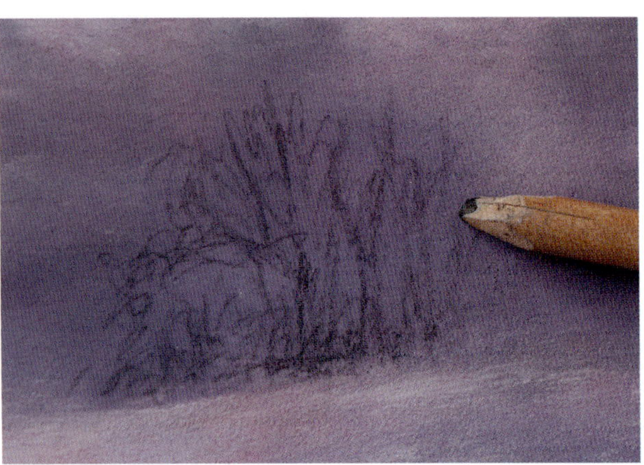

Trees

To draw convincing trees, build them up in multiple layers of lines, rather than in a single pass. Work lightly to avoid heavy lines, and always bear in mind that you're aiming to create the right impression, not copy a photograph. Too much detail can be counter-productive.

For a soft effect, hold the pencil with the thumb on one side and all four fingers on the other, so that you aren't able to put much pressure on the tip.

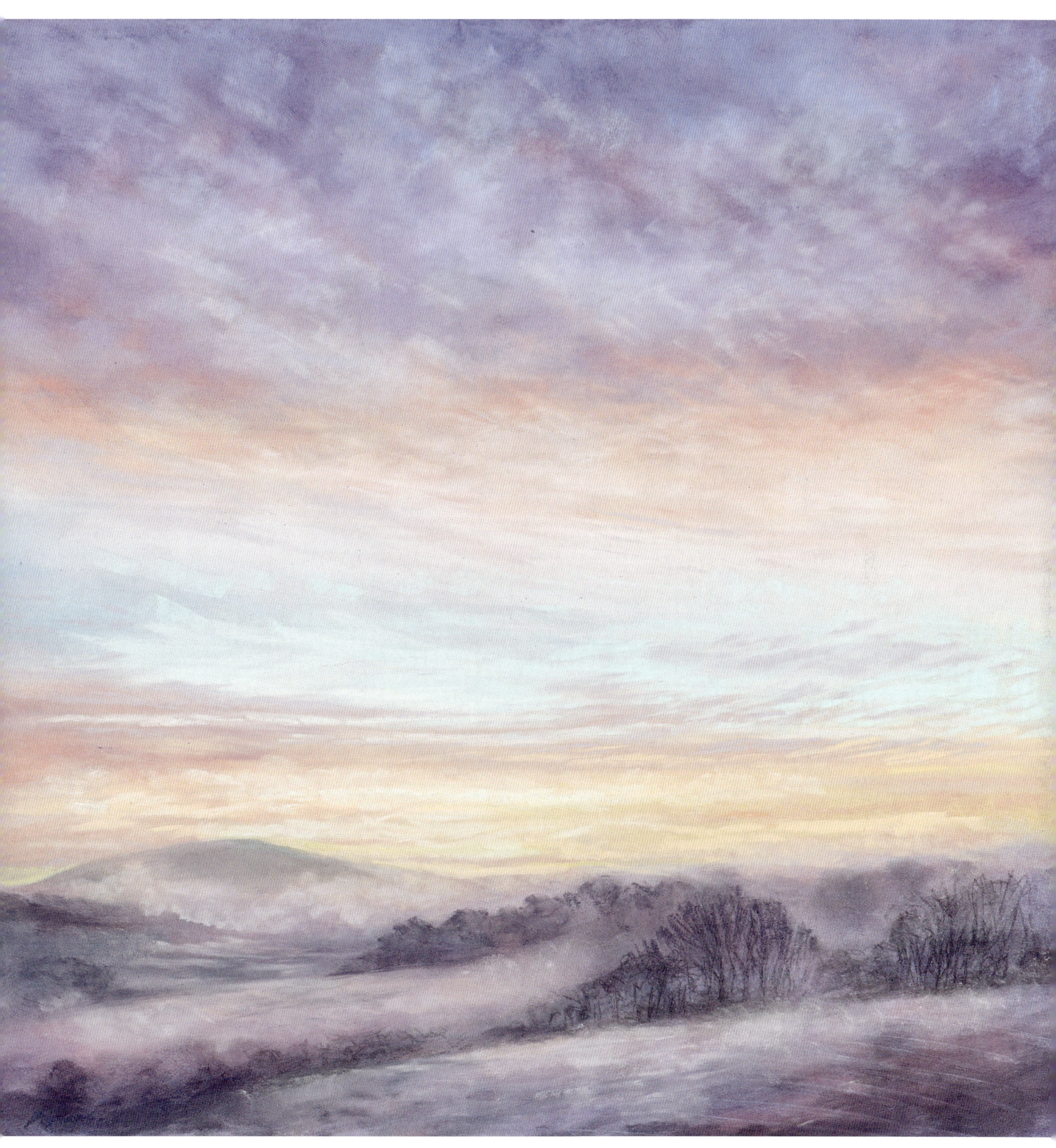

The painting at the end of stage 5.

The pastel sky clinic

THERE ARE SOME KEY ISSUES which crop up over and over when painting skies with pastels. Dip into this chapter to help with particular problems, or to gain insight and advice on a particular aspect of a sky you are working on. It is also a chance to practise key skills that will be useful to you, without having to commit to an entire painting.

MANAGING MISTAKES

There are some very common mistakes you can expect to encounter when working with pastels. For example, there will be times when you accidentally apply or mix the wrong colour. At other times, you may overfill the pastel surface: you can tell that this has happened if you try to apply a colour and it doesn't show up on the paper very well, or you just can't get the white 'bright' enough. One of the (many) great things about working with pastels on Pastelmat is how easy it is to correct when things got wrong.

With any mistakes you make, don't try and persevere; get a brush with firm bristles, carefully but firmly brush the mistake away and blow any excess dust off. The paper will remain tinted afterwards, but the tooth of the paper will be refreshed and you can work over the area as needed.

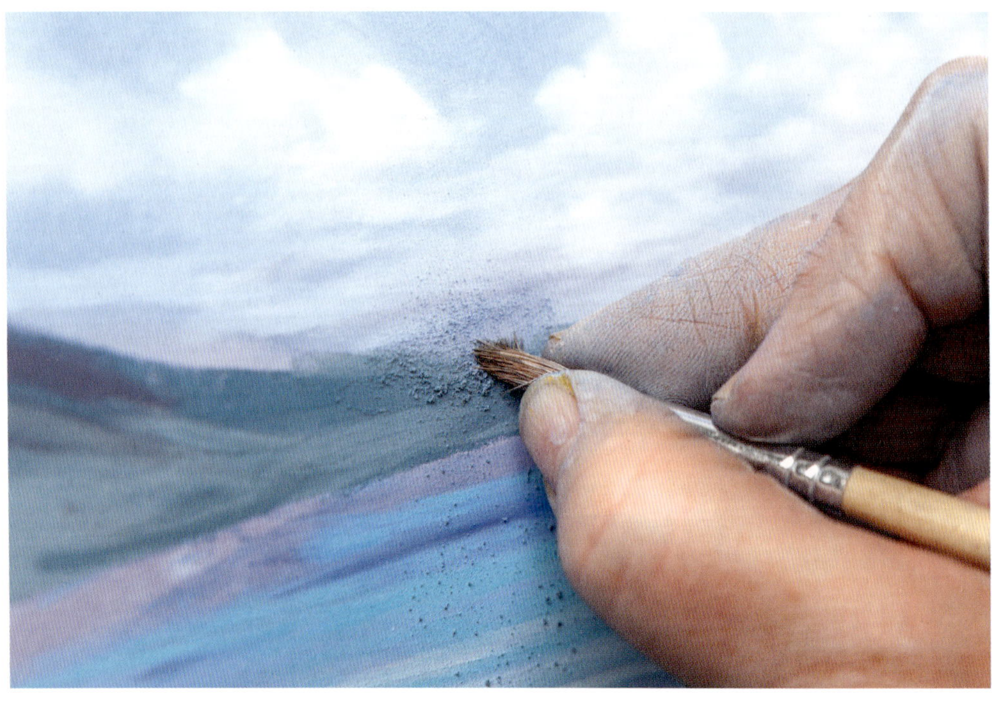

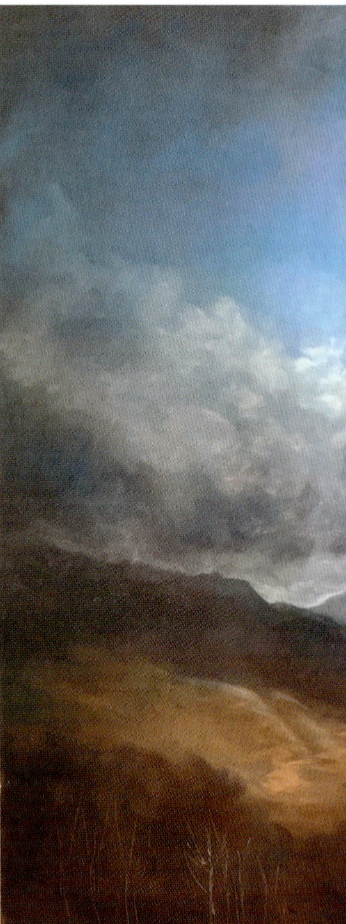

Using a bristle brush

If you place something in the wrong place – as with this hill – you can use a bristle brush to firmly brush away the pastel from the tooth of the paper. You can then work back over the area with the correct colour.

HOW DO YOU KNOW WHEN THE PAINTING'S FINISHED?

The eternal question! – and one I get asked a lot doing workshops. I wish there was a magic formula I could tell you about in answer to this. Unfortunately there is no definitive answer; rather it is something you feel your way towards.

Many artists will look at their work framed and hung on the wall, and yet still feel there was a bit more detail needed just there, or a touch of colour needed over there. I have learnt to live with these niggles – indeed, I believe that they are vital in driving us on to the next picture, and then the next, so we can revisit and push forward with our dream of pastel perfection!

What can help you make that judgment on whether you have reached the finish line is to consider the following:

Breathing room If you're unsure, stop. Put the painting to one side, and return to assess it with a fresh eye the next day (or the next week). This can help you see more clearly if something leaps out as unfinished. If nothing strikes you, then it could well be finished.

Look from a new viewpoint Take a photograph of your painting on your smartphone. Crop the edges so you can see it clearly without any studio detritus or the tape surrounding it. I do this regularly when approaching the end of a piece, as it helps me to see the work with a fresh eye.

Focal point Have you included an eye-catching focal point? How does it work with the composition of the piece? If you're not happy with the answers, you may need to carry on and refine.

Balance Think about the balance of the painting in terms of both colours and tone (relative lightness and darkness). Do they work together? Do you need a finishing touch of a complementary colour to enhance the piece? Do you need a final unifying colour added over much of the piece to pull it all together?

Does it say what you want? Bear in mind that you are trying to communicate something about the sky you are painting. What do you want to show the viewer? Is it the beauty of that swirl of cloud as it curls towards the horizon? It is the strength of that rich gold sunset as it moves from yellow to deep red behind that darkening cloud? Does it feel true?

The Mountain Pass
90 x 60cm (35½ x 23½in)

CREATING DELICATE WISPS OF CLOUD

There are many times where you will need to add some wispy clouds to your skies; perhaps on the edges of the main clouds, or as a major feature of the kind of sky you are creating. These wispy clouds can come in a variety of tints and colours – and although my step-by-step guide here uses pale colours, you can do this technique with dark as well as pale shades.

The big challenge here is to control where two strong colours meet. The trick is to use firm, controlled pressure and a shaper tool to maintain contrast in the edges.

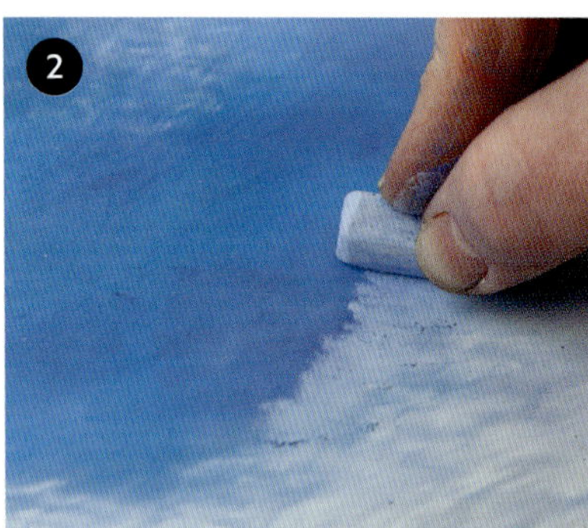

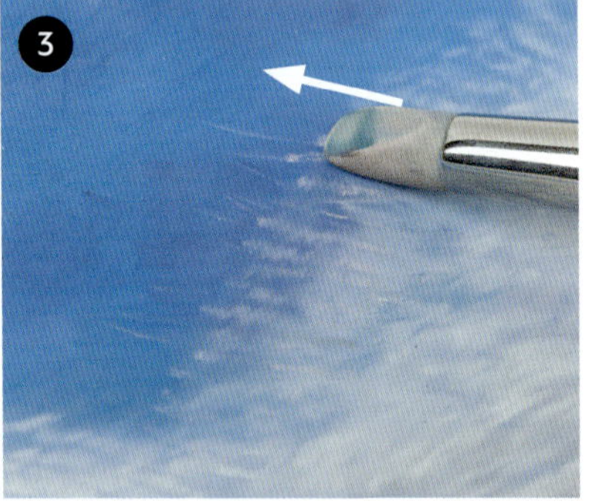

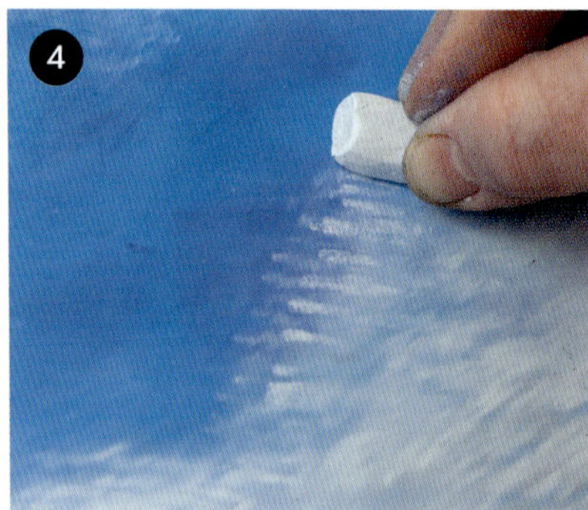

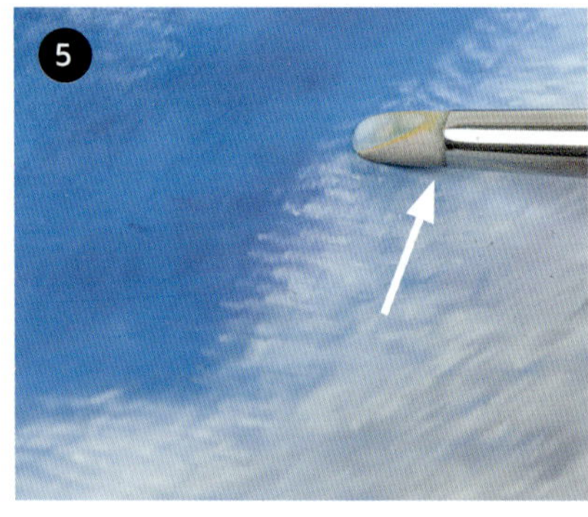

1 Start by building up blues in slicing movements near the edge of the cloud.

2 Blend the blue with a finger, then add pale (not white) pastels in slicing motions over the edge of the cloud, from the white cloud into the new blue area.

3 Using the shaper with firm pressure, pull the white edges off the cloud into the blue.

4 Refine the lines you've pulled out with further slicing movements of the white pastel.

5 Use light pressure to work across the marks with the shaper, subtly blending them.

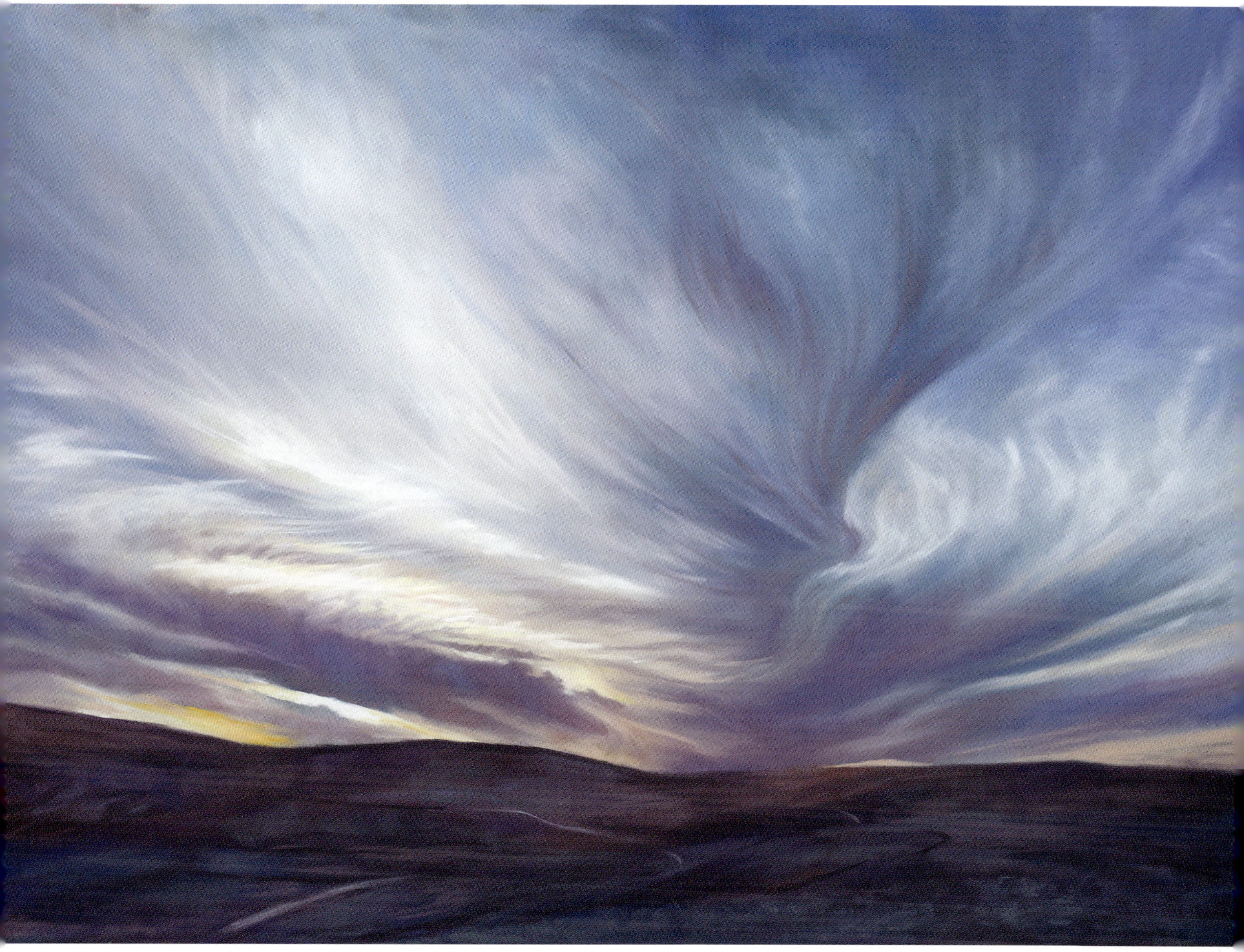

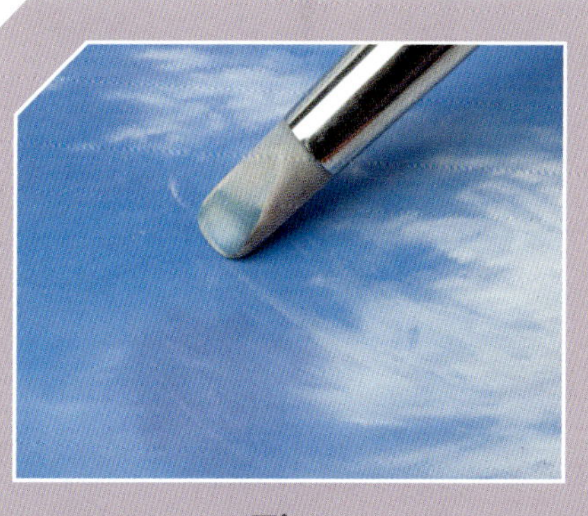

Sunset over Axe Edge
65 x 45cm (25½ x 17¾in)

Here, the wispy cloud effects have been created with stronger colours, after which the shaper tool has been used to pull the applied pastel colours out into the surrounding sky.

Tip

For looser, less structured wisps, simply apply your pastel with the slicing technique, then use the shaper with light pressure to draw it out from lighter areas of the cloud into the sky.

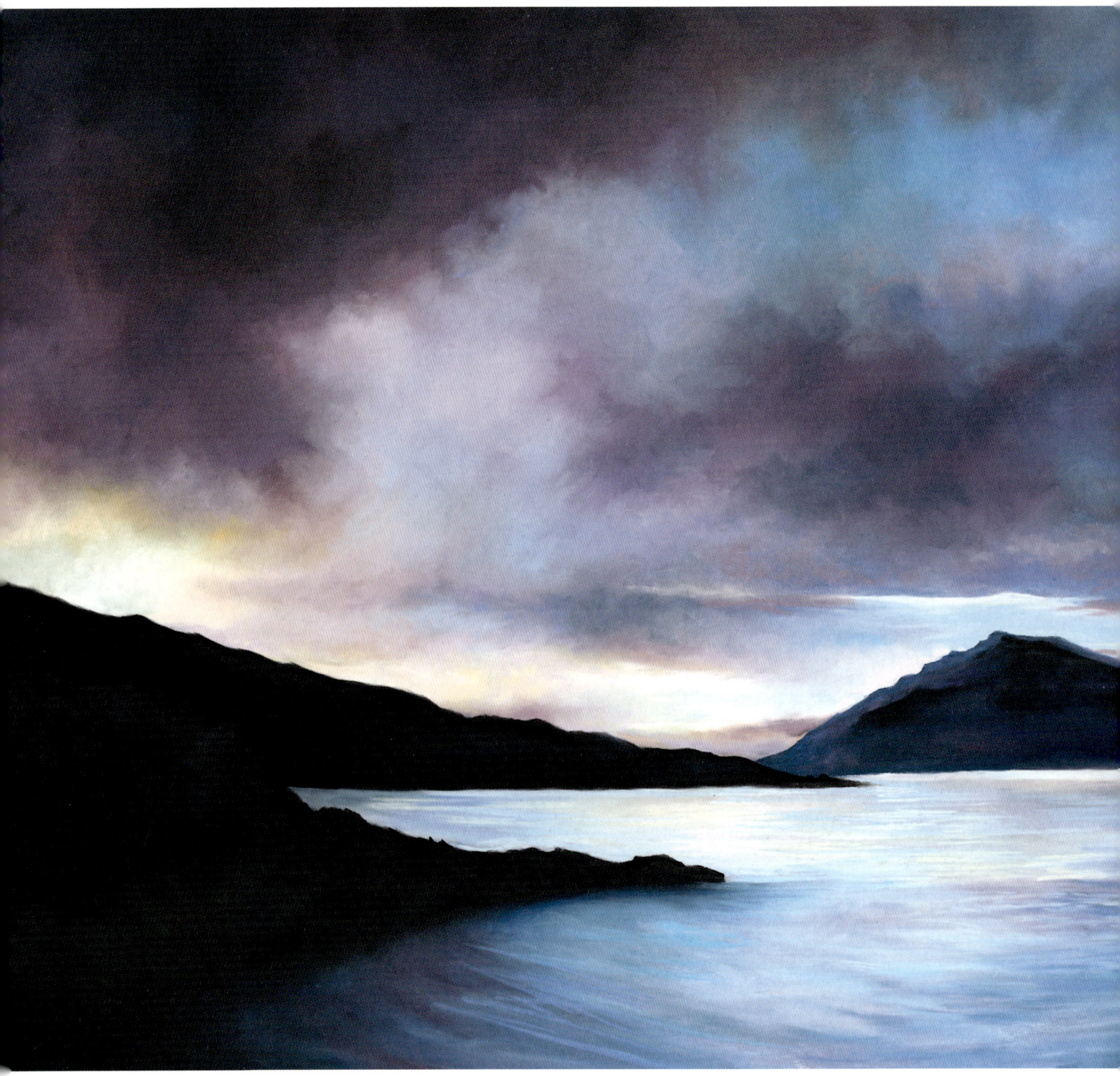

Lochside Evening

95 x 65cm (37½ x 25½in)

Sometimes dramatic dark clouds all merge and move together, but you can enhance their impact to greater effect in your artwork if you have detailed edges where these clouds meet brighter sky behind.

In this example, you can see how the sharp edges of the clouds above the mountains in the middle and on the right create a dramatic contrast to the stormy clouds above.

CONTROLLING CONTRASTS: DARK CLOUD EDGES

Sometimes it can be hard to control the dark colours on the edges of clouds when you have a pale sky behind them. There are a number of issues to focus on to ensure you don't spread the cloud too far into the pale areas. You also need to be aware of how different a dark colour can look next to a pale colour and adjust the tints you use accordingly. This tutorial will take you through the key factors to consider.

Start with a dark cloud base layer against a pale sky, built up using the rule of three and then gently blended.

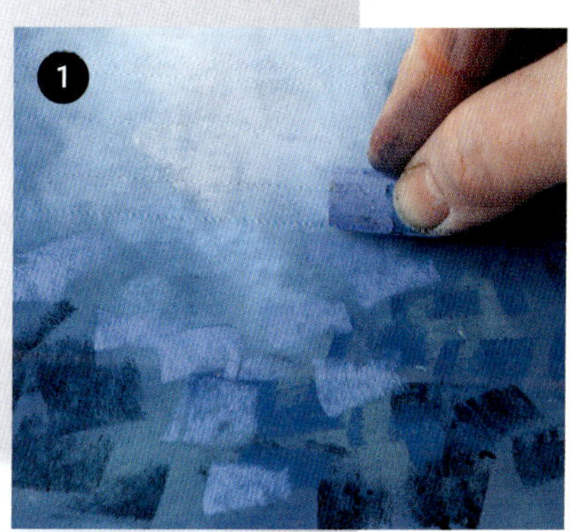

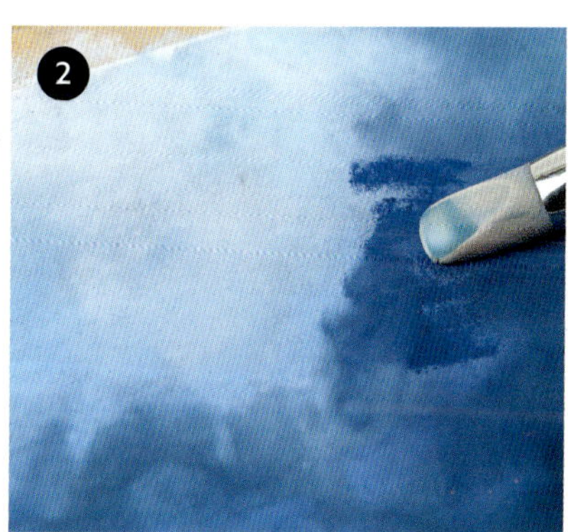

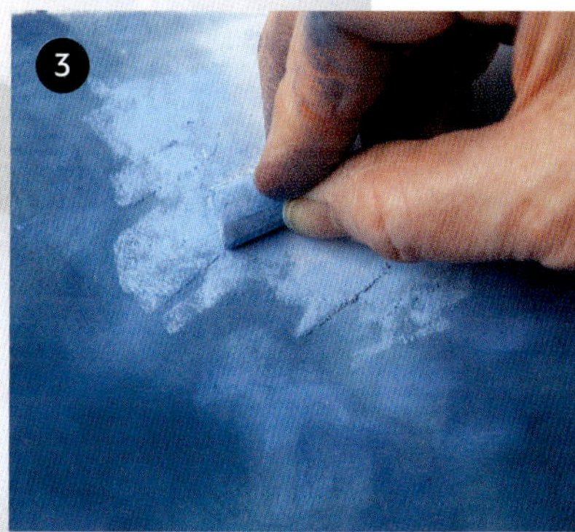

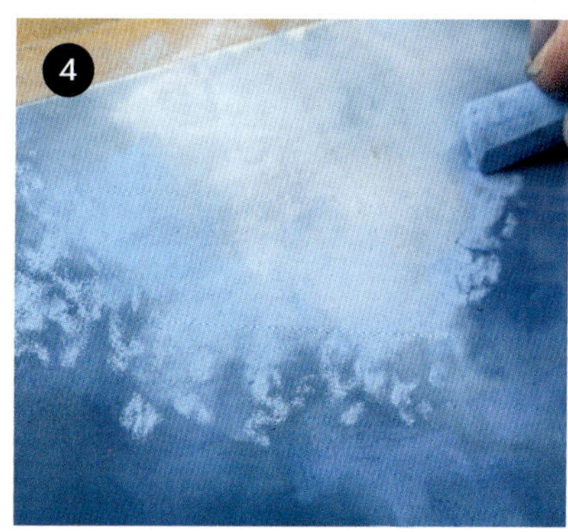

1 Add blocky marks to the dark cloud with criss-cross movements to build a sense of movement. As before, bear the rule of three in mind.

2 Blend the colours in with a fingertip, then add further dark tones as needed. Push the dark edge up to the edge of the pale area with the shaper.

3 Add lighter touches within the sky area and push back towards the dark. Gradually refine the shapes, using more controlled movements.

4 Push and pull these two areas, using the tips of the pastels for fine detail, and softening as necessary until you achieve the edge you want.

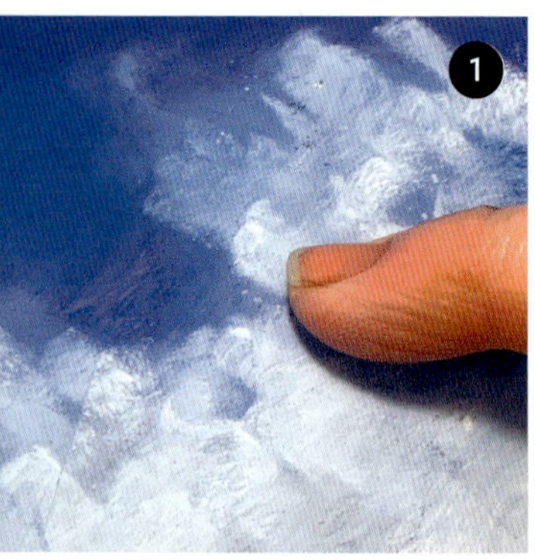
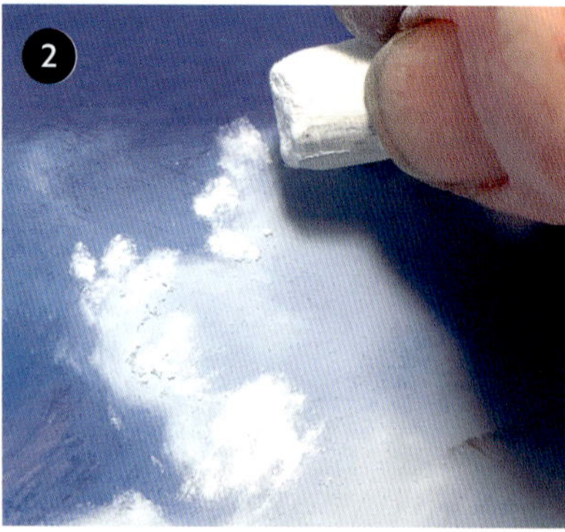

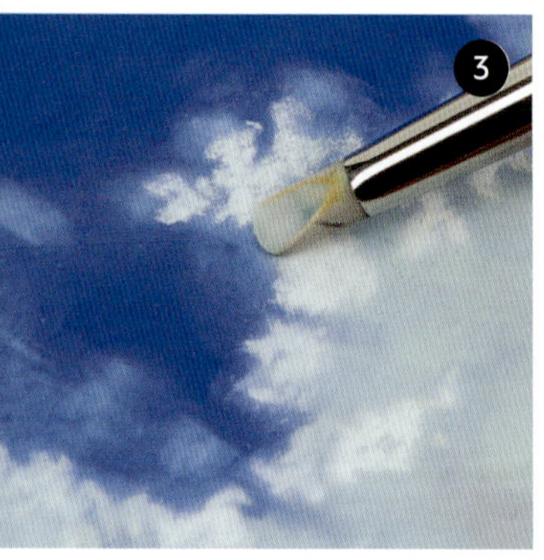
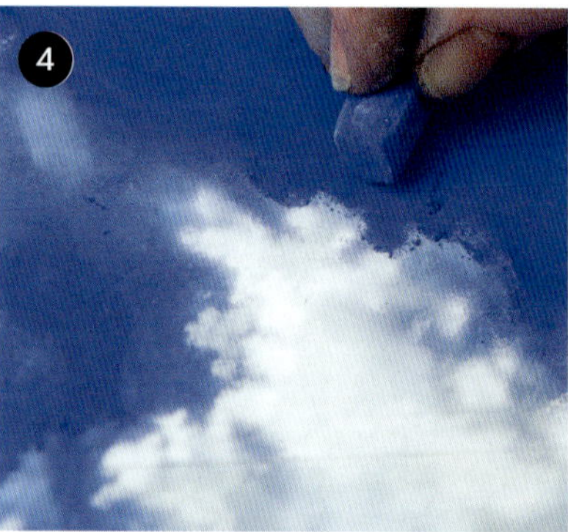

CONTROLLING CONTRASTS: EDGES OF PALE CLOUDS

When working with pale or bright clouds against a darker sky, there are some key points to bear in mind as you don't want to end up with a halo effect around the edge of your cloud. You need to build up the cloud gradually towards the brightest colour so you create a three-dimensional effect. This tutorial will take you through how to do this with white clouds, but the principle will remain the same for use with other bright colours.

Before you start, you'll need to have created a base layer of cloud using off-white colours – remember the rule of three! We use off-whites so we can build towards adding the very brightest colour last (white, in this example).

1 Add another layer of your off-white colours with blocking (see page 19) before blending lightly.

2 Add pure white with the tip of the pastel to the edge of the cloud where it meets the blue. Keep the edge erratic.

3 Use the shaper to soften the marks – this immediately darkens the white as it mixes with the colour underneath. Add a further layer of white to just the very lightest and sharpest areas, then blend. Repeat as needed.

4 Once happy, use the tip of your sky colour (blue in this example) to work back up against the white. To finish, add a final layer of white to the very brightest parts. Don't blend these – leave them as they are.

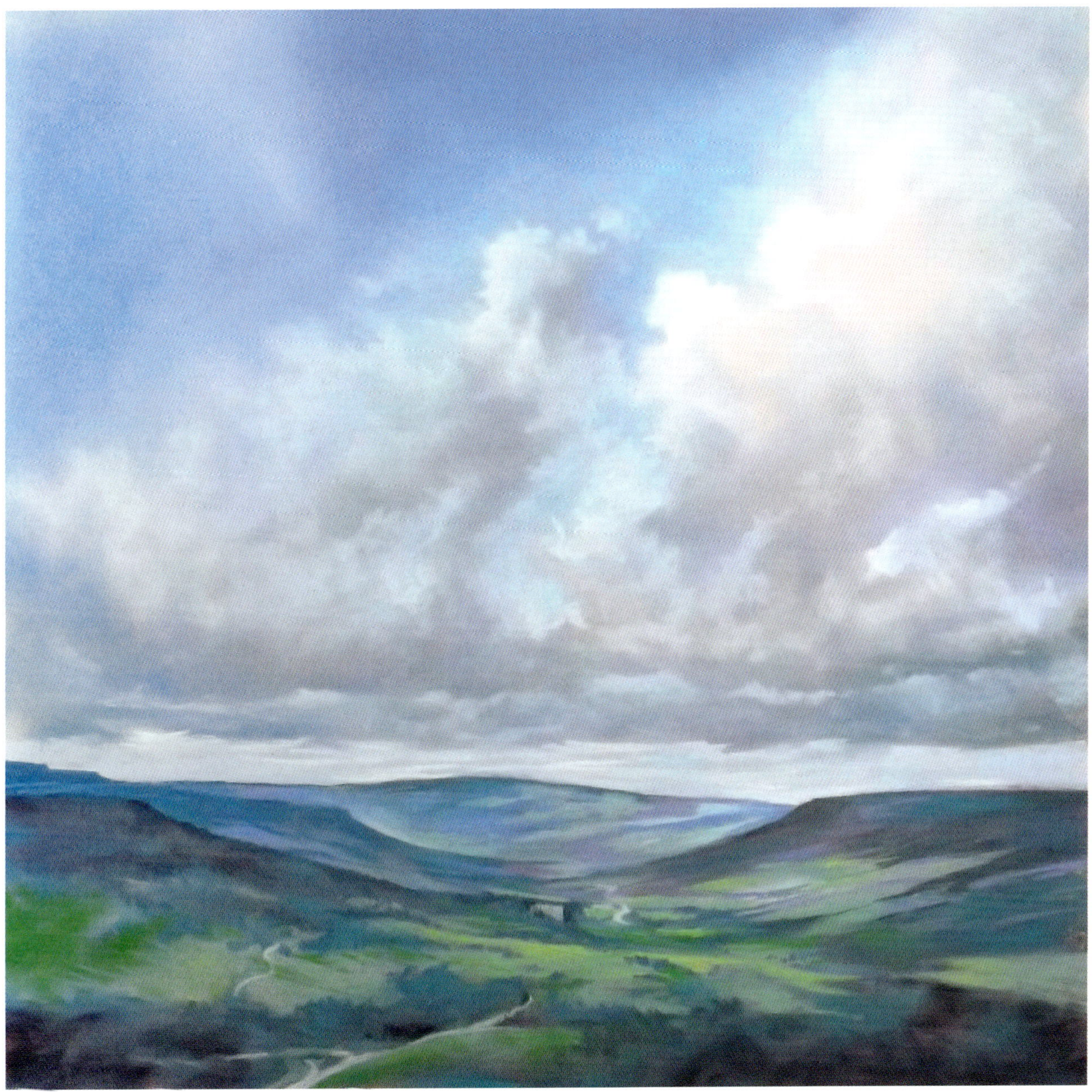

Chatsworth from Baslow Edge

40 x 40cm (15¾ x 15¾in)

When working with brighter edges, it is good to soften the edges in some areas, and leave others with stronger contrasts. This can occur on the edge of the clouds as they meet the sky, or within the clouds themselves. Use this technique to create strong three-dimensional cloud effects and to draw attention towards focal areas.

'Beyond these, again, rises a colossal mountain of grey cumulus, through whose shadowed sides the sunbeams penetrate in dim, sloping, rain-like shafts; and over which they fall in a broad burst of streaming light, sinking to the earth' **John Ruskin**

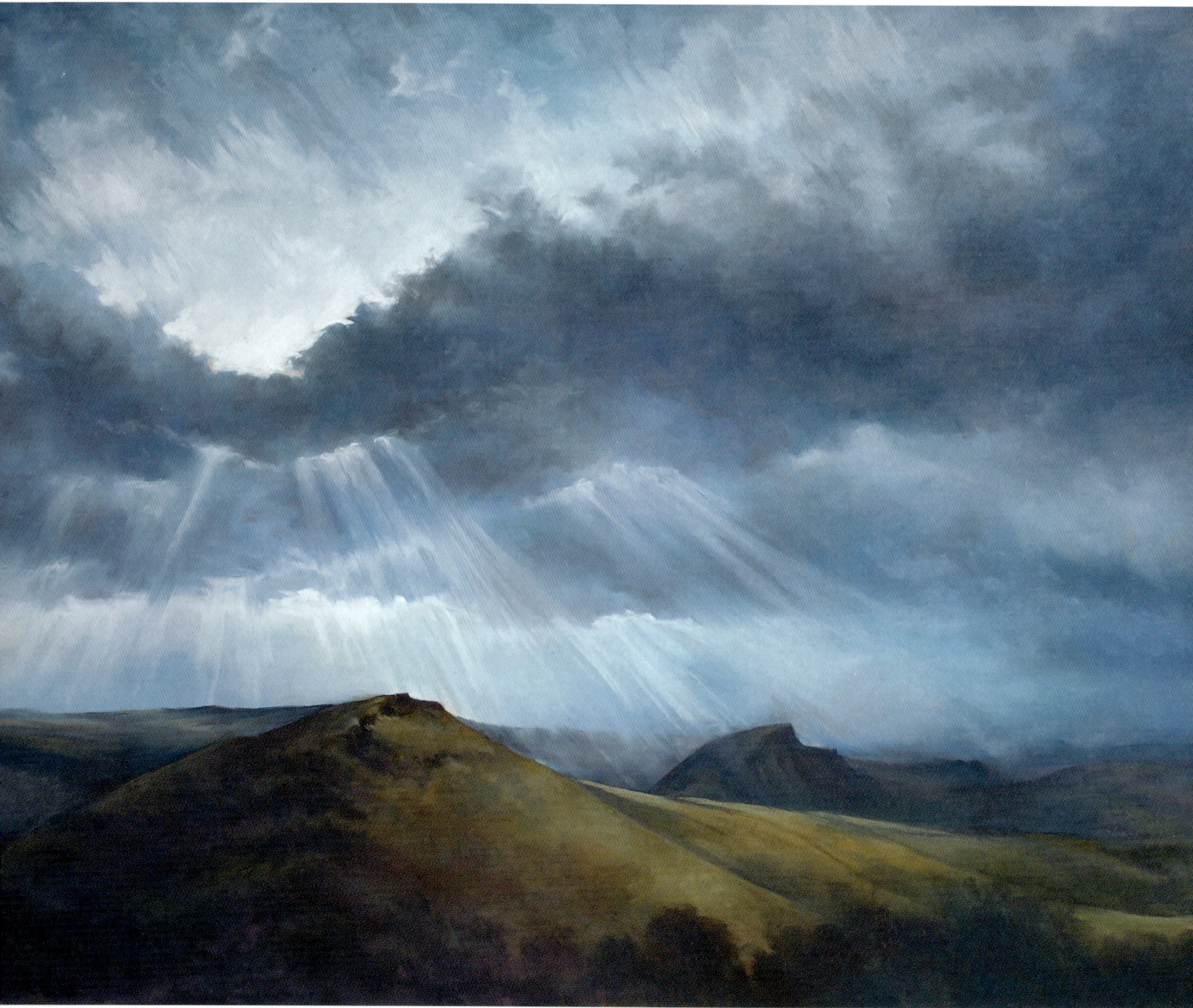

Summer Storm – Towards Chrome Hill

95 x 65cm (37½ x 25½in)

Beams will not always be at the same angle across a larger vista so be aware of this as you work – it's a common mistake to make on bigger scenes.

This painting shows how you can vary the angles of your sunbeams to show the position of the light source in the picture.

SUNBEAMS

Some of the most dramatic skies have beams of light slicing through clouds. These are often white or pale in colour, but can also occur at early morning or as the sun sets, when the clouds will be tinted with a variety of colours.

Once you have added the shafts of light, they are difficult to work over, so sunbeams will usually be one of the finishing touches at the end of a painting: you need the surrounding clouds or land/sea to be complete before you do this effect.

Start by building dark clouds as needed. Keep areas where beams are going to fall tinted but with only a thin layer of pastel.

1 When you are happy with the surrounding cloud, apply a heavy layer of white or yellow (or whatever colour the beam needs to be) with the tip of the pastel to the underside of the cloud.

2 Use your thumb or heel of your hand to firmly pull the colour down at the desired angle in one swift movement. Do not go back up and pull down again without adding more colour and cleaning your hand.

3 If desired, you can use the flat side of the pastel to create additional streaks, blending them in as before. Keep the angle at which you pull them consistent.

4 Once blended, you can slice through the sunbeams with the sharp edge of the colour shaper.

Before

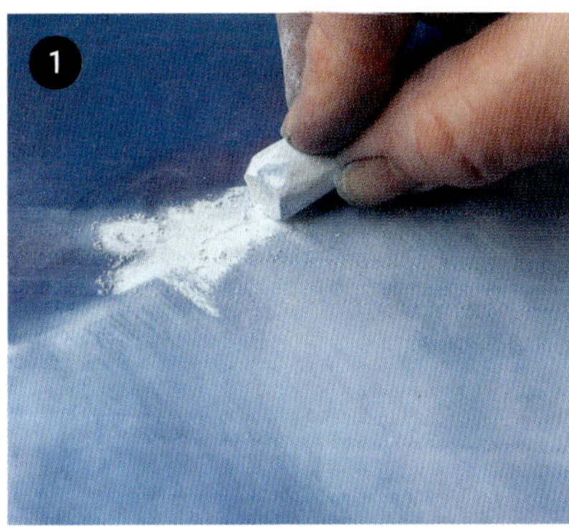

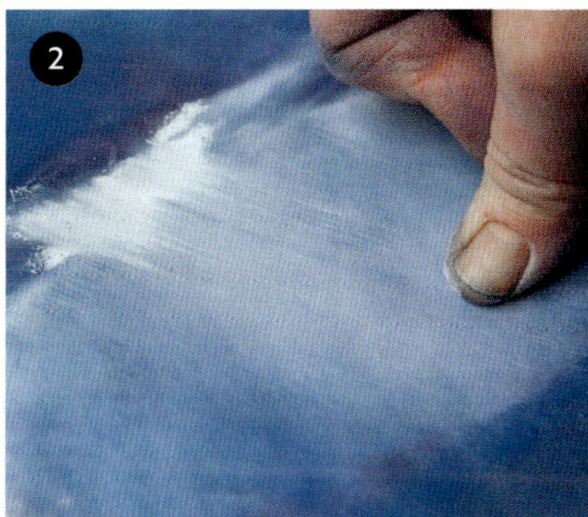

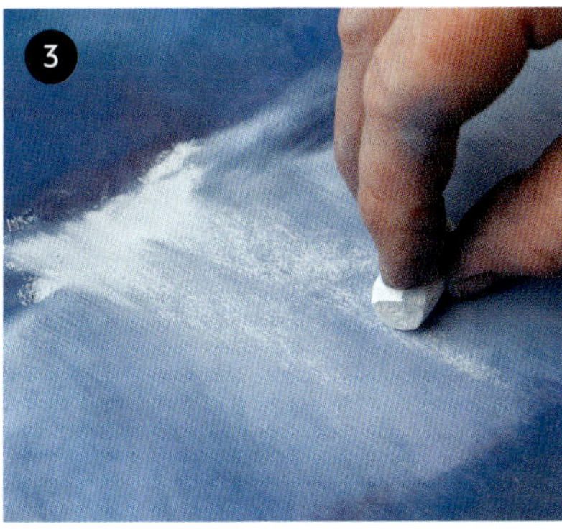

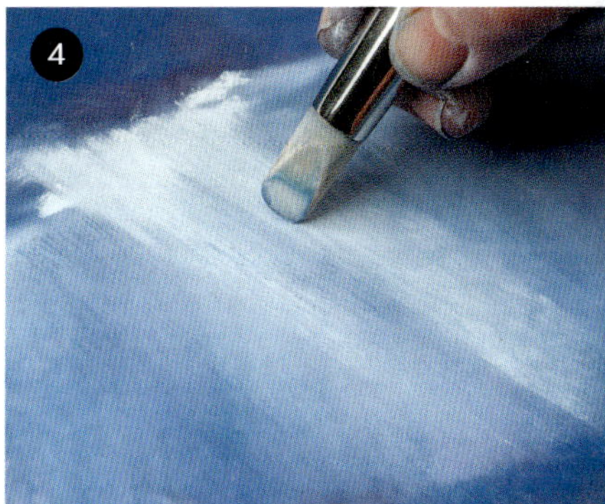

After

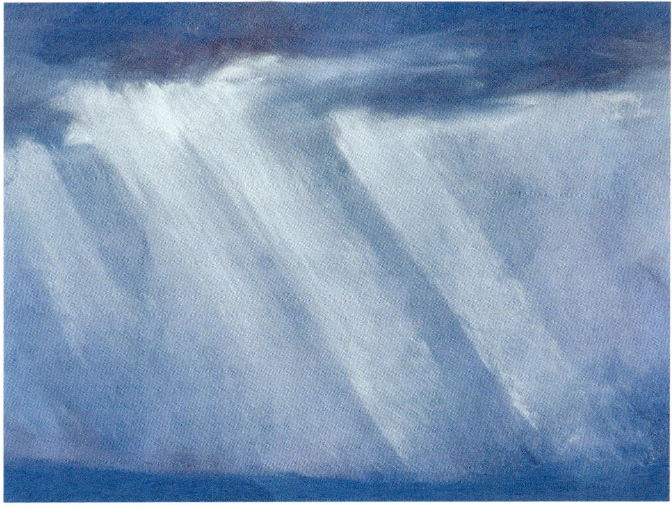

COLOUR TRANSITIONS IN SUNSETS/RISES

One of the more challenging things to control is the changes in colours from yellows and oranges into purples and blues. This is an area rife with problems, as it can lead to you inadvertently creating muddy or green colours. The most important thing to remember is to lay out your palette prior to working on this area, and ensure you have all the bridging colours you need.

Organize your colours to ensure you have clear bridging colours (see page 34) between key areas. For sunsets and sunrises, these will usually be lilac and pink. The pink will bridge from orange to lilac, and then the lilac transitions into blue. Be aware that some lilacs can be very blue-tinged, which is why having an intermediary pink is important when applying colour near orange tones.

As you work, test the colours with swatches on a test strip at the side of your painting (see page 36) prior to applying. It can be surprising how a colour that appears ideal can clash by being slightly the wrong tint – and a test strip will help you spot these potential problems.

Have your old bristle brush on standby and don't worry if things sometimes turn slightly green or brown. Brush away, look again at the subtle tints of the bridging colours, change your pastel and reapply fresh colour.

In the example shown here, you can see the importance of organizing your colours before you start, and ensuring you have the bridging colours in the correct places to avoid muddiness.

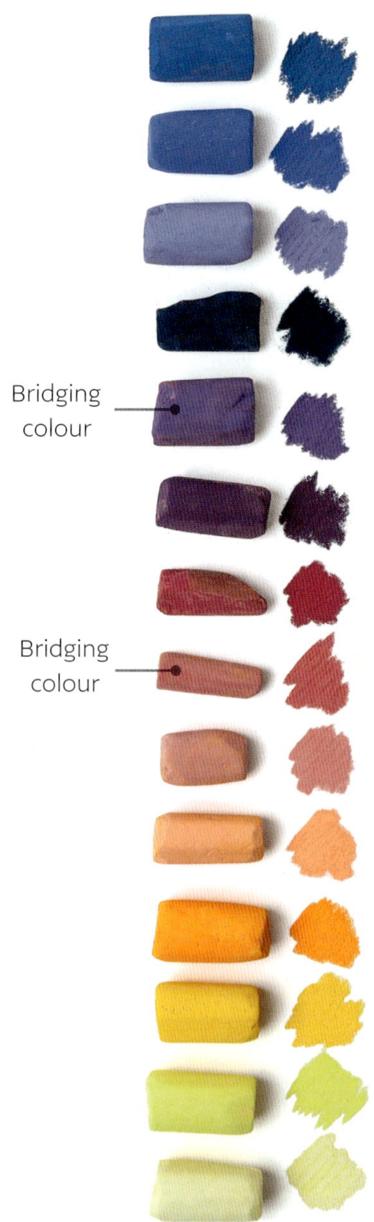

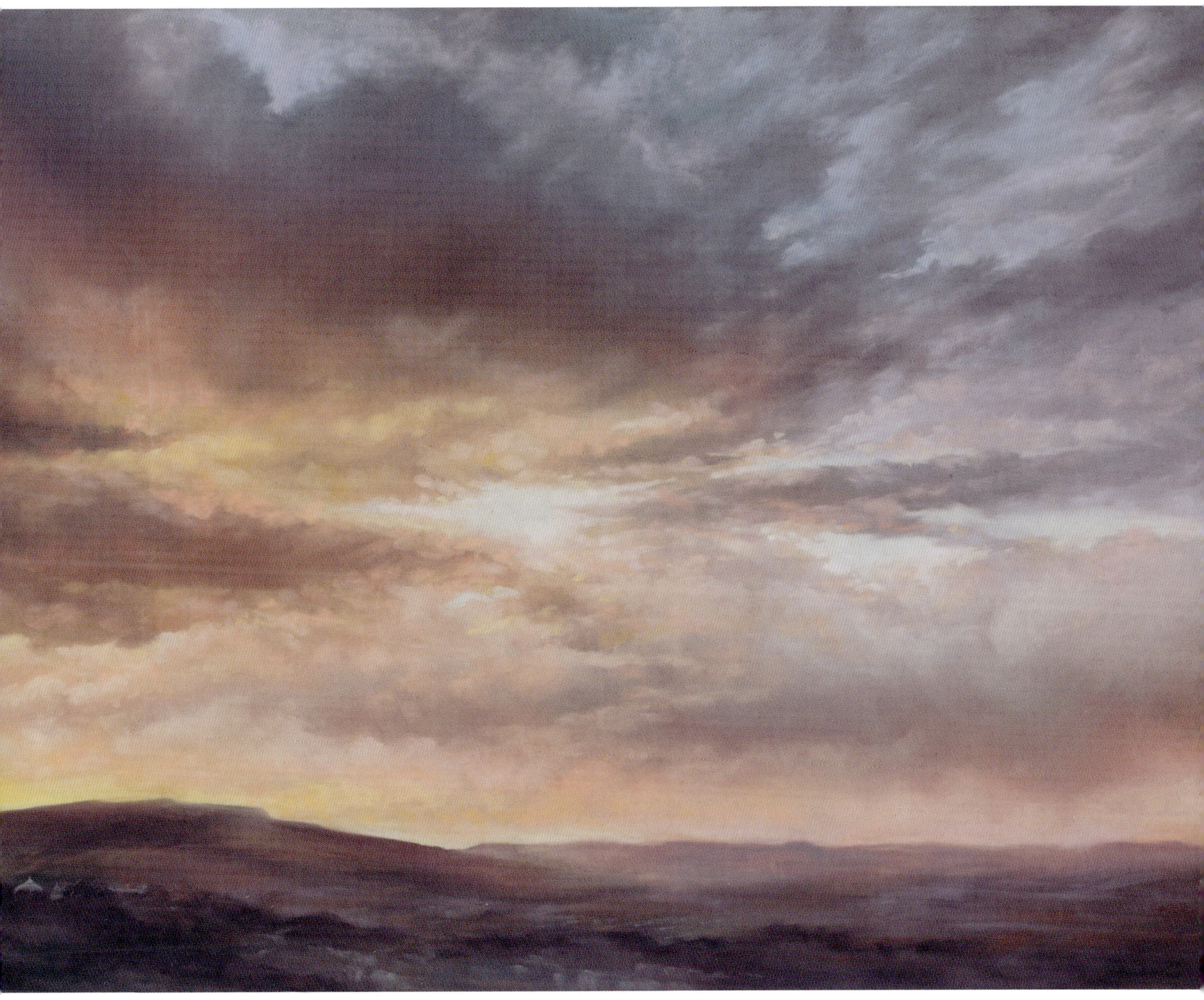

Summer Sunset over Buxton

95 x 65cm (37½ x 25½in)

For this painting, I laid out all my colours, from yellow to orange then pink, lilac and blue, before I began (see opposite). Note that as the landscape was added at the end, only the colours used in the sky are included.

I began by working upwards from the horizon, building the yellow and orange cloud, then the blue area. I blended these but kept them separate. Where blue areas met orange, I used lilac and pink to form buffer zones; overlapping these bridging colours into both areas. When blending, I was careful not to move from one zone to the other.

CREATING DEPTH IN DARK CLOUDS

Sometimes dark clouds can appear very flat and lack depth. If your cloud appears a bit lacking once you have added your basic colours (using the rule of three) and blended them in, there is a simple trick to help create a three-dimensional effect and add drama. This technique can be used for adding darker depth and also a vivid tint.

1 Choose a strong colour like dark purple or blue, and rub your finger gently over the pastel to pick a little up on your fingertip.

2 Lightly dab your finger across the cloud in a loose, semi-random pattern.

3 Do the same with a very dark colour like dark grey or black.

4 Clean your finger and blend gently, being careful not to spread the added colour too far, then repeat as needed to build up the tone.

Before

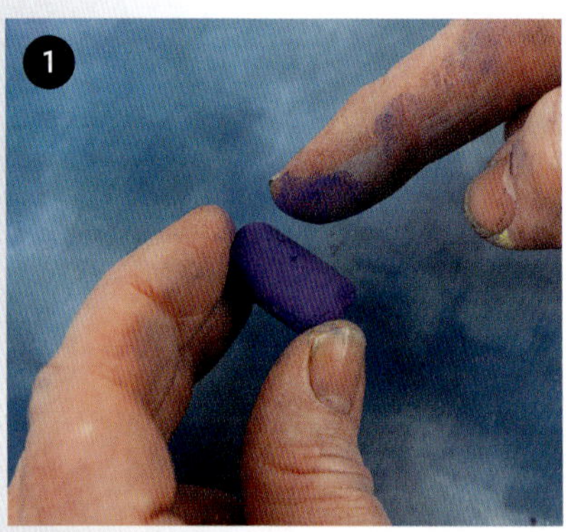

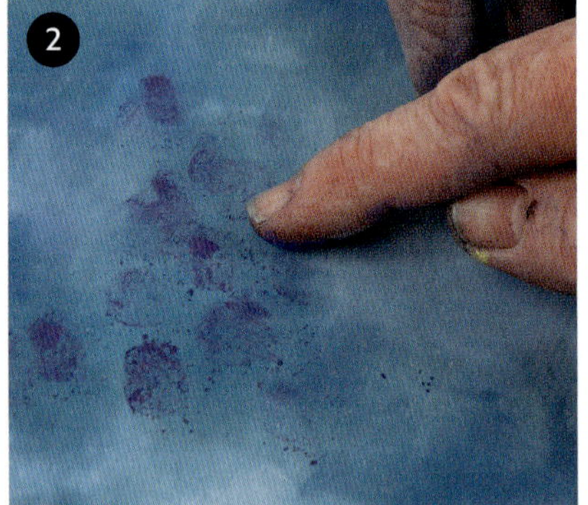

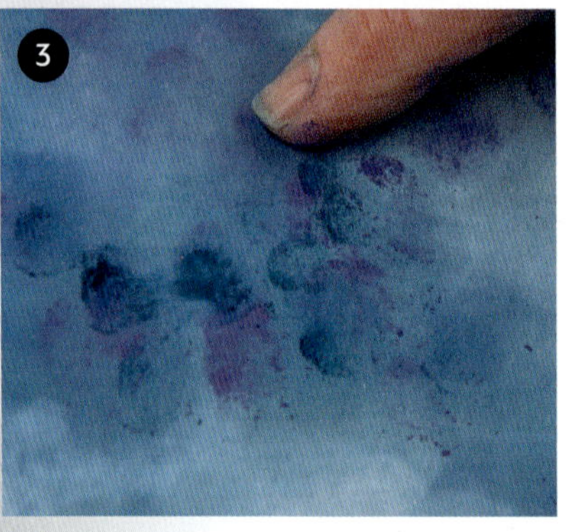

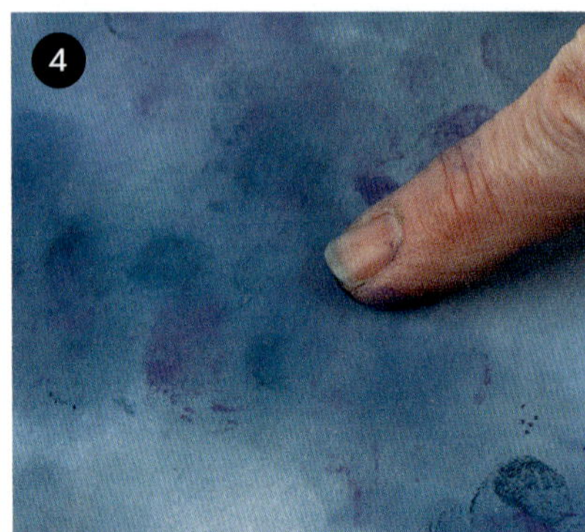

After

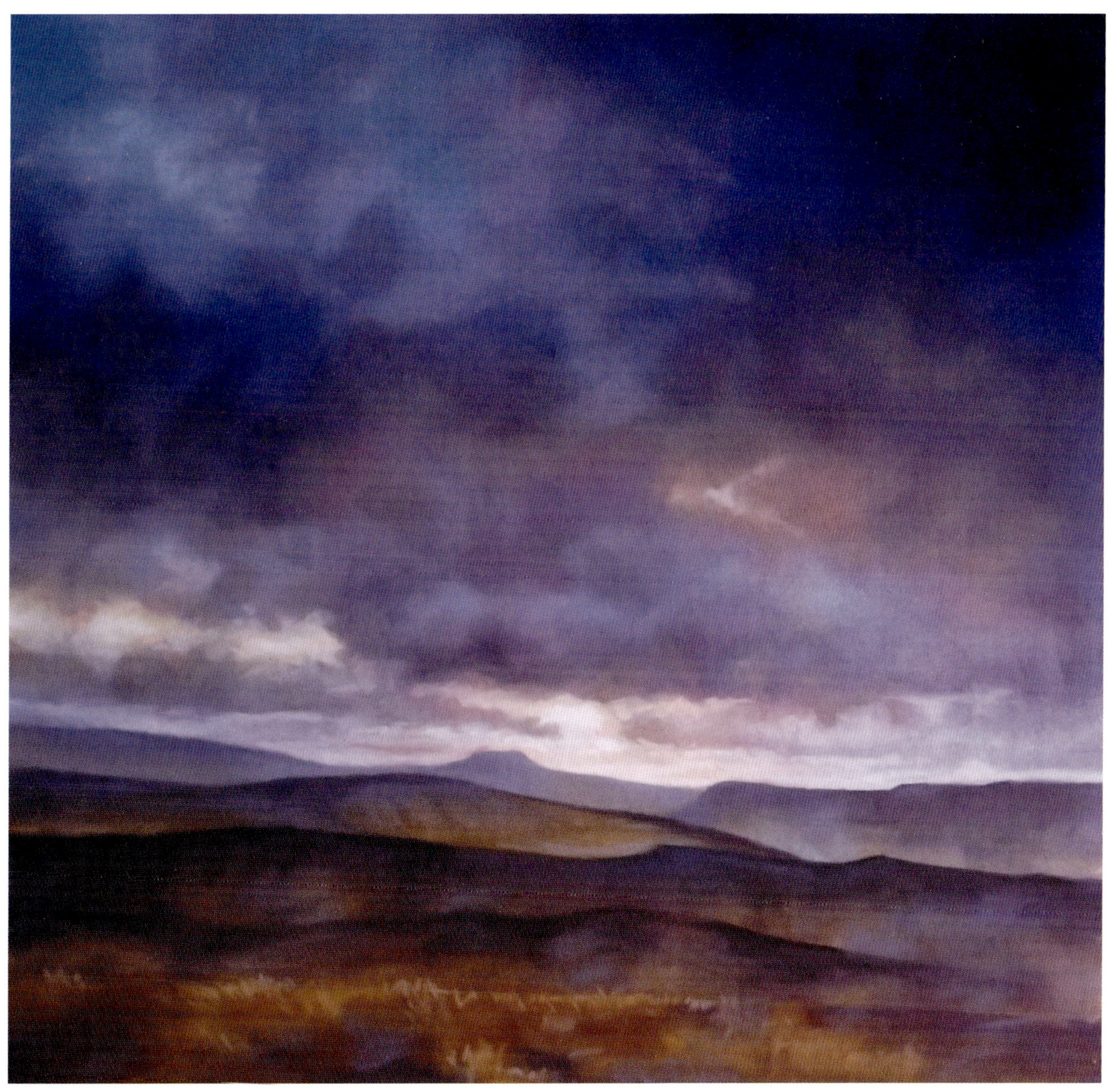

From the Tops, Axe Edge

40 x 40cm (15¾ x 15¾in)

In this piece I used dark purple, pink and hints of orange to add a warm glow and depth to these stormy clouds. These colours harmonize with the warmth of the moorland colours.

Explore doing this in your work. It will allow you to visually pull the piece together and avoid having the palette of the land (or sea) and the sky as two separate things.

DEALING WITH THE HORIZON

There are two main techniques involved here; one for a flat horizon (such as the sea), and one for varied topography. Whichever you use, don't try to add final horizon or hill edges until you are happy with the sky behind them.

Landscape

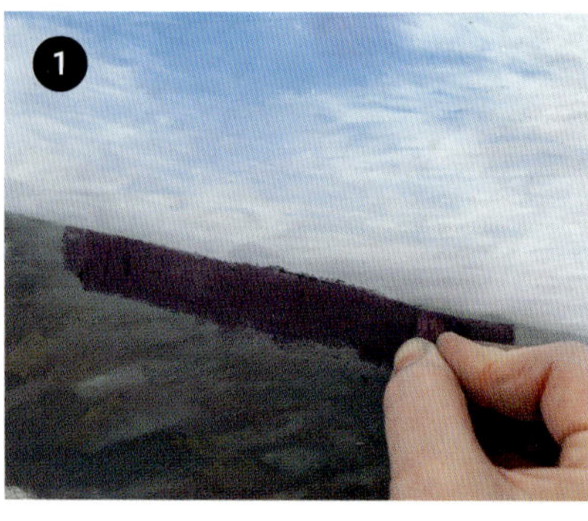 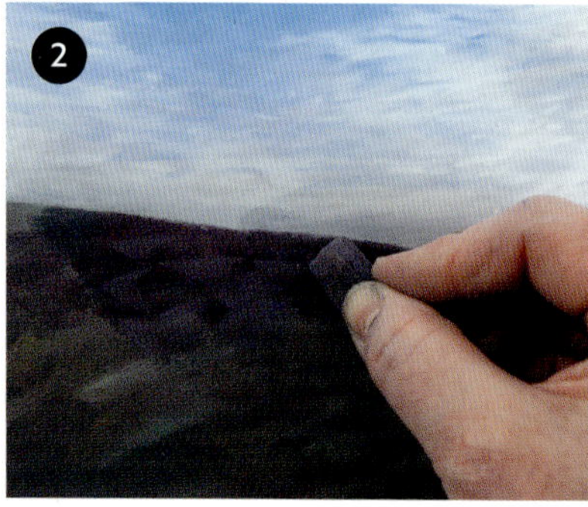 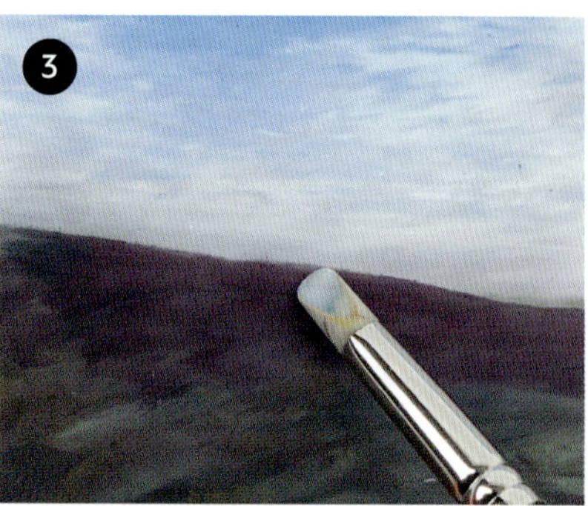

1 Once you are happy with the sky, choose a strong colour and use it on a flat edge. Press firmly and pull it along the desired shape. Overlap the edge of the existing sky.

2 Work down off the edge adding further colours, then blend as needed.

3 Use the colour shaper to add or keep texture as necessary.

Water

1 Lay framer's tape horizontally across the bottom of the sky. Make sure it is level – measure as needed to check. Overlap the edge of the sky so some part is visible beneath the tape.

2 Press firmly along the tape edge nearest the bottom. Choose sea colour and work firmly across the edge of the tape and into the sea below, always pulling the pastel down and along so it doesn't go back up under the tape.

3 Blend with your fingers, then add more colours as needed.

4 Remove the tape carefully to reveal the horizon line.

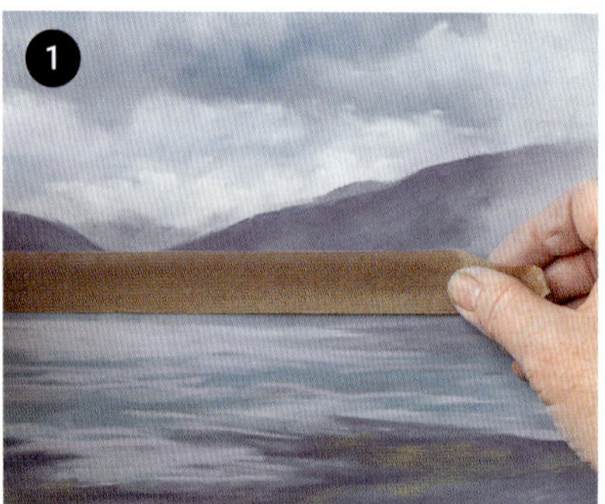 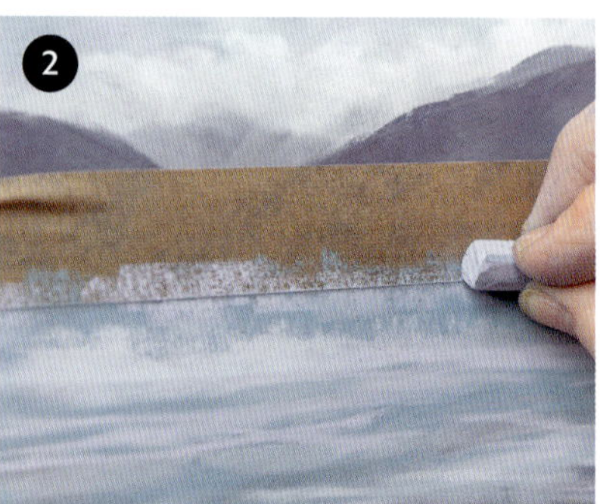

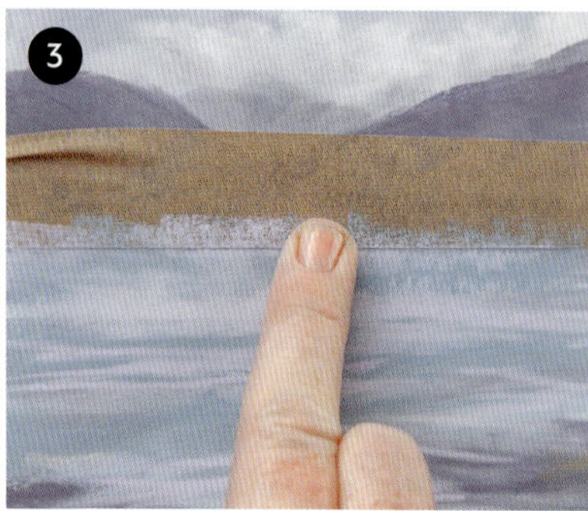 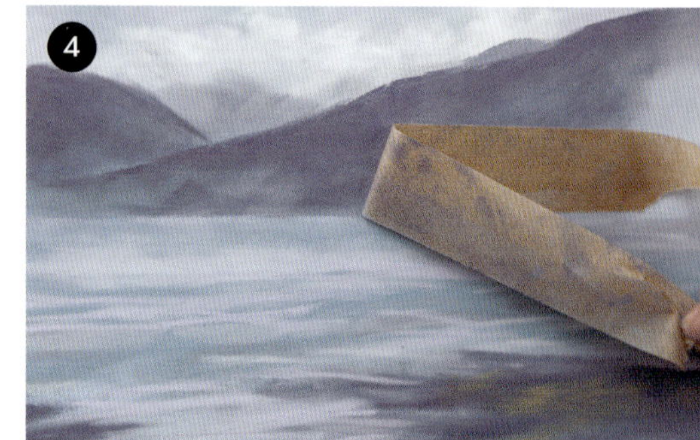

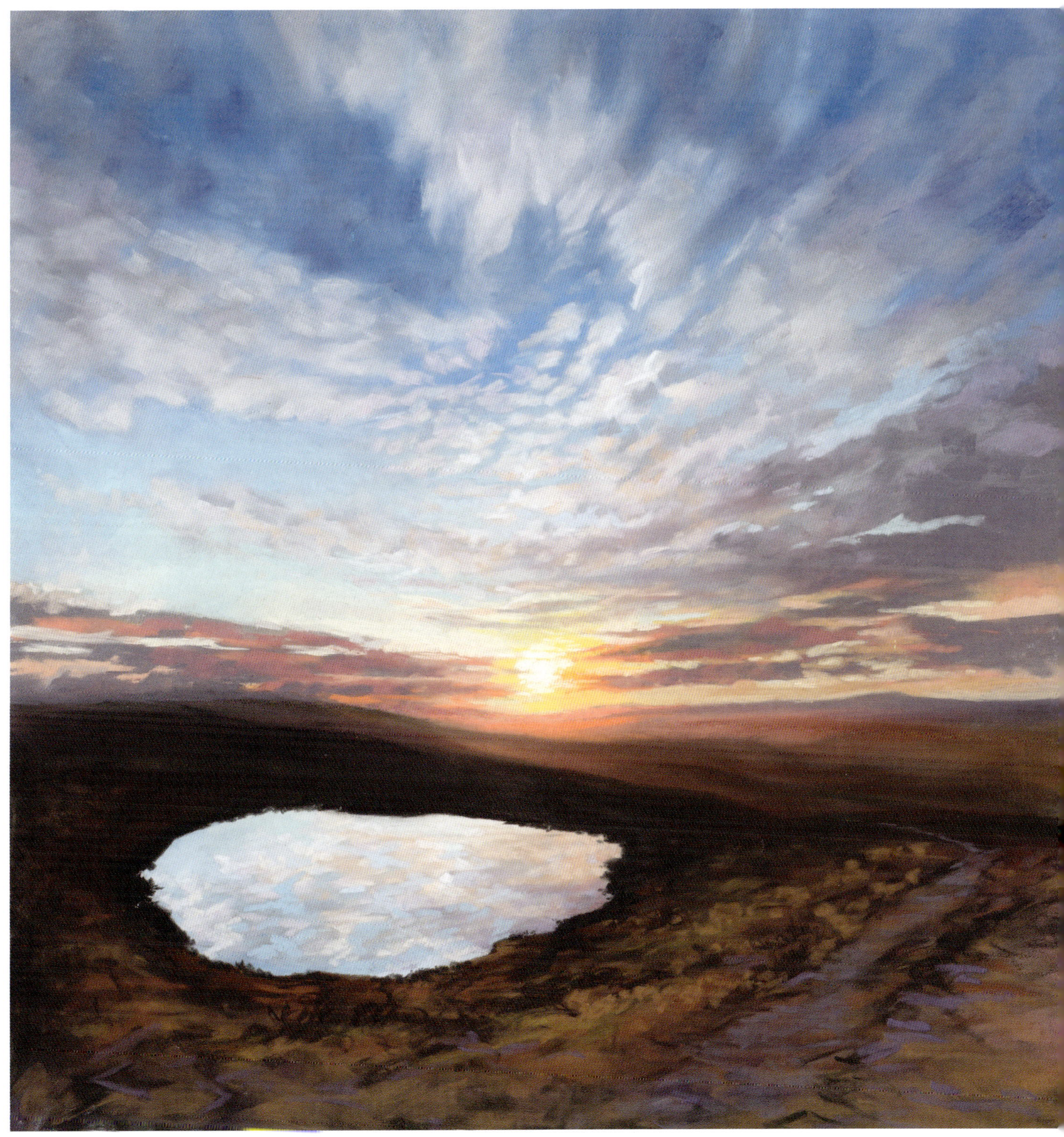

Sunset over Mermaid's Pool, The Roaches

50 x 40cm (19¾ x 15¾in)

Once you have mastered working with horizons, you can also play with the impact that they can have on the composition. This piece presented challenges with the horizon, as all the clouds merge and angle down towards it – plus there is the added complication of the sun itself just above the horizon. Here, I used a combination of warm purple and brown tints to draw the distant hills, deliberately creating areas on the left where the sky and land were cleanly divided, and merging them on the right so they were less clear cut. This helped to create a sense of distance.

ADDING MOVEMENT

There will be many times when you need to add movement to your clouds. It's the subtle variety of marks, colour and tone that creates the sense of movement. There are two main ways to do this, which can be used as and when needed.

Adding movement to start

The first, and ideal way, to add a sense of movement is through using the rule of three and blocky mark-making, followed by careful blending so you don't over-smooth and flatten the cloud. In these details of the painting opposite, blocking was used to build layers in the cloud. Careful attention was paid to using the rule of three. When you use the shaper tool, it can enhance or smooth as needed

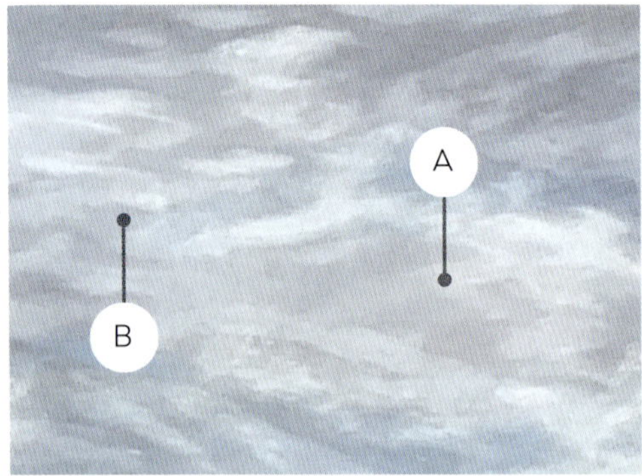

Here I used soft blending in areas (A), while retaining mottled movement elsewhere (B).

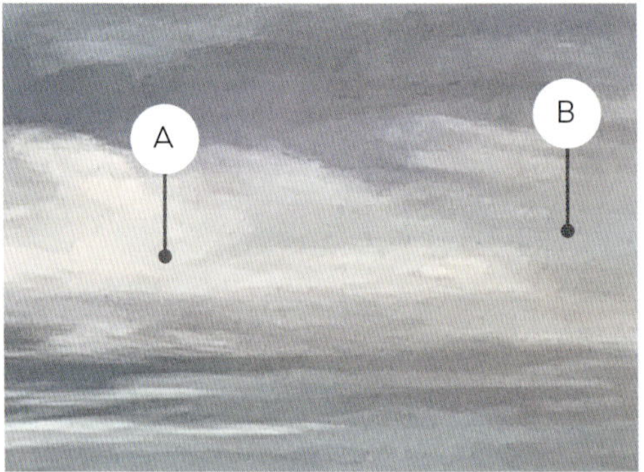

Firm, pulling movements were used here to create both more linear (A) and softer (B) effects.

Adding movement later

If you have already built your cloud layer and feel it is lacking in movement, you can add touches of colour then use the shaper tool to pull this colour firmly through the clouds. This will create dynamic marks. You might also add some dabs of colour with your finger first. Next, use the shaper to pull the pastel around the cloud. Blend only rarely, using circular and criss-cross random movements. Don't be heavy-handed here. This is where it is very common to lose movement and over-smooth the cloud.

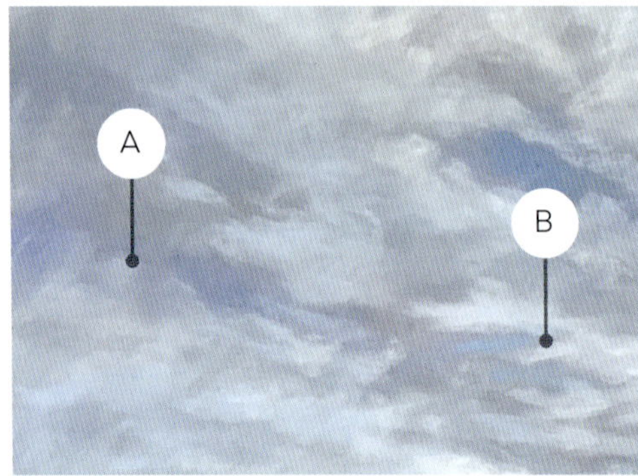

You can see in this detail where the shaper has been used to distort edges (A) and pull them across each other (B).

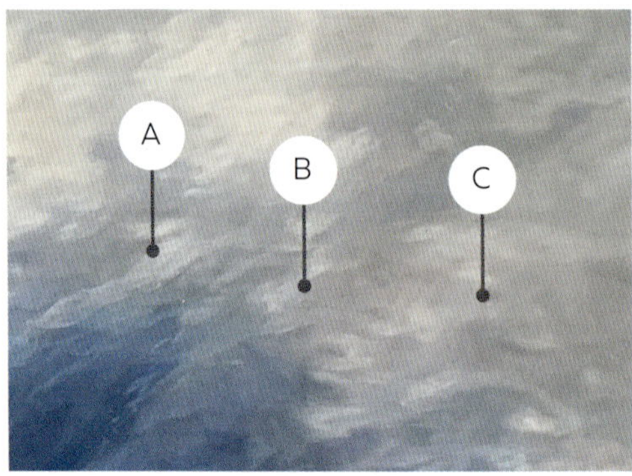

I have added dabs of white and used the shaper to pull them in the direction of the wind in this detail (A, B and C).

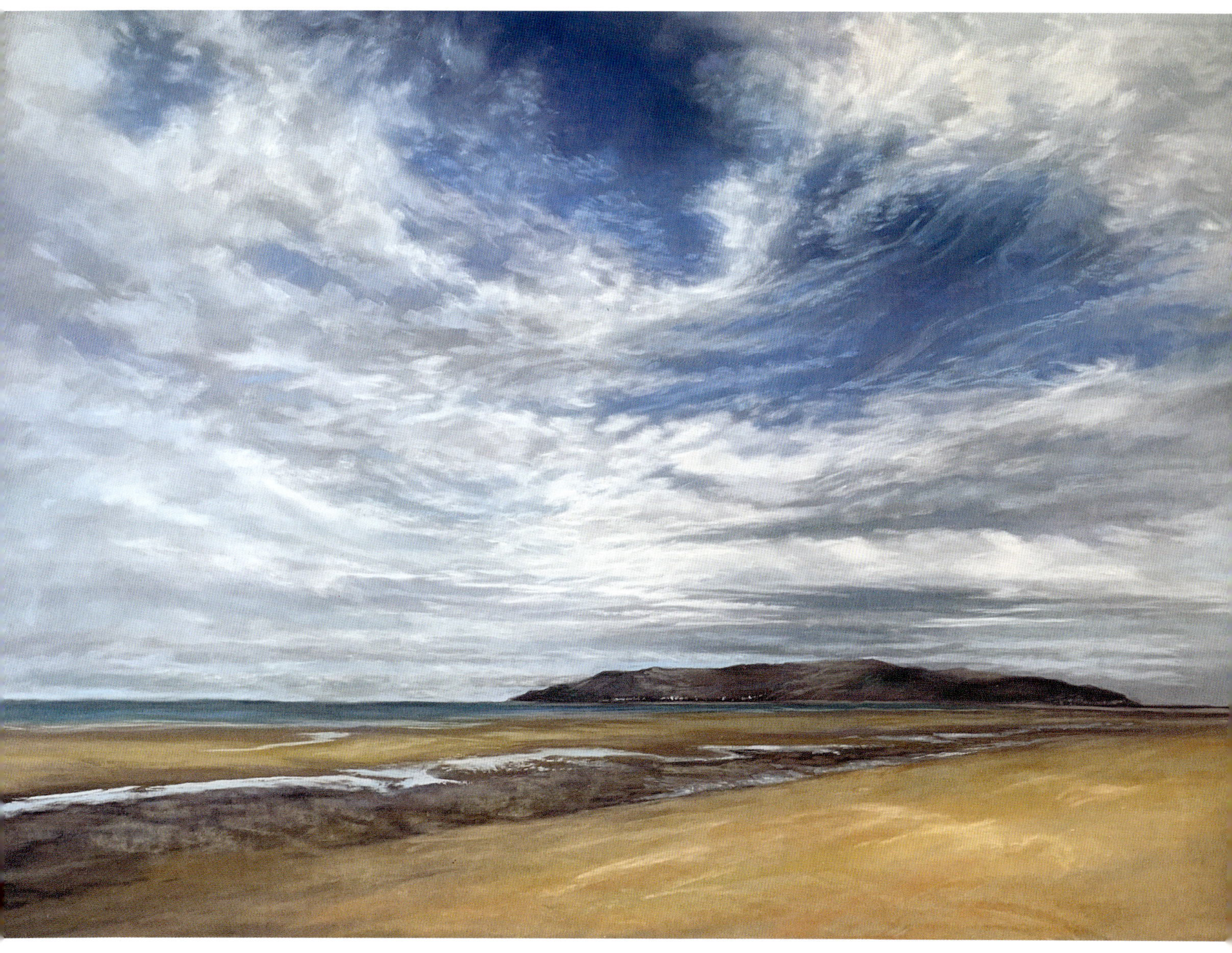

Windy Day, Great Orme's Head

95 x 65cm (37½ x 25½in)

A dramatic and wild sky can be created with a limited palette. In this piece the colours used for the clouds range from greys to pales and white, along with the blue of the sky behind. Depsite this, the attention paid to controlling and creating movement evokes the complex twisting and turning of these clouds on a windswept day.

Index

First published in 2023

Search Press Limited
Wellwood, North Farm Road,
Tunbridge Wells, Kent TN2 3DR

Text copyright © Sandra Orme, 2023
Photographs by Mark Davison at Search Press studios, except for page 86 (top) by Lee Montgomery-Hughes, and pages 1, 2–3, 15, 17, 27, 35, 111, 114, 115, 117, 118, 121, 123 and 127 by Chris Farrow.

Photographs and design copyright © Search Press Ltd. 2023

ISBN: 978-1-78221-989-7
ebook ISBN: 978-1-78126-984-8

Suppliers
For details of suppliers, please visit the Search Press website:
www.searchpress.com

You are invited to visit the author's website: www.sandraorme.com

Publisher's note
All the step-by-step photographs in this book feature the author, Sandra Orme, demonstrating pastel painting. No models have been used.

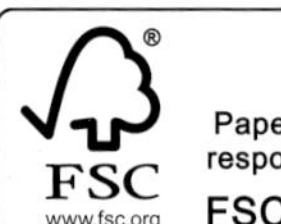